# ...cs:
# ...oncise guide

BARRY HARRISON

LONGMAN
LONDON AND NEW YORK

Longman Group UK Limited,
Longman House, Burnt Mill, Harlow,
Essex CM20 2JE, England
*and Associated Companies throughout the world.*

Published in the United States of America
by Longman Inc., New York



First published 1991

**British Library Cataloguing in Publication Data**
Harrison, Barry 1951–
Economics : a concise guide.
1. Economics
I. Title
330

ISBN 0–582–05726–4

**Library of Congress Cataloging-in-Publication Data**
Harrison, Barry.
Economics : a concise guide / Barry Harrison.
p. cm.
Includes bibliographical references and index.
ISBN 0–582–05726–4 : $9.99
1. Economics—Examinations, questions, etc. I. Title.
HB171.5.H32634 1991
330′.076—dc20 90–26152
CIP

Set in Melior 10/13 pt

Printed in Malaysia
by Percetakan Anda Sdn. Bhd.,
Sri Petaling, Kuala Lumpur

# Contents

# Preface

This book aims to provide a concise and modern introduction to economics. The topics covered are common to most syllabuses including 'A' level. However, a great number of people now take professional examinations in economics and must combine study with a full-time occupation and, in some cases, an active family life. I have had the needs of such people uppermost in mind in preparing this text.

Throughout the text I have made liberal use of diagrams as an aid to understanding. I have also used sub-headings to break down each chapter into manageable sections. At the end of each chapter, review questions are included to provide a regular check on progress and understanding.

I have tried, I hope with success, to make the text interesting by showing the relevance of theory to real world behaviour. In addition I have taken every opportunity to include examples from the real world. I have also included up-to-date statistics so as to illustrate the contemporary relevance of theory.

I am grateful to my wife Lea who typed most of the manuscript and who, along with my children Paul, Matthew and Simon, provided much encouragement. While I am also grateful to the entire team at Longman, I must place on record my particular thanks to Chris Harrison and Joy Cash for their patience and help.

# Study skills

## Introduction

Experience repeatedly shows that many students fail to achieve their full potential in examinations. This is not always through lack of effort or determination. Instead it is often due to failure to study effectively and to show the necessary level of knowledge and understanding to achieve success in the examination. The aim of this section is to outline some basic study skills that will help promote thorough understanding of the subject matter and to provide some advice on examination techniques.

## Essay writing techniques

Writing essays of a consistently high standard is not an easy task. During your course there will usually be the opportunity to submit assignments for assessment by your tutor. Take advantage of this opportunity and use it to develop good practice. Here are some tips.

### Plan your essay

Before you begin writing it is important to plan what you are going to include in your essay and how you are going to organise your material to form an answer. In your plan make a list of the following:

*What to put in your introduction.* In general this should be brief and to the point. It should *not* be an outline of the material you intend to cover. Instead it should include a basic definition of the topic you intend writing about or the central relationships to be covered. One or two sentences is usually sufficient for this purpose.

*What to put in the body of your essay.* Note down the major items you will be dealing with. Consider how to divide these up into separate paragraphs. In general each separate item should be dealt with in a separate paragraph.

*What to put in the conclusion.* A conclusion provides an opportunity to summarise the basic argument that you have covered in the body of the essay and to outline the implications of your argument.

### Learn from your mistakes

When an assignment is returned to you it is important to have a look at any comments made by your tutor. Think about them and read through your assignment again trying to identify ways in which it could be improved and your understanding increased.

### Exam preparation

Although examinations usually last only two or three hours, exam preparation should start when you begin your course. Many students leave revision for the examination until the two or three weeks preceding it. This is very unwise and is probably the major reason for poor performance in the examination. Knowledge and understanding are best accumulated over a period of time and certainly not when the pressure of the examination is growing.

Ideally you should regard revision as an integral part of your weekly routine. Try and set aside a small amount of time each week, perhaps half an hour, and revise a topic making sure you fully understand it. A topic which is understood is easy to remember. A topic which is not, is very difficult to remember!

### Revision

When to begin final revision is a matter of personal preference. However, it is important to begin early enough to allow the full syllabus to be covered. It is also important to remember that in the early stages of revision you will work quite quickly and find it relatively easy to retain information. As revision proceeds the whole task becomes more difficult. Take heart if you find revision becomes more and more difficult, it is the same for everybody else! If you stick at it you will make progress.

#### Make a revision plan

It is a good idea to begin by making a revision plan. Write down the topics you are going to cover and the dates when you will do this. Try not to be too ambitious when making your plan. Allow some free time in your plan in case you fall behind in your revision. Having made your plan, try to stick to it.

#### Making summaries

One technique favoured by many students is to make summaries of course notes. This can be a useful exercise, but make sure your summaries are just that. All too often students simply end up re-writing their notes instead of summarising them.

#### Practice

It is important to give yourself plenty of practice at writing essays under examination conditions. It is easy to underestimate how difficult it is to write a comprehensive answer in the time you will have available in the examination. There is no substitute for practice but try to ensure you have no prior knowledge of the question you are going to attempt. Pick a question at random from a past examination paper or ask someone else to pick one for you. Stick to the amount of time available in the examination.

#### In the examination

Before you attempt any questions in the examination you must read and make sure you understand the rubric on the front of the examination paper. Pay particular attention to the number of questions you are required to attempt and the time allowed for completing the paper. Here are some tips to help you choose and answer examination questions.

**Choosing questions**

Before you decide to attempt any question read through all of the questions on the paper and, as you do so, mark those you *think* you can answer. From this list select the questions you are going to attempt. You must take great care when selecting these questions. Make sure you can answer all parts of the question fully and remember questions which initially look quite easy can sometimes be very difficult and vice versa.

**Plan your answer**

Think about what you are going to put in your answer and how you are going to organise the material. Make *brief* notes so that you remember all of your points. Think carefully about the question and make sure as far as possible that your answer will be full and comprehensive. Make sure you only include material which is relevant.

**Refer back**

As you write periodically refer back to the question and your plan. It's very easy under examination conditions to wander off the point and to include irrelevant material. It only takes a short while to check that you are following your plan and that what you have written is relevant to the question.

# Acknowledgements

The publishers are grateful to the following for permission to reproduce copyright material:

The Bank of England for fig. 14.1, tables 15.2 and 18.3 and the Controller of Her Majesty's Stationery Office for tables 6.1, 6.2, 9.1, 9.2, 12.2, 17.1 and 18.2

# Further reading

Barry Harrison, *Studying Economics at 'A' Level*, (Lon
(Available direct from: Longman Resources Unit, 62 H
Layerthorpe, York, YO3 7XQ.)

Although primarily written for students of 'A' level economics, this book provides a comprehensive discussion of study skills that will be useful to those taking professional examinations in economics.

# 1 The economic problem

## Scarcity and choice

The economic problem is summed up in two key words, *scarcity* and *choice*. To the economist scarcity has a very specific meaning and does not simply mean *rare* as many people often assume. To the economist something is scarce if society desires more of it than is currently available. On this definition most goods and services are scarce because the desires of society for material consumption seem unlimited, whereas the resources, such as land, labour and capital from which output is produced, are strictly limited.

Because society cannot have all the goods and services it desires at any moment in time, it is forced to make choices. These choices are:

1. *What output will be produced?* Because society cannot have all the output that it desires, it must choose which goods and services to produce from the available resources.
2. *How shall the output be produced?* There are various ways of producing *any given output*. Sometimes economists refer to *labour-intensive* production where large amounts of labour are used *relative* to other resources and *capital-intensive* where large amounts of capital are used *relative* to other factors of production. These are simplistic terms and the point to emphasise is that all production requires a combination of resources but the proportion in which these resources are used in the production of any given output is variable. In industry computers and robots now perform tasks which once employed hundreds of thousands of individuals!
3. *For whom shall the output be produced?* Society must also choose the method through which its output is to be distributed to consumers.

Although the fundamental economic problem confronting any societies is the same, they do not always adopt the same means of dealing with it. For example, it is clear that in some societies more decisions – about what, how and for whom – are made by the government than in others. In other words, different economic systems have evolved for dealing with the same economic problem. These economic systems are considered later. First we consider the important concept of *opportunity cost*.

## Opportunity cost

Because *all* output is created from scarce resources, it follows that these resources have alternative uses. How many uses can you think of for timber, steel, electricity and labour for exampl... urse we can think of many differe... ey have been used to p... able to produce somethi... will be produced from s... goods and services it ... o the economist and, in ... next most desired alte... s the *opportunity cost* o...

Opportunity co... s in economics. In taki... tion, both policy-makers ... the concept of opportu... nits resources to an ex... oes society forego as a re... ves that any government... this nature. For example ... rease hospital provision, education ... delence establishments and so on. Society does not do without all of these since there are insufficient resources to have more of everything. Opportunity cost is simply the next most desired alternative foregone. In this case, if the decision to increase the motorway network is financed by a lower level of expenditure on hospital provision, then the latter is the opportunity cost of the former.

opportunity cost –

choosing what to produce..

Most desired alternative foregone or sacificed, is referred to as the oppurtunity cost of what is produced.

This is a relatively simple example but in reality there are few aspects of our lives that are not touched by ... portunity cost. As individuals ... of our income to spend ... d our income on certai... Whether to spend our ti... school earlier or later. ... n. Similarly firms consta... nd take decisions about ... whether to use differe...

## Production possibility curves

One w... ces available to society ... Such a curve is illustrat... ned that society can only...

Becau... ces, there is an

Production possibility curves.
represents the range of possible choice.

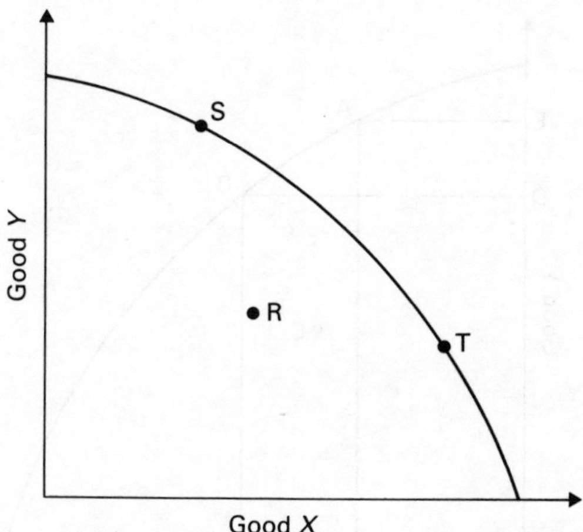


*Figure 1.1* A production possibility curve

upper limit on the amount of output that can be produced at any moment in time. A production possibility curve therefore shows the maximum output that society can produce given its existing resources. In other words, all points *on* the curve represent points at which the economy is operating at full productive capacity, that is, full employment. Any point *inside* the curve must, therefore, indicate that there are unemployed resources in the economy. Thus at point R in Figure 1.1 there are unemployed resources in the economy, whereas at points S and T there is full employment.

A production possibility curve shows what society can produce with *existing resources* at any moment in time. However, over time, society's ability to produce output will increase because of improvements in the productivity of labour, greater technological progress, an increase in the size of the labour force and so on. Whatever the cause, if society's ability to produce output increases, this will be represented by an outward movement of the entire production possibility curve.

It is also important to note that the shape of the production possibility curve indicates that the opportunity cost of any *given* increase in the output of one good will change as we move along the production possibility curve. For example, in Figure 1.2 we can see that the opportunity cost of increasing the output of good X by AB units when we move from an output of OA of good X to an output of OB of good X, is CD of Y. However, if we increase the output of good X from zero to OA, roughly the same increase in the output of good X, the opportunity cost is much lower at only EC of good Y. In other words, opportunity cost increases as the output of any good increases. There are several reasons for this, but the most obvious is that not all resources are equally well suited to the production of both goods. Some resources are better suited to the production of certain goods than others and, when resources specialise where they are most efficient, higher levels of output will be produced.

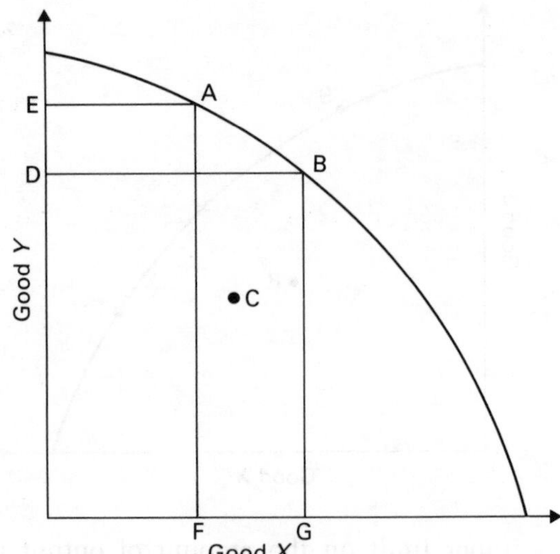


*Figure 1.2* The change in opportunity cost as the output of one good increases

## Externalities, private costs and social costs

One important aspect of production and consumption in modern economies is that they frequently give rise to *externalities*. These are the spillover effects of production and consumption which affect society as a whole rather than just individual producers or consumers. Externalities might impose costs on society, such as air pollution from the operation of motor vehicles or river pollution from the dumping of waste materials. Equally, they might confer benefits (negative costs) such as the general increase in property values in a particular street that results from individual improvements to property. To derive the full *social costs* of production, we must add the costs (or benefits) of these externalities to the *private costs* of production, that is, the monetary costs incurred by the individual undertaking production (or consumption), such as labour costs, raw material costs and so on. We shall see later that the existence of externalities has an important bearing on the allocation of resources.

## Private goods, public goods and merit goods

Economists sometimes find it useful to distinguish between *private goods*, *public goods* and *merit goods*. Private goods are simply those goods bought by individuals or organisations for their private use. This might include extending the use of such goods to others, as for example when a person lends a neighbour his car. In such cases the owner has control over who uses the good and its use can be restricted to particular individuals or institutions.

The same is not true of public goods. Public goods have two main characteristics: *non-exhaustibility* and *non-excludability*. The former implies that consumption of an extra unit by one person does not diminish the amount available for consumption by others, while the latter implies that it is often difficult to prevent a person from consuming an additional unit. For example, street-lighting, lighthouses and defence are often cited as examples of public goods. Once they are available, the extra cost of extending their availability to an additional person is zero and it is impossible to prevent consumption by any individual or group.

Merit goods are so-called because they add to the quality of life but would tend to be under-consumed if they were not provided through the state. Education and health care are often cited as examples of merit goods because a healthy and better educated labour force will be more productive. The absence of education and health care would therefore seriously reduce living standards. Because of these wider benefits to society certain merit goods are provided freely or at subsidised prices through the state to encourage consumption to the optimum level so that society gains maximum benefit.

## Test your understanding

1. Distinguish between *scarcity* and *rarity*.
2. Which of the following would an economist classify as a scarce good? Explain your answer in each case.
   (a) A motor car in the UK.
   (b) Ice at the south pole.
   (c) Fish in the sea.
3. Insert the missing words to complete the following sentence correctly. Opportunity cost is the ____ ____ ____ ____ ____ foregone.
4. Does the fact that some countries can produce goods more efficiently than others imply that there is less of an economic problem in these countries than in others?
5. If an individual is vaccinated against a contagious disease what positive externality is conferred on society?
6. What negative externalities does cigarette smoking impose on society?
7. Figure 1.2 on page 4 shows a production possibility curve for a particular economy.
   (a) How much of good X and good Y is produced when the economy is at (i) point A and (ii) point B on the production possibility curve?
   (b) What is the opportunity cost of moving from point A to point B?
   (c) What is the opportunity cost of moving from point C to point B?
   (d) How would the production possibility curve be affected if this economy experienced economic growth?

# 2 Economic systems

## The market economy

Whilst the nature of the choices confronting all societies is the same, they sometimes adopt different methods of dealing with them. One method is to allow choices to be resolved by the free play of *market forces* (supply and demand), and in this case we say that resources are allocated through the *price mechanism*. In this case individuals, as consumers, freely choose which goods and services they will purchase, and producers freely decide which goods and services they will provide.

In market economies production is undertaken for *profit* and resources are allocated through the *price mechanism*. There is a very limited role for the government which is perhaps restricted to the provision of law and order, thus creating a framework of rules within which the business sector can operate.

## The operation of the price mechanism

This is the most important feature of market economies because it is the mechanism through which resources are allocated. Decisions about consumption are undertaken by millions of different people, each freely expressing their preferences for different goods and services. Decisions about production, on the other hand, are undertaken by tens of thousands of producers who freely decide which goods and services they are going to provide. There is little or no direct communication between each of these groups, and yet any change in the preferences of consumers is accurately and quickly transmitted to producers via its effect on the prices of goods and services which producers provide. These price changes ensure that the decisions of producers and consumers, although taken independently, are usually compatible with one another.

How do price changes achieve this? Consider as an example the case of a good which suddenly becomes more popular so that there is a market shortage at the *existing price*. In these circumstances the price of the good will rise so as to ration the available supply. However, the rise in price will make production of that commodity more profitable. Output will therefore increase as producers are now able to attract resources away from alternative uses by the offer of higher rewards. The process will operate in reverse when a product becomes less popular. It is particularly important to note that, because of their impact on price, changes in consumer demands lead to changes in the allocation of resources. Because of this, the consumer is said to be '*sovereign*' in market economies.

*Advantages of market economies*

1. An important advantage of market economies is that producers respond to the demands of consumers. In other words, consumers dictate what is produced. We can be sure of this because production is undertaken for profit and only those goods which consumers demand will be profitable to produce.
2. Since production is undertaken for profit, producers have an incentive to respond quickly to changes in consumer demands. Any producer that does not respond quickly will lose business to those producers who do, and the more rapid the response the greater the profit.
3. Consumers are assumed to be price conscious buyers and this encourages firms to produce at the lowest possible cost. Firms which fail to do this will lose business to other firms which offer a lower price and here again the end result will be a lower level of profit. To avoid this firms will produce in the least cost way.
4. Resources are allocated to their 'Pareto optimum', or most efficient, use. An allocation of resources is said to be a Pareto optimum when it is no longer possible to make any member of society better off, by reallocating resources, without at the same time making someone else worse off. If it is possible to make some members of society better off and no one else worse off, by reallocating resources, then clearly by doing this total welfare can be increased. Only when we can no longer do this have we reached a Pareto optimum.

But why does a market economy lead to a Pareto optimum allocation of resources? The answer is simple. It is assumed that the price consumers are willing to pay for a commodity represents their valuation of the resources used to produce that commodity. In other words, price is a measure of the value consumers place on a commodity. On the other hand, the cost of producing a commodity is the cost producers pay to attract resources away from other uses. In other words, financial costs of production are a measure of the opportunity cost of production. An optimum allocation of resources exists when the value society places on another unit of the commodity (shown by the price they are willing to pay for it) exactly equals the cost of attracting resources away from alternative uses (i.e. its opportunity cost). This must be so because, if alternatives were more highly valued, resources would move into their production because entrepreneurs would offer higher rewards for them. This is precisely what happens when demand for a good increases. Its price is bid up and production expands as resources are attracted away from alternatives. When price equals opportunity cost, a Pareto optimum allocation of resources is said to exist and this simply means that it is impossible to make one person better off without simultaneously making someone else worse off.

## *Disadvantages of market economies*

In practice it is unlikely that the advantages of market economies as outlined above would always materialise. There are also disadvantages of market economies.

1. An efficient or optimum allocation of resources can only exist when all prices in the economy fully reflect the social costs of production and consumption. However, prices in market economies are based entirely on private costs of production. Thus, if a product imposes relatively large social costs on society, then the free operation of the price mechanism will not lead to an optimum allocation of resources. This is simply because the social costs of production will be greater than the private costs, and hence market price will be less than the real opportunity cost of production. This will encourage over-consumption of these commodities in relation to the optimum and under-consumption of others where private costs are more closely related to social costs.
2. Public goods and merit goods present a particular problem in market economies. These goods often confer benefits on society far in excess of their costs. However, public goods would not be provided through the market mechanism because their characteristics (non-exhaustibility and non-excludability) would mean that no one would ever pay individually to consume such goods and therefore no firm could earn a profit from their production. The same is not true of merit goods which might be provided for a few privileged members of society, but they would most certainly be under-provided in relation to the optimum level. Because of this the market mechanism might again fail to allocate resources efficiently.
3. Free market economies would tend to be unstable because as consumer demands changed production would change. When demand for a particular good fell the unemployment consequences might be quite serious for particular industries and even whole regions if that industry is localised. This is quite a serious criticism because unemployed resources imply that production is not at its maximum level. Since the standard of

living in a country partly depends on the amount produced, the implication is that living standards are below their maximum attainable level.

4. Free market economies are also criticised because they lead to considerable inequality in the distribution of income and wealth. Those who own land and capital derive incomes from hiring them out, but the vast majority of people have nothing but their labour to sell. In addition, when instability in the economy leads to unemployment, the limited role for the government implies an absence of state aid in the form of supplementary benefit, for example.

## The centrally planned economy

An alternative method of allocating resources is for the government to issue directives or instructions to firms indicating what they should produce, the quantities that should be produced and so on. In some cases this might be accompanied by complete physical rationing among consumers, but it is more rational to allow consumers a large degree of choice over the items they purchase.

## The problems of planning

One obvious problem for this kind of system is to ensure that the demands of consumers match the output of firms. We have seen that the price mechanism performs this function in free enterprise economies, but in centrally planned economies producers will only follow the instructions they are given. In this type of system the mechanism which 'signals' shortages of some commodities is often the existence of long queues and empty shelves; whilst the signal for surpluses of other commodities is often the accumulation of stocks.

Another problem faced by the planners is to ensure that the target levels of output assigned to various industries are compatible with each other. For example, when giving the steel industry a target level of output, the planners must take into consideration the target levels of output assigned to other industries which use steel, such as car manufacturing and ship building. Similarly, when assigning a target to the steel industry, the planners must ensure that a sufficient supply of coal is available to the steel industry. Hence the target given to the coal industry must take account of the target given to the steel industry and so on. These target levels of output should largely reflect the likely demands of society for consumption.

It is clear that the planners face an extremely difficult task, and although plans are normally expected to run for several years, in practice they are often revised more frequently to take account of changes in consumer demands, technological change, the effects of the weather on agricultural production and so on. Nevertheless, it is sometimes claimed that centrally planned economies have many advantages over market economies. The most commonly suggested advantages and disadvantages are summarised below.

*Advantages of centrally planned economies*

1. Because production is not undertaken for profit, it is argued that there is **greater likelihood of both public goods and merit goods being provided** (see p. 8). The government simply has to issue a directive to ensure production.
2. The **production and consumption of demerit goods**, which impose relatively large social costs on society, can be **limited** or prevented altogether. This might be done by using taxes (or subsidies) to bring prices more fully into line with social costs, or by direct restrictions on production and consumption.
3. It is sometimes suggested that there is likely to be **greater equality in the distribution of income and wealth** in centrally planned economies. Since the factors of production, with the exception of labour, are owned by the state, it is impossible for anyone to derive incomes from hiring out land and capital. Similarly, in a fully centrally planned economy, there are no private individuals who derive profits from combining the factors of production.
4. It is claimed that centrally planned economies are likely to be far **more stable than market economies**. Economic management is entirely in the hands of the government, and consumers have far less power to influence production. Thus, if consumer demand for a particular good falls, it will not necessarily lead to unemployment in the industry. The planners might initially maintain production at existing levels and gradually reduce it over time by not replacing workers who leave the industry through retirement, etc. Any surplus output accumulated as a result of this might be sold abroad at reduced prices. It is clear that this could not happen where production is undertaken for profit, since such a policy will undoubtedly reduce the profitability of an industry.

*Disadvantages of centrally planned economies*

1. There is general agreement among the critics of this system that an important disadvantage of centrally planned economies is the loss of consumer sovereignty. In other words the state decides what is to be produced, and consumers have much less influence over production than in market economies. Because of this there are likely to be shortages of certain commodities and surpluses of others, with no automatic mechanism for their removal.
2. There may be a tendency towards larger bureaucratic structures. It is government planning departments, rather than decentralised markets, which govern resource allocation in such economies. The opportunity cost of employing people to gather information, process it and formulate plans, etc., is the alternative output these people could otherwise have produced.
3. Another important criticism of centrally planned economies is that, because the profit motive is absent, organisations are less likely to operate efficiently. In market economies any increase in

the efficiency of firms will lower costs of production and increase profits. This provides a powerful incentive to increase efficiency, encourages the use of the latest advances in technology in the production process (i.e. process innovation) and the quest for new processes and products via research and development expenditure. However, production is not undertaken for profit in centrally planned economies, so that there is less incentive to increase efficiency. Indeed, it is sometimes suggested that, because any increase in efficiency will lead the planners to raise the target levels of output assigned to an industry, industries in such economies have an incentive *not* to increase efficiency. Whatever the truth of this, there is no doubt that a great deal of industry in centrally planned economies is considerably less efficient than industry in the West where the profit motive guides producers.

4. It is also suggested that **the absence of competition** in centrally planned economies is a disincentive to efficiency. There is less competition among firms in such economies, since each firm simply responds to the instructions it receives from the planners. So long as planners issue instructions for the continued production of any good or service this will be provided, even if firms make a loss, that is, costs of production exceed sales revenue. Any loss that does arise will be underwritten by the state. The absence of competition might therefore discourage moves towards greater efficiency which, in a competitive market economy, would be necessary for the firm to survive. The ultimate sanction against inefficient firms in a market economy is that if they do not earn profits they will eventually be forced into liquidation.
5. There is evidence that, while high and stable levels of employment exist in certain Comecon countries, this is achieved by overmanning and inefficiency in the allocation of resources. Indeed the problem is exacerbated because factory managers tend to hoard labour partly because targets are often raised suddenly and without warning.
6. Price controls are frequently used to achieve greater equality. However, relatively low prices encourage over-consumption in relation to the optimum level and this is one of the main reasons for shortages, for example of foodstuffs in many Eastern-bloc countries. Here again the result is inefficiency in the allocation of resources. The problem is further compounded in some Eastern-bloc countries because inefficiency in production means that a great deal of agricultural produce rots in the fields before it even reaches the market.

There is a another problem. Shortages create a demand for imports, but allowing the free import of goods and services is likely to be inconsistent with the plan for the economy. Hence trade is likely to be restricted in centrally planned economies and, as we shall see in chapter 16, international trade has an important effect on the efficiency with which resources are used and therefore on the growth of living standards.

These disadvantages are reflected in relatively low living standards in some Eastern-bloc countries.

## Reform in Eastern Europe

The widespread reforms currently taking place in Eastern Europe suggest that central planning has been discredited as an economic system. Shortages of many goods and the relatively slow growth of living standards compared to rates of growth achieved in the West have increased pressure for change. These difficulties have made Eastern Europe particularly receptive to Mr Gorbachev's ideas of *glasnost* (greater openness) and *perestroika* (restructuring of the Soviet economy).

There is a shortage of empirical material relating to Eastern Europe but it seems that a major problem in these countries is low investment in capital equipment (machinery, etc.) and low productivity (output per unit of input). In planned economies growth of output has been achieved largely by increasing inputs, with less emphasis on changing the techniques of production than occurs in the West where the substitution of capital for labour is common. This is a major reason for low productivity in East European countries and identifies increased investment as a major feature of the reform process. However, while higher productivity is a major aim of reform, other major aims include eliminating shortages and queues by producing more of those goods and services which consumers demand and improving the quality of output.

The reforms introduced are quite far-reaching and can be summarised under the following headings:

- *Decentralisation of decision-making.* At the core of the reform process is the decentralisation of decision-making with individual enterprises being given more responsibility to decide what to produce and how to produce it so as to encourage greater responsiveness. Remember that one of the advantages of the price mechanism is that it encourages firms to respond quickly and efficiently to changes in consumer demands. However, enterprise managers will only take economically efficient decisions if they operate in an 'enterprise culture'. To achieve this, measures are being introduced to allow liquidation of enterprises, and state subsidies are being reduced to ensure that managers are aware of market prices for inputs, labour and their output.

- *Self-financing enterprises.* In addition, to encourage greater efficiency, enterprises are to become self-financing and will have more influence in determining output levels and the price at which their output is sold. However, this does not imply that the price mechanism will operate freely. It is simply intended that henceforth prices will more closely reflect private costs of production. In order that enterprises can become more self-financing, all reforming countries have plans for restructuring their banking systems to give banks greater freedom in deciding what loans to make and to ensure that interest rates are more closely influenced by supply and demand.
- *Increased foreign trade.* Foreign trade is also to be encouraged by an easing of regulations, with the aim of increasing exports. Joint ventures with foreign companies are to be allowed. One reason for this is of course to encourage increased investment but it is also anticipated that such investment will lead to the introduction of technologically superior equipment than is currently available within Eastern Europe.

## The mixed economy

We have seen that both free enterprise and centrally planned economies have their respective advantages and disadvantages. For this reason neither is found in its extreme form in the economies of the world. Instead all economies are more properly described as *mixed economies* in which some resources are allocated through the state and some through the market. The difference is the extent to which resources are allocated through the state and through the market. The main functions performed by the government in a mixed economy include the following, but remember the extent of government involvement will differ from country to country.

- *The provision of public goods.* This is a very important role for the government because certain public goods are essential for the operation of developed economies. However, we have already seen that public goods would not be provided through the market because there is no way of avoiding the problem of *free-riders*. In other words, once a public good is available there is no way of denying its use to those who refuse to pay. Such goods must therefore be provided through the state and be made available to everyone without distinction, or they will not be provided at all.
- *The provision of merit goods.* As well as providing public goods, the government also undertakes to provide many other goods and services which add to the quality of life but which are not pure public goods. Merit goods do not possess the same characteristics as public goods. They could therefore be provided through the

market mechanism. However, many are provided free of charge through public bodies because their consumption confers relatively large social benefits on society which far outweigh their cost of provision. Examples of merit goods include state education, public health care, municipal housing and so on.

*Control of the economy*

One of the most important functions governments now perform is that of economic management to achieve certain economic objectives, such as a high and stable level of employment and a relatively low rate of inflation. Governments attempt to achieve their aims by using a variety of policies, such as varying the rate of interest, the money supply, the rates of taxation and government expenditure (See Ch. 19).

- *Redistribution of income.* Governments intervene in economies to create greater equality in the distribution of income and wealth than would otherwise exist. The most obvious way in which this is done is through a system of taxation where the higher income earners are taxed more heavily than the lower income earners. Greater equality could also be achieved by the government providing certain goods free of charge or at a subsidised rate. Thus, for example, medical care is provided free of charge in the UK, whilst drugs issued on prescription are heavily subsidised. Finally, greater equality might be achieved through a social security system which provides payments from the state for the sick and aged, as well as for the unemployed and low income earners.
- Modifying the system. Governments sometimes place taxes and subsidies on goods and services to influence their prices and hence the volumes produced and consumed. A tax on a product usually raises its price and so reduces consumption and hence production, while a subsidy usually lowers its price and stimulates consumption and hence production.

## Cost-benefit analysis

In mixed economies governments sometimes use *cost-benefit analysis* to assist in their expenditure decisions. This is a technique which attempts to assess the full social cost or social benefit that society will derive from a particular project. This has a clear advantage over a simple consideration of private costs and benefits since externalities are also considered by assigning an estimated money value to their worth. If, after all costs and benefits have been considered, social benefits outweigh social cost, society will apparently benefit if the project goes ahead.

However, the technique is fraught with difficulties. An obvious problem is that of estimating the value of externalities. Whatever figure is assigned to these, it represents a value judgement and is not necessarily accurate. Another problem is that benefits usually occur in the future whereas costs are incurred in the present. Economists use the process of discounting to present value (see pp. 110–111) to compare future benefits with current costs, but the choice of the appropriate discount rate is a value judgement. A higher discount rate will reduce the present value of future benefits and vice versa.

## Test your understanding

1. What indicates the existence of shortages in:
   (a) market economies?
   (b) centrally planned economies?
2. What is meant by a 'Pareto optimum' allocation of resources and why is the concept important?
3. What factors might prevent the price mechanism from achieving a 'Pareto optimium' allocation of resources?
4. Classify the following as either private goods, public goods or merit goods. Explain your classification.
   (a) National defence.
   (b) A season ticket for a football club.
   (c) A motorway.
   (d) A motor car.
   (e) Public libraries.
5. Why is it argued that the price mechanism leads to an optimum allocation of resources but the operation of price controls does not?
6. In a market economy, which of the following would lead to a change in the allocation of resources?
   (a) A change in the distribution of income.
   (b) An increase in negative externalities.
   (c) An increase in unemployment.
7. Free market economies are free of what?
8. What is planned in a centrally planned economy?
9. Why does an attempt to fully plan an economy have an opportunity cost?

# 3 Production

## The factors of production

Factors of production are usually thought of as *resources* or *inputs*. Anything which is used in the process of production is therefore a factor of production. For analytical purposes economists have found it convenient to classify all factors of production as either land, labour, capital or enterprise. Each is considered in turn.

### *Land*

Land was defined by early economists to include 'all the free gifts of nature'. It therefore includes the surface area of the planet as well as its mineral and ore deposits. As a factor of production, land has special characteristics. It has no cost of production, is completely fixed in supply, that is, cannot be reproduced, and cannot be moved from one place to another.

### *Labour*

As a factor of production, labour is defined as the physical and mental human effort used to create goods and services. The supply of labour to an economy is therefore very important in determining the level of output an economy is able to produce and depends on such factors as size of the population, length of the working week, number of hours worked per day and so on. However, the quality of labour is also important and this depends on general health and well-being, as well as on education and training. More is said about the supply of labour to an economy in Chapter 5.

### *Capital*

Capital is defined by economists as any man-made asset which is used in the production of further goods and services. In general, it is the use to which a particular asset is put which determines whether it is capital. For example, a motor car used by a salesman would be classed as capital, but a car used for social and domestic purposes would be classed as a consumer good.

Economists distinguish between *fixed* capital and *circulating* capital. The former can be used time and again in the production process and therefore includes such things as machinery and factory buildings, the road and rail networks, hospitals and educational buildings and so on, whereas the latter, circulating capital (also commonly known as working capital), consists of raw materials and work in progress, and can only be used once.

Capital is created from scarce resources and therefore has an opportunity cost. In order to create more capital it is necessary to consume less so that resources can be released for the production of capital. In other words, in order to accumulate capital a community must forego current consumption, that is, the community as a whole must save. This fact is expressed in the often quoted phrase, *capital accumulation depends on abstention from current consumption.*

### *Enterprise*

This factor of production is more commonly referred to as the *entrepreneur*. The entrepreneur performs two important roles:

hiring and combining the other factors of production, risk-taking by producing goods and services *in anticipation* of demand.

## Production and productivity

The terms *production* and *productivity* are frequently confused. Production simply refers to creation of output and includes any economic activity which uses scarce resources to create that output. Economists therefore make no distinction between the production of goods and the production of services. To the economist then, the chain of production is complete when output is sold to the ultimate consumer. Productivity, on the other hand, refers to the amount of output produced per unit of input. For example, labour productivity is measured as average product per worker.

## Division of labour

Division of labour refers to the way in which jobs are broken down into their various component parts so that each worker performs only a small part of the entire operation. Because of this, division of labour is often referred to as *specialisation*. In the production of many goods and services, each worker specialises in a single task or small group of related tasks.

Division of labour is widespread in industry and its major advantage is that it leads to higher productivity than is possible in the absence of specialistaion. There are many reasons for this but the main one is undoubtedly the fact that specialisation of labour makes possible the use of specialised units of capital. In the motor industry for example, we see the use of assembly lines and a great deal of work carried out by robots. Society benefits considerably from this because higher levels of productivity make possible lower prices.

Division of labour clearly makes mass production possible, but for this to be profitable a mass market must exist. Indeed the major factor limiting the division of labour is the size of the market. Where the market is small there is less scope for division of labour. Many factors might limit the size of the market. In the case of certain goods, such as luxury cars, the market is limited by the size of consumers' incomes. In other cases transport costs might be high in relation to the value of the product so that only local markets are served.

## Mobility of the factors of production

The benefits of specialisation are clear. However, a major problem with increased specialisation is that it is likely to reduce the *mobility* of labour. Economists identify two types of mobility: *geographical mobility* and *occupational mobility*. The former refers to a physical movement of a factor of production from one geographical location to another whereas the latter refers to a factor of production moving from one occupation to another. Clearly when labour possesses specialised skills it will not be easy to move from one job to another as the pattern of consumer expenditure changes. This is an important point. Remember from Chapter 2 that a disadvantage of the price mechanism is that changes in consumer demands can sometimes lead to unemployment.

This partly explains why a high degree of labour mobility is considered important. The more mobile the labour force the easier it will adapt to changing circumstances. For example, if demand for a particular good falls and demand for a different good simultaneously increases, the more mobile the labour force, the easier it will be for workers to transfer from one job to the other.

However, the employment of labour is not the only important issue. Over time the techniques of production change and only if the labour force is mobile will it be possible to take full advantage of changes in technology. This is important because using the latest technology is an important means of increasing productivity. This, as we shall see on p. 220, is a major reason why the standard of living increases. It also has an important influence on the competitiveness of exports and this again has important implications for the standard of living in a particular country.

## The short run and the long run

When considering the causes of changes in output, economists frequently distinguish between the *short run* and the *long run*. These are not fixed time periods, but instead are defined in terms of the time required to bring about changes in the input of various factors of production.

Specifically, the *short run* exists when there is *at least one* fixed factor of production. In other words, the short run refers to a period of time when it is possible to vary the input of some factors of production but impossible to vary the input of at least one other factor. For example, sometimes it is impossible for firms to recruit skilled labour until more workers have been trained, but they usually have little difficulty in recruiting unskilled workers. It is important to note that any factor of production can be fixed in the short run. In contrast, the *long run* is the time period required to bring about a change in the input of *all* factors of production. In other words, there are no fixed factors of production in the long run.

## Total, average and marginal product

When firms change the input of factors of production the effect on output can be measured in different ways. In its own way each is important for the information it reveals. There are three main concepts to consider:

1. *Total product.* Total product or total output is simply the amount of output a firm produces within a given period of time such as 1,000 units per week. When firms change the input of factors of production there will almost certainly be a change in total product.
2. *Average product.* This is usually measured in relation to a particular factor of production such as labour or capital. Thus the average product of labour is measured as Total product/Number of workers. For example, if the total product of the firm is 1,000 units per week and ten workers are employed, average product per worker is 1,000/10, that is, 100 units per week. Changes in average product are referred to as changes in productivity and we shall see on pp. 27–29 that changes in productivity have an important impact on the firm's costs of production.
3. *Marginal product.* This is the *rate at which total product* changes as an additional unit of a *variable factor* is employed. For instance, the marginal product of labour is usually measured as the change in total product when *one more* worker is employed. Thus, if total product when the firm employs ten workers is 1,000 units per week, and this rises to 1,080 units per week when the firm employes an additional worker, the marginal product of the last worker is 80 units per week.

## The law of variable proportions

The effect on output of changing the input of variable factors can be explained in terms of the *law of variable proportions*. This law can be broken down into two component laws. These are the *law of increasing returns* and the *law of diminishing returns*. Each is considered in turn.

1. *The law of increasing returns.* This law states that, in the early stages of production, as successive units of a variable factor are combined with a fixed factor, both marginal and average product will initially rise. In other words, total output will rise *more than in proportion* to the rise in inputs.
2. *The law of diminishing returns.* This law simply states that as successive units of a variable factor are combined with a fixed factor, after a certain point both marginal product and average product will fall. In other words, total output will rise *less than in proportion* to the rise in inputs. Eventually total output will even diminish as marginal product becomes negative.

*Table 3.1*

| No of workers | Total product | Average product | Marginal product |
|---|---|---|---|
| 1 | 4 | 4 | 4 |
| 2 | 10 | 5 | 6 |
| 3 | 20 | 6.7 | 10 |
| 4 | 35 | 8.8 | 15 |
| 5 | 50 | 10 | 15 |
| 6 | 60 | 10 | 10 |
| 7 | 65 | 9.3 | 5 |
| 8 | 65 | 8.1 | 0 |
| 9 | 55 | 6.1 | −10 |

### An illustration of the laws of returns

The changing nature of returns to the variable factor can be seen in Table 3.1. We assume that an increasing amount of labour works on a fixed quantity of land, that each worker is homogeneous, that is, identical to all other workers, and that the techniques of production are unchanged.

It can be seen that up to the employment of the fourth worker marginal product is rising. When marginal product is rising, total product is rising at a *faster rate* because each additional worker employed makes possible an increase in total product that is greater than that achieved from the preceding worker. This means that total product rises *more than proportionately* and therefore the firm is experiencing *increasing returns.*

With the employment of the fifth worker the situation changes, because marginal product is constant. Employing the fifth worker results in an increase in output that is exactly the same as the increase in output that occurs when the fourth worker is employed. In these circumstances we say that the firm experiences *constant returns* because total output rises at a *constant rate.*

After the employment of the sixth worker marginal product begins to fall. This implies that the *rate* at which total output rises, as more workers are employed, begins to fall. In these circumstances we say that the firm experiences diminishing returns.

The concepts of increasing, constant and marginal returns are illustrated in Figure 3.1 which is based on Table 3.1.

### Returns and the division of labour

The laws of returns discussed and illustrated above are widely known. However, we have not yet explained the *causes* of increasing and diminishing returns. In fact, increasing returns are due to the *division of labour*. It was suggested earlier that the major advantage of division of labour is that it makes possible an increase in productivity. If productivity does rise as more workers are employed, this implies that output per worker increases. Increasing returns therefore stem

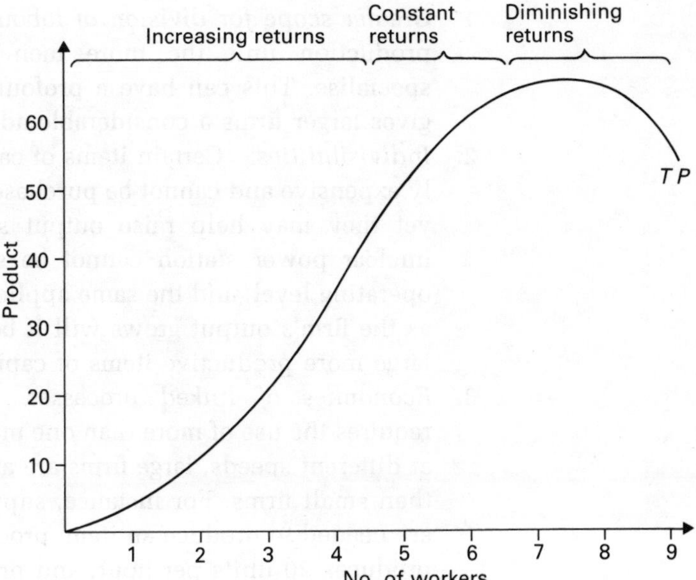


*Figure 3.1* The behaviour of total product as more workers are employed

from increased specialisation. Conversely, when productivity falls as a result of employing more workers, the implication is that there is some limit to the gains from specialisation. Falling productivity therefore indicates that the proportion in which the factors are employed has become less favourable.

## Returns to scale

In the long run, there are no fixed factors and firms can vary the input of *all* factors of production. When this happens there has been a change in the *scale of production*. If a change in the scale of production leads to a *more than proportional* change in output, firms are subject to *increasing returns to scale*. For example, if all factor inputs are increased by 10 per cent and output grows by more than this, firms experience increasing returns to scale. These are more generally referred to as *economies of scale*.

Despite this fairly precise definition, firms are most unlikely to vary equi-proportionately the input of all factors of production. A more useful definition of economies of scale is those aspects of increasing size, brought about by a change in all factor inputs, which lead to falling average costs, that is, cost per unit produced (see p. 28). Diseconomies of scale are those aspects of increasing size, brought about by an increase in all factor inputs, which lead to rising average costs.

## Sources of economies of scale

The sources of economies of scale are many and varied, but they are usually grouped into certain categories.

### Technical economies

These are common in manufacturing, since they relate to the scale of the production unit. There are several reasons why costs might fall as the scale of production increases, including:

1. *Greater scope for division of labour.* The larger the size of the production unit the more men and machines are able to specialise. This can have a profound effect on productivity and gives larger firms a considerable advantage over smaller firms.
2. *Indivisibilities.* Certain items of capital expenditure are relatively expensive and cannot be purchased in smaller or cheaper units, yet they may help raise output substantially. For example, a nuclear power station cannot be scaled down below a certain operating level, and the same applies to a car assembly line. Only as the firm's output grows will it be able to afford and use these large more productive items of capital.
3. *Economies of linked processes.* Most manufacturing output requires the use of more than one machine. Where machines work at different speeds, large firms are able to operate more efficiently than small firms. For instance, suppose two processes, A and B, are needed to produce an item; process A needs a machine which produces 20 units per hour, and process B a machine producing 50 units per hour. Only if output is as high as 100 units can both machines be fully used – with five machines in process A and two machines in process B. It is likely that, because of the cost involved, small firms will be unable to purchase machines in sufficient quantities to achieve full utilisation of machinery.

**Marketing economies**

Marketing embraces many activities, but the main economies of scale from marketing include:

1. *Economies from bulk purchases.* Large-scale production requires the large-scale input of raw materials. When firms place large orders for raw materials, they are able to negotiate bulk discounts which substantially reduce the cost of each unit purchased.
2. *Economies from bulk distribution.* Where large quantities of output are to be transported, firms can often gain economies. For example, the average cost of transporting a given quantity of oil by sea is much lower when a single super tanker is used than when several smaller tankers are used. Similarly, the increasing use of articulated lorries is evidence that it is cheaper to transport in bulk when using the road network.

**Financial economies**

Large firms are frequently able to obtain finance more easily and on more favourable terms than smaller firms. Even a small reduction in interest rates charged on borrowing yields substantial savings where relatively large sums are involved.

**Risk-bearing economies**

A number of advantages can lead to large firms experiencing risk-bearing economies. However, the underlying factor is that large firms frequently engage in a range of *diverse* activities, so that a fall in the return from any one activity does not threaten the viability of the whole firm.

**Managerial economies**

This source of improved efficiency stems from the fact that large firms are able to offer the rewards necessary to attract the most capable staff whose ability and expertise may well lead to lower average costs.

**Sources of diseconomies of scale**

While increases in scale frequently confer advantages on firms, in many cases there is a limit to the gains from growth. In other words, there is an optimum level of capacity and increases in scale beyond this level lead to diseconomies of scale which manifest themselves in rising average costs of production. Diseconomies of scale have several sources including:

1. *Managerial difficulties.* There is no doubt that the increasing complexity of managing large-scale enterprises is a major source of inefficiency as firms grow beyond a certain size. As firms grow it becomes increasingly difficult to control and coordinate the various activities of planning, product design, sales promotion and so on. This is especially true where a diverse range of products is produced.
2. *Low morale.* Organisations which employ large numbers of people sometimes suffer from low morale, perhaps because individuals feel they have little influence on decisions in large firms. It is thought that this encourages high rates of absenteeism and poor punctuality. It may also lead to a lack of interest in the job which inhibits the growth of productivity and leads to a higher incidence of spoiled work.
3. *Higher input prices.* As the scale of production increases firms require more inputs, and increasing demand for these might bid up factor prices. Additionally, when firms produce on a large scale and rely on full capacity utilisation of capital equipment to gain economies of scale, the power of trade unions is substantially increased. This might enable unions to negotiate wage awards in excess of the growth of productivity, thus increasing average labour costs.

**Test your understanding**

1. Who is the entrepreneur in a large corporation?
2. Capital accumulation is impossible without ____. What is the missing word?
3. What are the main functions of the entrepreneur?
4. Why is there less scope for division of labour in television repair than in television assembly?
5. The more specialised a factor of production the greater its productivity but the lower its mobility. Why is this?
6. Why does the size of the market limit the scope for division of labour?
7. If marginal product is falling what is happening to average product?

8. If average product is rising what is happening to marginal product?
9. If marginal product is constant what is happening to total product?
10. A firm reduces the size of the working week from 40 hours to 32 hours, increases the number of workers employed by 10 per cent and as a result experiences a rise in total weekly output from 1,000 units to 1,050 units.
    (a) What happens to productivity?
    (b) If the hourly rate of pay is unchanged, what happens to labour costs per unit?
11. The following table shows how the weekly output of a firm varies with different combinations of labour and capital.

Output per week (thousands)

| | | Units of labour | | |
|---|---|---|---|---|
| | | 1 | 2 | 3 |
| Units of capital | 3 | 36 | 60 | 80 |
| | 2 | 22 | 38 | 52 |
| | 1 | 10 | 18 | 24 |

In each of the following cases, choose the word which correctly completes the sentence. This firm is experiencing:
    (a) increasing/decreasing returns to capital,
    (b) increasing/decreasing returns to labour,
    (c) economies/diseconomies of scale.
12. Complete the following table by inserting the missing values:

| No. of workers employed | Total product | Marginal product | Average product |
|---|---|---|---|
| 1 | 4 | | |
| 2 | | 5 | |
| 3 | 16 | | |
| 4 | | | 7 |
| 5 | | 10 | |
| 6 | | | 6.67 |

After the employment of which worker does the firm experience diminishing:
    (a) marginal returns?
    (b) average returns?

13. Which of the following would the economist classify as production?
(a) Retailing.
(b) Car assembly.
(c) Consumption.

# 4 Costs of production

## The short run

In the short run it is possible to categorise the firm's costs as either fixed costs or variable costs. Clearly fixed costs are incurred on fixed factors of production and variable costs on variable factors.

### Fixed costs

Because it is impossible to vary the input of fixed factors in the short run, fixed costs do not change as output increases. Additionally, it is important to realise that fixed costs are incurred even when the firm's output is zero. Fixed costs include mortgage or rent on premises, hire purchase repayments, local authority rates, insurance charges, depreciation on assets and so on. None of these costs is directly related to output and they are all costs which are still incurred in the short run, even if the firm produces no output. They are therefore sometimes referred to as *indirect costs* or *overheads*.

Because total fixed costs are constant with respect to output, *average fixed costs*, that is, total fixed costs divided by output, decline continuously as output expands (see Table 4.1 page 29).

Diagrammatically, the behaviour of total fixed costs and average fixed costs as output expands are shown in Figure 4.1.

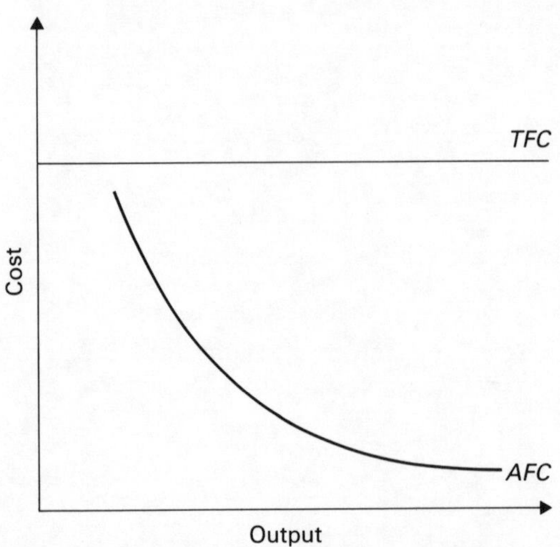


*Figure 4.1* The behaviour of total fixed costs and average fixed costs as output changes

## Variable costs

Unlike fixed costs, variable costs are directly related to output. When firms produce no output they incur no variable costs, but as output is expanded variable costs are incurred. Because they vary directly with output these costs are sometimes referred to as *direct costs* or *supplementary costs*. Examples of these costs include costs of raw materials and power to drive machinery, wages of direct labour and so on.

## The relationship between marginal costs and variable costs

Marginal cost is the change in total cost when one more unit is produced, and is therefore entirely a variable cost. Because in the short run only the input of variable factors can be changed, it is clear that the sum of the marginal costs of producing each unit equals the total variable cost of production. Reference to Table 4.1 on page 29 will confirm this.

Additionally, although variable costs vary directly with output, they are unlikely to vary proportionately because of the effect of increasing and diminishing returns. Figure 4.2 shows the general shape of the total variable cost curve.

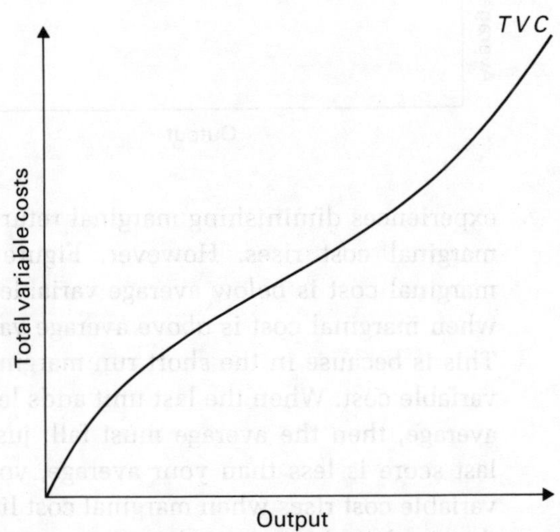


Figure 4.2 The behaviour of total variable costs as output changes

It is clear that total variable costs at first rise less than proportionately as output expands and the firm experiences increasing returns. Subsequently, as the firm experiences diminishing returns, total variable costs rise more than proportionately as output expands.

The changes in total variable costs brought about by increasing and diminishing returns also imply changes in *average variable costs*. The relationship between average and marginal product and average variable and marginal cost is shown in Figure 4.3.

When the firm experiences increasing marginal returns, marginal product rises and marginal cost falls. Conversely, when the firm

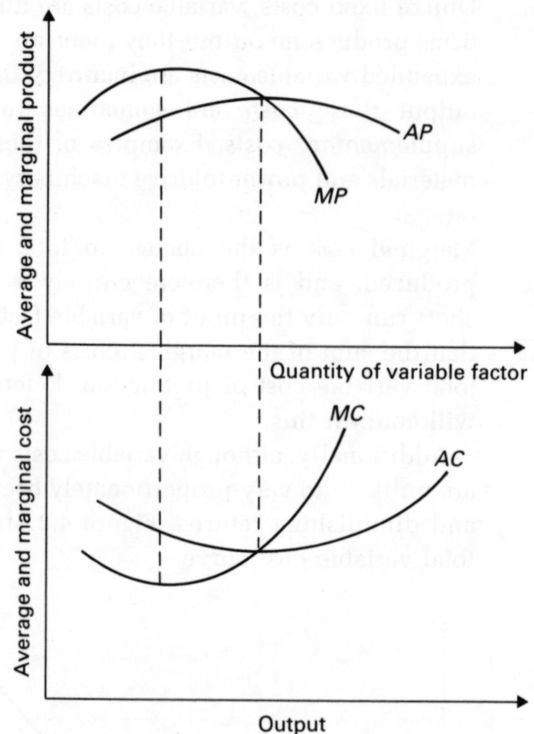


*Figure 4.3* The effect of changes in marginal and average product on marginal and average cost

experiences diminishing marginal returns, marginal product falls and marginal cost rises. However, Figure 4.3 also shows that, when marginal cost is *below* average variable cost, the latter is falling, and when marginal cost is *above* average variable cost, the latter is rising. This is because in the short run marginal cost is the *addition* to total variable cost. When the last unit adds less to the total than the current average, then the average must fall; just as in any game, when your last score is less than your average, your average must fall. Average variable cost rises when marginal cost lies above it. The implication of this is that the marginal cost curve cuts the *average variable cost* curve at its *minimum* point.

Similar reasoning explains why average product rises when marginal product is above it and falls when marginal product is below it, and why the marginal product curve cuts the average product curve at its maximum point.

## Average total costs of production

These are more generally referred to simply as average costs, and for any given level of output they are obtained by dividing the total cost of producing that output by the level of output itself. We know that *average fixed costs* fall continuously as output expands and that initially, because of increasing average returns, *average variable costs* fall. It follows that *average total costs* will initially fall. However, beyond a certain point average variable costs will begin to rise because of diminishing average returns, and, once the rise in average variable costs more than offsets the fall in average fixed costs, average total costs will rise. This is clearly shown in Figure 4.4 which also shows that the marginal cost curve cuts the *average total cost curve* at the *minimum* point for exactly the same reason that it cuts the average variable cost curve at the minimum point.

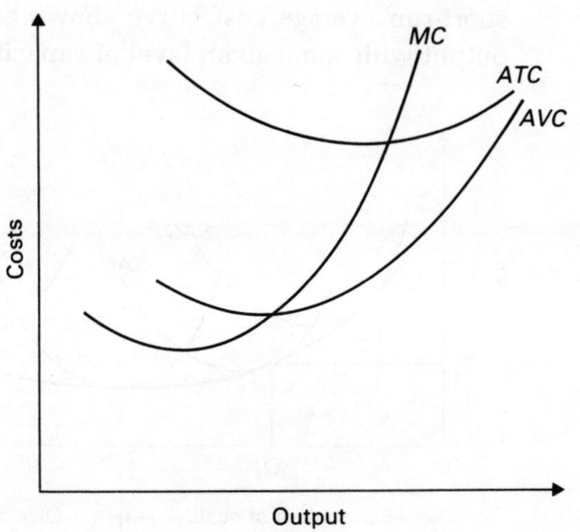


*Figure 4.4* The behaviour of costs as output changes

Table 4.1 provides an arithmetic example of how costs change in the short run as output expands.

*Table 4.1*

| Output | Fixed cost | Total cost | Total cost | Marginal cost | Average variable cost | Average fixed cost | Average total cost |
|---|---|---|---|---|---|---|---|
| 0 | 100 | 0 | 100 | | 0 | | |
| 1 | 100 | 50 | 150 | 50 | 50 | 100 | 150 |
| 2 | 100 | 95 | 195 | 45 | 47.5 | 50 | 97.5 |
| 3 | 100 | 135 | 235 | 40 | 45 | 33.3 | 78.3 |
| 4 | 100 | 165 | 265 | 30 | 41.3 | 25 | 66.3 |
| 5 | 100 | 180 | 280 | 15 | 36 | 20 | 56 |
| 6 | 100 | 190 | 290 | 10 | 31.7 | 16.7 | 48.3 |
| 7 | 100 | 195 | 295 | 5 | 27.9 | 14.3 | 42.1 |
| 8 | 100 | 205 | 305 | 10 | 25.7 | 12.5 | 38.1 |
| 9 | 100 | 225 | 325 | 20 | 25 | 11.1 | 36.1 |
| 10 | 100 | 265 | 365 | 40 | 26.5 | 10 | 36.5 |
| 11 | 100 | 325 | 425 | 60 | 29.5 | 9.1 | 38.6 |
| 12 | 100 | 410 | 510 | 85 | 34.2 | 8.3 | 42.5 |

*Note:* Because of rounding AFC + AVC might not always equal ATC.

## The long run

In the short run the existence of fixed factors means that firms can only increase output by increasing the input of variable factors. In other words, firms have limited capacity. However, in the long run, it is possible for firms to increase capacity. The most obvious reason for doing this is to make possible a greater level of output. However, when firms gain economies of scale, they might also increase capacity because this will lead to lower average costs of production. Figure 4.5 shows the effect on costs of changes in capacity. Each SAC curve is a short-run average cost curve showing how average cost varies with output with some *given* level of capacity (i.e. the fixed factor capital).

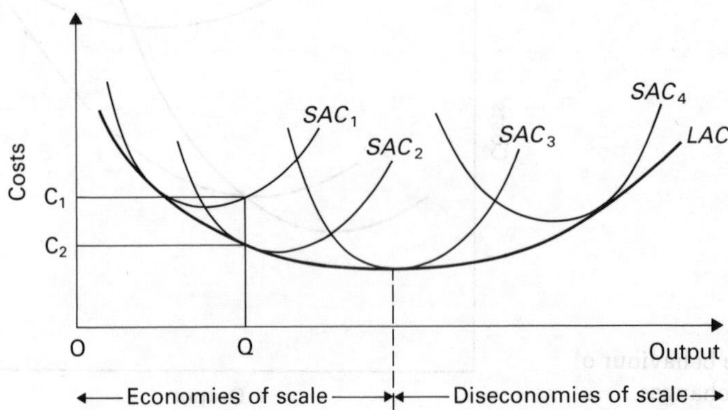


*Figure 4.5*

If we consider an output OQ, it is clear that the firm can produce this with the level of capacity implied in $SAC_1$ at an average cost of $OC_1$ per unit. Alternatively, it could increase capacity to the level implied in $SAC_2$ giving an average cost of producing OQ units of $OC_2$. By increasing capacity the firm lowers its average cost of producing a *given* output.

More generally, by adjusting capacity in the long run, firms can minimise the cost of producing any *given* level of output. Indeed, the firm's long-run average cost curve (*LAC*) shows the minimum average cost of producing any given level of output after adjustments in capacity. It is therefore tangential to all the short-run average cost curves. For this reason the long-run average cost curve is sometimes referred to as an 'envelope curve', because it supports an infinite number of short-run average cost curves each reflecting a different level of capacity.

## The least-cost combination

All production requires the input of resources or factors of production. However, these can often be combined in a variety of ways, sometimes using more of one factor relative to another, and vice versa (see page 1). Profit-maximising firms, that is, firms which aim to make as large a profit as possible, will combine the factors of production so as to minimise the cost of producing *any given output*.

So far, we have implicitly assumed that firms will aim to produce any given level of output in the cheapest possible way. This is a perfectly valid assumption when the ultimate aim of firms is to maximise profit. The combination of factor inputs which minimises the cost of producing any given level of output is referred to as the *least-cost combination*. It is achieved when firms have adjusted their inputs in such a way that, for any factor of production, the ratio of marginal product to price is exactly equal to the ratio of marginal product to price of all other factors of production. In other words, when:

$$\frac{\text{Marginal product of factor A}}{\text{Price of A}} = \frac{\text{Marginal product of factor B}}{\text{Price of B}}$$

and so on, for all factor inputs.

When this condition is satisfied the last pound spent on each factor input yields exactly the same return in all cases. It follows that the cost of producing *any particular output* is at a minimum when this condition is satisfied. It would only be possible to reduce the total cost of producing that level of output if the last unit of one variable factor added more to total product than the last unit of any other variable factor, *per pound spent*. This is impossible when the marginal product/price ratios of all factor inputs are equal.

It follows from this that any change in the productivity or the price of a factor of production will lead to factor substitution. For example, if a firm uses two factors, labour and capital, and the price of labour rises while all other things remain equal, firms will cut back on their use of labour and increase their use of capital. This factor substitution will continue until equality between the marginal product/price ratios of both factors is restored.

## Deciding whether to increase capacity

An important decision firms are often forced to take is whether to increase capacity in response to an increase in demand for their product. The most fundamental issue here is whether the increase in sales is expected to be permanent, or whether it is simply a temporary increase caused by exceptional factors. Only in the former case will the firm have to decide whether to increase capacity by building an additional plant.

If the firm's aim is to maximise profit, its decision about whether to expand capacity will depend on the behaviour of costs as output expands. In the short run the crucial factor is whether the firm experiences increasing returns or diminishing returns as output expands. If the firm is currently experiencing increasing average returns, average cost will be falling and in these circumstances there might be no cost advantage to the firm in changing the level of capacity. The firm is more likely to seek ways of raising output *within* the current level of capacity. This might involve expanding its existing plants, in the sense of using more labour, raw materials, etc. to raise output.

However, if the firm is experiencing diminishing average returns, average cost will be rising. Diminishing returns set in because it is impossible to increase the input of fixed factors in the short run. In the long run, however, it is possible to increase the input of all factors of production, and the option of increasing capacity by building an additional plant might well be the option the firm chooses. This will make economic sense if the increase in capacity leads to lower average costs of production, that is, if the firm experiences economies of scale.

## Test your understanding

1. What is meant by capital depreciation and why does it occur?
2. Given that TC = total cost, complete the following: $TC_n - TC_{n-1} =$
3. How are fixed costs defined?
4. Why are there no fixed costs in the long run?
5. Classify the following as fixed or variable costs in the short run: (i) Insurance charges, (ii) depreciation of capital, (iii) raw materials, (iv) electricity, (v) waste disposal.
6. Typically we assume that the firm's marginal cost is 'U' shaped. Why is this?
7. If marginal cost falls as output expands, what happens to total cost as output expands?
8. Complete the following table.

| Output | Total cost | Fixed cost | Variable cost | Average total cost | Average variable cost | Marginal cost |
|---|---|---|---|---|---|---|
| 0 | | 100 | | | | |
| 1 | | | | | | 40 |
| 2 | | | | 85 | | |
| 3 | | | 90 | | | |
| 4 | | | | | 25 | |
| 5 | | | 120 | | | |
| 6 | | | | | | 50 |

At what level of output does the firm begin to experience diminishing marginal returns?

# 5 Demand, supply and price determination

### The market

This chapter is about the determination of market prices. A market can be defined as any arrangement which brings buyers and sellers of particular products into contact. The collective actions of buyers for a particular product establishes the market demand for that product, and the collective actions of sellers establishes the market supply. The interaction of these forces of demand and supply, i.e. market forces, establishes the market price for any given product.

### Demand

In economics the term *demand* has a particular meaning. It does *not* simply mean the desire to possess something. This desire to possess something must be backed up by the willingness and ability to pay for it. To emphasise this economists refer to *effective demand*. However, to say that effective demand for something is a thousand units has little meaning. It is essential that we know how many units are demanded at a given price within a given period of time.

### Utility and consumer equilibrium

Utility simply means satisfaction derived from consumption. It is important in any consideration of consumer demand because we assume, quite reasonably, that only those commodities which give satisfaction will be demanded. Additionally, economists assume that consumers 'act rationally' and this implies that they aim to maximise their total utility, that is, gain as much utility as possible, given the limited income they possess and the prices they face.

### The law of diminishing marginal utility

The *law of diminishing marginal utility* simply states that, as consumption of a product increases, each successive unit consumed confers less utility than the previous unit. In other words, as consumption increases, marginal utility falls.

### Consumer equilibrium

Equilibrium can be thought of as a state that exists when there is *no tendency to change*. In the present context equilibrium will exist when consumers achieve their aim, that is, maximise satisfaction given their limited income. When this is the case they will have no incentive to change the quantities of the different goods and services they currently purchase because to do so will result in a reduction in the amount of satisfaction they receive from their purchases. In other words consumer equilibrium exists when a consumer *cannot* increase his total utility by reallocating his expenditure. This occurs when the following condition is satisfied:

$$\frac{MU_A}{P_A} = \frac{MU_B}{P_B} = \ldots \frac{MU_n}{P_n}$$

This condition simply implies that consumer equilibrium exists when the ratios of marginal utility and price are equal for all goods consumed.

When this condition is satisfied, it is impossible for the consumer to increase his total utility by rearranging his purchases because the last pound spent on each good yields the same addition to total utility in all cases. This must maximise total utility because, for example, if the last pound spent on product B yielded *more* utility than the last pound spent on product A, then the consumer could increase his total utility by buying more of B and less of A. This is impossible when the ratios of marginal utility and price are equal, as is illustrated in Table 5.1. It is assumed that only two goods, A which costs £2 per unit and B which costs £4 per unit, are available, and that the consumer has a total budget of £18.

*Table 5.1*

| | Good A | | | Good B | | |
|---|---|---|---|---|---|---|
| Quantity consumed | Price (£) | Total utility | Marginal utility | Price (£) | Total utility | Marginal utility |
| 1 | 2 | 15 | 15 | 4 | 25 | 25 |
| 2 | 2 | 27 | 12 | 4 | 48 | 23 |
| 3 | 2 | 37 | 10 | 4 | 68 | 20 |
| 4 | 2 | 46 | 9 | 4 | 86 | 18 |
| 5 | 2 | 53 | 7 | 4 | 102 | 16 |
| 6 | 2 | 56 | 3 | 4 | 116 | 14 |
| 7 | 2 | 57 | 1 | 4 | 128 | 12 |
| 8 | 2 | 55 | − 2 | 4 | 139 | 11 |

Given the consumer's budget, the existing prices and the levels of utility available from consumption, equilibrium is achieved when three units of good A and three units of good B are purchased, i.e.

$$\frac{MU_A\ (10)}{P_A\ \ (2)} = \frac{MU_B\ (20)}{P_B\ \ (4)}$$

With a budget of £18 it is impossible to achieve a higher level of utility by varying the combination of A and B consumed. For example, if we bought one *less* B and two *more* A with the income released, total utility would fall from 105 to 101.

## The individual's demand curve

Once achieved, equilibrium can only be disturbed if there is a change in some factor that influences the level of satisfaction that can be achieved, such as a change in the consumer's income, a change in the prices of other goods and services available to consumers, a change in the range or quality of goods and services available and so on. However, since at any moment in time all factors that affect demand, other than price, are assumed to be constant, it is changes in price which are important to us at present. More specifically the question we have to answer is, if all other things remain unchanged, how will a change in the price of one good affect the amount of that good a consumer purchases?

We can answer this question by looking again at Table 5.1. Using the information given here let us consider what would happen to the amount of good B consumed if there was a reduction in its price from £3 per unit to £2 per unit, and all other things remained unchanged. Because the consumer's aim is to maximise utility, his reaction to the price reduction is predictable. He will simply rearrange his purchases so as to achieve equilibrium following the price reduction. Applying the equilibrium condition:

$$\frac{MU_A}{P_A} = \frac{MU_B}{P_B}$$

leads to the conclusion that (with income still £18) the consumer will increase his consumption of good B to seven units, and cut consumption of A to two units. When this is done the equilibrium condition is satisfied because:

$$\frac{MU_A}{P_A}\frac{(12)}{(\ 2)} = \frac{MU_B}{P_B}\frac{(12)}{(\ 2)}$$

This rearrangement of purchases occurs because, as the price of one product falls, the price of obtaining a given level of satisfaction from consuming that product also falls. The price per unit of satisfaction (i.e utility) obtained from a product therefore becomes cheaper after a price reduction, and a consumer will react by increasing consumption of the product whose price has fallen. The implication is that, for the individual consumer, price and quantity demanded vary inversely and this general relationship is illustrated in Figure 5.1. So widely applicable is the inverse relationship between price and quantity demanded that we refer to Figure 5.1 as a normal demand curve. Any other demand curve is referred to as *exceptional* since it is an exception to the general rule that price and quantity demanded vary inversely. Exceptional demand curves are considered on pages 38–39.

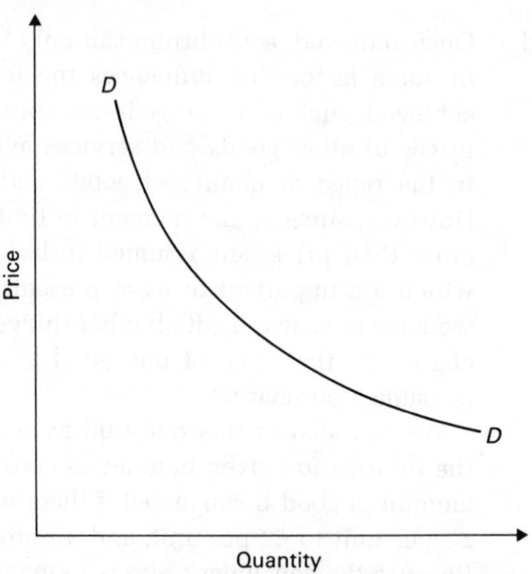


Figure 5.1 A normal demand curve

## Market demand curves

The total market demand for a commodity at any given price is simply the total amount demanded by each consumer at that price. Market demand curves are therefore simply the horizontal summation of each individual's demand curve. Since, for each individual, quantity demanded varies inversely with price, this general relationship will be embodied in the market demand curve. A typical, or normal, market demand curve therefore has the same general shape as the individual's demand curve illustrated in Figure 5.1.

## A change in quantity demanded and a change in demand

Great care must be taken in the use of these terms because, although they appear similar, they imply entirely different things.

### A change in quantity demanded

For any product a change in quantity demanded is *always caused by a change in its price*. A change in quantity demanded therefore refers to a movement along an *existing* demand curve. Figure 5.2 is used as a basis for illustration.

If price rises from OP to $OP_1$ quantity demanded falls from OQ to $OQ_1$. This is referred to as a reduction in quantity demanded or a *contraction* of demand, that is, demand contracts from OQ to $OQ_1$. No other term can be used to describe this. Conversely, if price falls from $OP_1$ to OP, quantity demanded rises from $OQ_1$ to OQ. This rise in quantity demanded can also be referred to as an *extension* of demand, since demand extends from $OQ_1$ to OQ. Again, either of these terms is acceptable, but no other term can be used in this context.

### A change in demand

A change in demand, on the other hand, is caused by a change in some factor other than price. So far we have assumed that at any moment in time price is the only factor that affects demand, all other

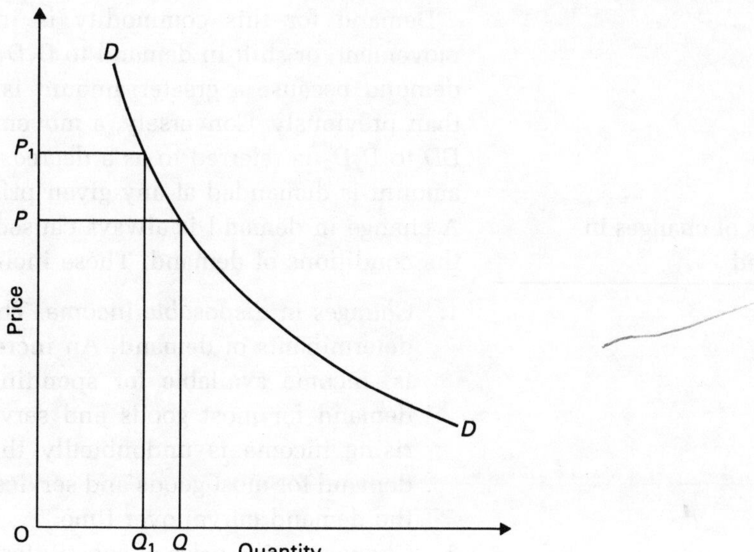


Figure 5.2 A movement along an existing demand curve

factors remaining constant. These factors which are assumed to be constant are referred to as the *conditions of demand*, or the parameters of demand. A change in demand is caused by a change in the conditions of demand and means that either more or less of a commodity is demanded at *each and every price*. Figure 5.3 is used as a basis for illustration.

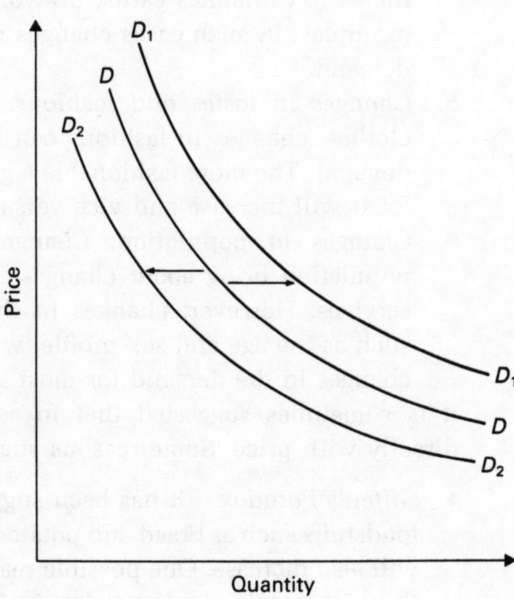


Figure 5.3 A change in the conditions of demand

Demand for this commodity is initially represented by *DD*. A movement, or shift in demand to $D_1D_1$ is referred to as an *increase in demand* because a greater amount is demanded at any given price than previously. Conversely, a movement, or a shift in demand from *DD* to $D_2D_2$ is referred to as a *decrease in demand* because a smaller amount is demanded at any given price than previously.

## Causes of changes in demand

A change in demand is always caused by a change in at least one of the conditions of demand. These include:

1. *Changes in disposable income.* This is one of the most important determinants of demand. An increase in disposable income, that is, income available for spending will lead to an increase in demand for most goods and services. There are exceptions but rising income is undoubtedly the most important reason why demand for most goods and services increases (an outward shift of the demand curve) over time.
2. *Changes in the price of substitutes.* Many goods are substitutes for one another and in this case a change in the price of one good will lead to a change in the demand for goods which are substitutes. For a detailed explanation see p. 43.
3. *Changes in the price of complements.* Certain goods are jointly demanded. Here again a change in the price of one good will lead to a change in the demand for goods which are complements. For a detailed explanation see p. 44.
4. *Changes in the weather.* Some goods are demanded seasonally and at certain times of the year demand for these goods will increase. Christmas cards, fireworks and Easter eggs are obvious examples. In such cases changes in the seasons cause changes in demand.
5. *Changes in tastes and fashions.* For certain products, such as clothes, changes in fashions can bring about marked changes in demand. The more fashionable a good becomes, the more demand for it will increase and vice versa.
6. *Changes in population.* Changes in the *size* of a country's population bring about changes in demand for most goods and services. However, changes in the *structure* of the population, such as the age and sex profile, will also lead to quite substantial changes in the demand for most goods and services.

## Exceptional demand curves

It is sometimes suggested that in some cases demand might vary directly with price. Some reasons suggested for this include:

- *Giffen's Paradox.* It has been suggested that, if the price of basic foodstuffs such as bread and potatoes increases, quantity demanded will also increase. One possible reason for this is that as price rises the higher price makes it impossible for consumers to purchase better quality foodstuffs. They therefore substitute the poorer quality foodstuffs despite the fact that the price of these has increased! This has an appealing logic but is unconfirmed by empirical evidence.

- *Veblen goods.* In this case it is argued that some goods are purchased for ostentatious purposes and as their price rises so does their attractiveness because they provide a means of displaying superior wealth. Again the logic is appealing but it is difficult to conduct tests which will confirm the existence of Veblen goods.

## Market supply

The total market supply of any commodity at a particular price is equal to the total amount that all individual firms which produce that commodity will supply at that price. The market supply curve is therefore the horizontal summation of all individual firms' supply curves. In other words we simply add the amount that every firm supplies at each and every price. Like demand curves, supply curves are drawn on the assumption that all factors that affect supply, except price, are constant.

Economic theory indicates that market supply and price vary directly. In other words, that a greater amount is supplied at higher prices than at lower prices. There are two main reasons for this:

1. It is assumed that firms produce for profit, and, other things being equal, at higher prices it becomes more profitable to expand output.
2. At higher prices it becomes possible for *marginal firms*, that is firms which cannot cover their costs at lower prices, to undertake production. As price rises, more firms enter the industry and market supply rises.

A normal supply curve is illustrated in Figure 5.4.

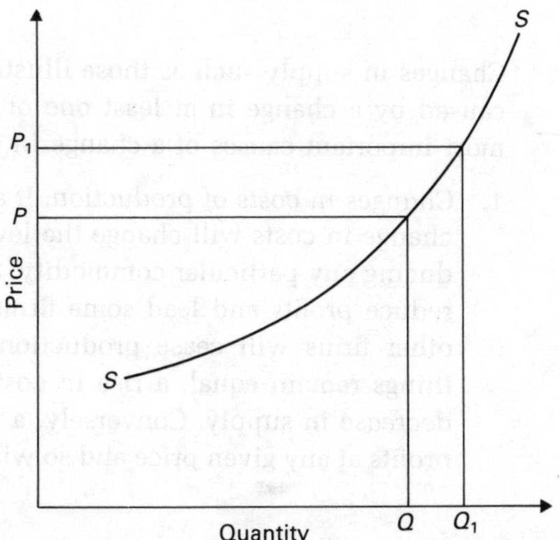


Figure 5.4 A normal supply curve

It is important to stress that the same rules used when describing demand apply when describing movements along a supply curve and movements of a supply curve. Thus when price rises in Figure 5.4 from OP to $OP_1$ there is an *expansion* or *extension* in the quantity supplied from OQ to $OQ_1$. Conversely, a fall in price from $OP_1$ to OP leads to a *contraction* in quantity supplied from $OQ_1$ to OQ.

## A change in supply

A change in supply implies a *complete shift of an existing supply curve*. When more is supplied at any given price than previously we refer to an *increase* in supply. This is illustrated in Figure 5.5 by a movement of the supply curve from SS to $S_1S_1$. When less is supplied at any given price than previously we refer to a *decrease* in supply. This is illustrated by a movement of the supply curve from SS to $S_2S_2$ in Figure 5.5.

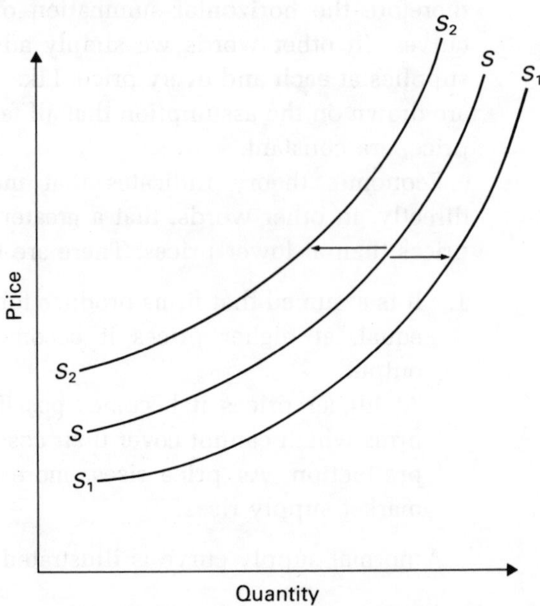


*Figure 5.5* A change in conditions of supply

## Causes of changes in supply

Changes in supply such as those illustrated in Figure 5.5 can only be caused by a change in at least one of the conditions of supply. The most important causes of a change in supply are considered below.

1. *Changes in costs of production*. If all other things remain equal, a change in costs will change the level of profit available from producing any particular commodity. Specifically, a rise in costs will reduce profits and lead some firms to cut back on output, while other firms will cease production altogether. Thus, if all other things remain equal, a rise in costs of production will lead to a *decrease* in supply. Conversely, a fall in costs will lead to higher profits at any given price and so will lead to an *increase* in supply.

Despite this, it is possible to pay a higher reward to any factor of production and yet leave average costs of production unchanged. For example, a 5 per cent increase in wages which is accompanied by a 5 per cent increase in productivity will leave average labour costs unchanged and therefore the supply curve will not move. However, when costs rise by *more than productivity*, this will lead to a decrease in supply, and when costs rise by *less than productivity* there will be an increase in supply.

2. *Changes in the prices of other commodities.* Some goods such as beef and hides are jointly supplied. This simply means that it is impossible to supply one good without also supplying the other good. In these circumstances, a rise in the price of one good will lead to an *increase* in the supply of the other. For example, if the price of beef rises, there will be an *expansion* in the quantity of beef supplied. This in turn will lead to an *increase* in the supply of hides, since *at any given price* of hides more hides are now being supplied.
3. *Changes in the weather.* This can have important repercussions on the supply of certain agricultural commodities. Favourable weather conditions can produce a bumper harvest of certain commodities and a consequent increase in supply. Conversely, unfavourable weather conditions will lead to a poor harvest and a decrease in supply.
4. *Changes in indirect taxation and subsidies.* A rise in indirect taxation such as a higher rate of VAT, will have the same effect on producers as a rise in costs of production. It will reduce the profit available to producers at any given price, and will consequently lead to a *decrease* in supply. A subsidy has the opposite effect.

## The determination of market price

In free markets, prices are determined by the interaction of demand and supply. With given demand and supply functions only one price is sustainable. This is the equilibrium price, and it is the only price at which demand and supply are equal. This is illustrated in Figure 5.6.

With demand and supply given by *DD* and *SS* respectively the equilibrium price is O*P*, because it is the only price at which supply and demand are equal. At prices above O*P*, supply exceeds demand and there is a market surplus of this commodity. The existence of this surplus will cause price to fall. As price falls producers will cut back production (supply contracts) and consumers will purchase more (demand expands) until supply and demand are equal at quantity O*Q*. Conversely, at prices below O*P* there is a market shortage and this shortage will cause price to rise. The higher price will persuade producers to expand output. Only when price is O*P* is there equilibrium in the market, with no tendency for producers **or** consumers to revise their decisions.

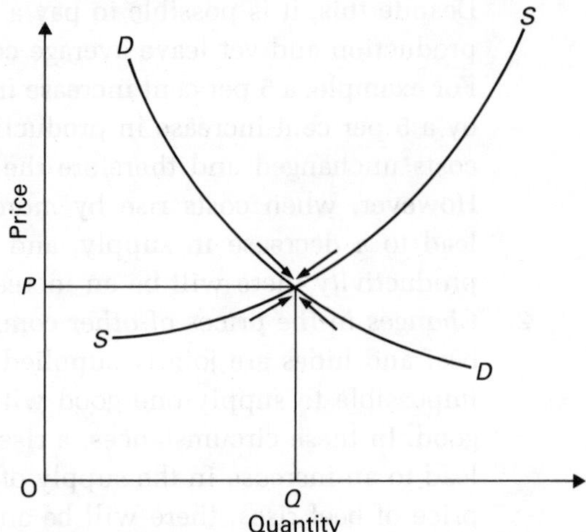


Figure Figure 5.6 Market equilibrium

## Changes in market price

We have seen that prices are determined by demand and supply. It follows that, once equilibrium has been established, prices can only change if there is a *change* in the conditions of demand and/or supply. This is fairly straightforward. However, it is essential to be clear about the *causes* of changes in price, otherwise it is impossible to predict the *effects*.

Figure 5.7 shows that it is possible for different causes of a rise in price to have different effects.

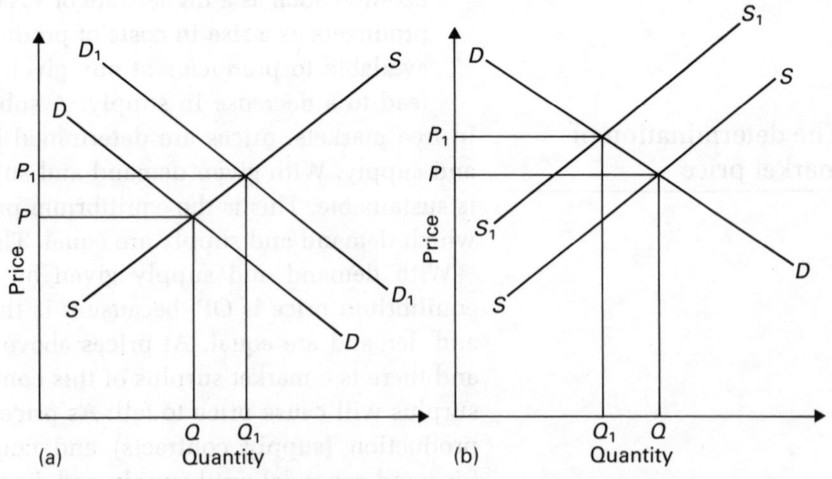


Figure 5.7a The effect of an increase in demand

Figure 5.7b The effect of a reduction in supply

Figure 5.7a shows the effect of an *increase in demand* from *DD* to $D_1D_1$. Price rises from its original equilibrium of *OP* to $OP_1$ and there is a rise in the equilibrium quantity demanded and supplied from OQ to $OQ_1$. Figure 5.7b, on the other hand, shows the effect of a *decrease in supply* from *SS* to $S_1S_1$. Again, there is a rise in price from OP to

$OP_1$ but this time there is a fall in the equilibrium quantity supplied and demanded from OQ to $OQ_1$. Clearly, the effect of a rise in price on equilibrium output depends on the cause.

## Some applications

### Substitutes in consumption

When goods are substitutes in consumption they compete against each other. Tea and coffee are often quoted as examples but there is undoubtedly more competition between different brands of coffee and different brands of tea. The more closely goods are regarded as substitutes, the greater the effect of a change in the price of one good on demand for the other. Figure 5.8, in which good A and good B are substitutes, is used to illustrate this point.

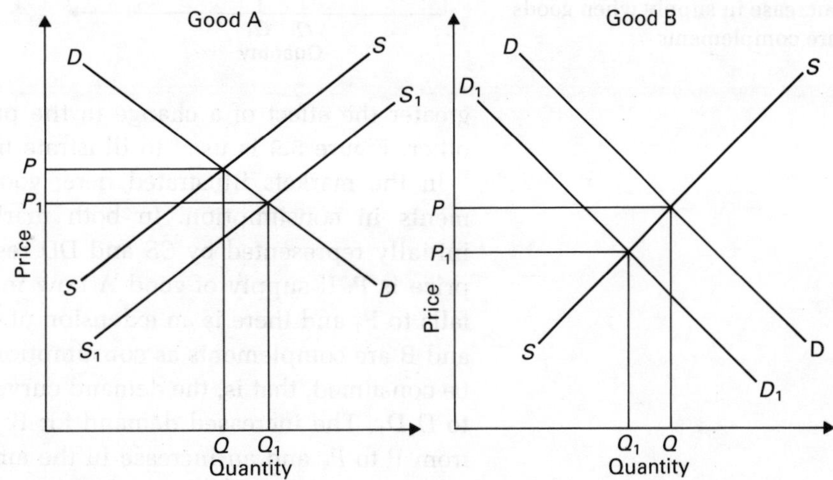


*Figure 5.8* The effect of an increase in supply when goods are substitutes

In the markets illustrated here, supply and demand are initially represented by *SS* and *DD* respectively and the equilibrium price is *P*. If the supply of good A now increases (perhaps because of a reduction in the cost of raw materials) to $S_1S_1$, the price of A will fall to $P_1$, and there is an extension of demand from *Q* to $Q_1$. However, since A and B are substitutes, the fall in the price of A will result in some consumers increasing their consumption of A and reducing their consumption of B. Since the change in demand for good B is *not* caused by a change in the price of B, this implies a complete shift in the demand curve for B from *DD* to $D_1D_1$. This causes a fall in the price of B from *P* to $P_1$.

### Complements in consumption

Goods which are complements in consumption are jointly consumed. Examples include fish and chips, cars and petrol and so on. Many goods are complements in consumption but some are more closely related than others. For example, bricks and mortar are often purchased together but the relationship between pens and writing paper is less strong. The stronger the relationship between goods, the

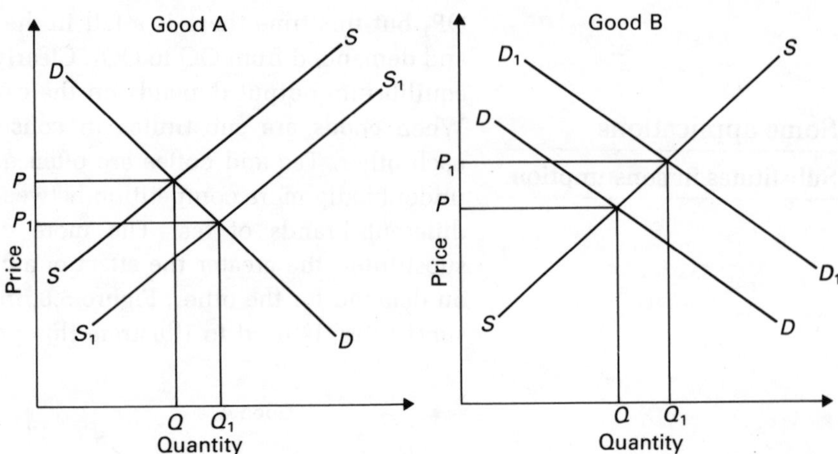


Figure 5.9 The effect of an increase in supply when goods are complements

greater the effect of a change in the price of one on demand for the other. Figure 5.9 is used to illustrate how complements are related.

In the markets illustrated here, good A and good B are complements in consumption. In both markets supply and demand are initially represented by SS and *DD* respectively and the equilibrium price is P. If supply of good A now increases to $S_1S_1$, the price of A falls to $P_1$ and there is an extension of demand from Q to $Q_1$. Since A and B are complements as consumption of A increases more of B will be consumed, that is, the demand curve for B shifts outwards from *DD* to $D_1D_1$. The increased demand for B causes an increase in its price from P to $P_1$ and an increase in the amount consumed from Q to $Q_1$.

## Complements in production

Some goods are jointly supplied such as wheat and straw. When wheat is harvested the stalks on which it grows are left behind as straw. Figure 5.10 is used to illustrate the way in which goods which are jointly supplied interact.

Supply and demand are initially represented by SS and *DD* respectively and the equilibrium price is P in each case. If demand for wheat now increases from *DD* to $D_1D_1$ this will pull up the price of wheat to $P_1$ and cause an extension of supply from Q to $Q_1$. However, increased production of wheat implies an increase in the supply of straw which shifts the supply curve to $S_1$ $S_1$ and pulls down the price of straw to $P_1$.

## Taxes and subsidies

The effect of an indirect tax will be to shift the entire supply curve vertically upwards by the full amount of the tax. This is because the imposition of a tax on a product will be treated as an increase in costs of production by suppliers. The example in Table 5.2 illustrates this, and for simplicity we assume the imposition of a lump sum tax of £1 per unit.

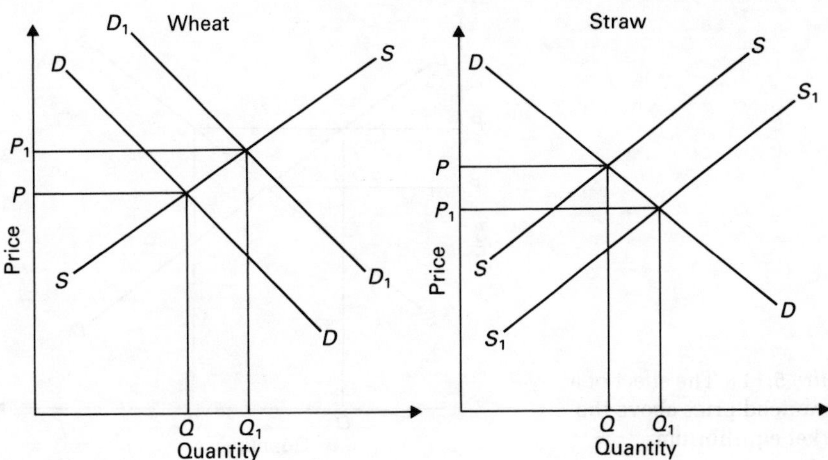


*Figure 5.10* The effect of an increase in demand when goods are jointly supplied

*Table 5.2*

| Price (£)m. | Quantity supplied before tax | Quantity supplied after tax |
|---|---|---|
| 7 | 145 | 125 |
| 6 | 125 | 105 |
| 5 | 105 | 90 |
| 4 | 90 | |

After the tax is imposed, producers receive £1 less than previously at any given price. They will therefore supply at each price the amount they would have previously supplied at a price of £1 less. For example, when producers receive £4 per unit, they will supply 90 units. After the tax is imposed, producers actually receive £4 per unit when the market price is £5. They will therefore only supply, at a market price of £5, what would previously have been supplied at a market price of £4.

A subsidy has exactly the opposite effect. It represents a payment to suppliers in addition to any revenue received from sales and therefore raises the amount of profit obtained from supplying any given level of output. In the case of a specific subsidy, such as £1 per unit, the effect will be to shift the supply curve vertically downwards by the full amount of the subsidy.

## Minimum price

Governments sometimes establish minimum prices for certain products. The aim of such schemes is usually to ensure the continued production of the product. An example of such a scheme is the Common Agricultural Policy (CAP) operated by the EC. A simple example of a minimum price scheme is illustrated in Figure 5.11.

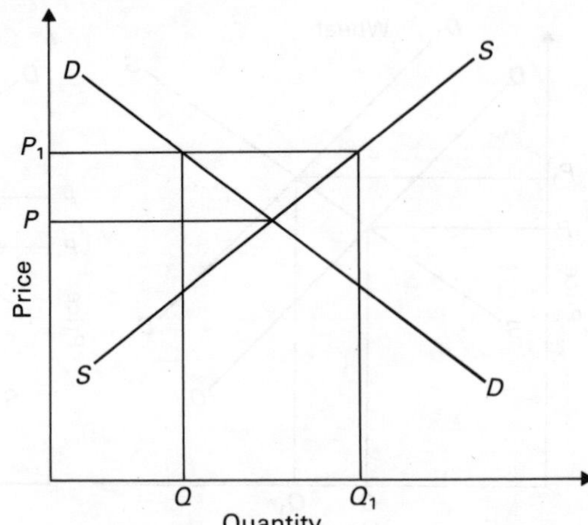


Figure 5.11 The effect of a guaranteed price above the market equilibrium

Supply and demand are given by *SS* and *DD* respectively and the free market price would be *P*. However, if the government has implemented a minimum price guarantee of $P_1$ there will be a market surplus of $QQ_1$ at the guaranteed price. To maintain the guaranteed price the government must purchase this surplus and dispose of it perhaps by destroying it or selling it abroad.

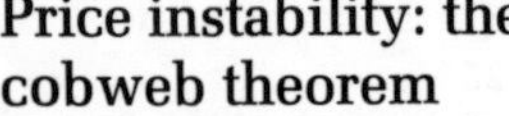

## Price instability: the cobweb theorem

The cobweb theorem is useful in explaining the circumstances when disequilibrium in a free market might be temporary or permanent. Figure 5.12 is used to illustrate this point.

In Figures 5.12a and 5.12b *SS* and *DD* represent the long-run supply and demand conditions for a particular commodity. Let us consider the effect in both cases of an increase in price above the long-run equilibrium price caused by a temporary reduction in supply perhaps

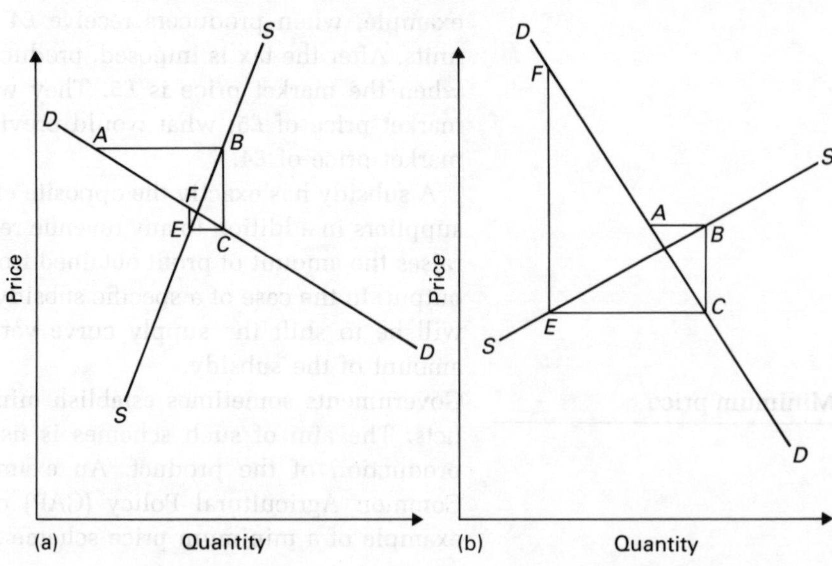


Figure 5.12 The cobweb theorem

because of an unusually poor harvest. We begin at point A. The higher price encourages increased production of AB. However, since there is no change in demand, the excess supply will force price down and we move to point C. This represents a lower price than anticipated and consequently producers will cut back on production and we move to point E. The reduction in the amount supplied implies a market shortage at the lower price and so price rises. We move to point F and so on. Note that Figure 5.12a shows a *converging* cobweb so that each change in production results in a move closer to long-run equilibrium, while Figure 5.12b shows an explosive cobweb where each change results in a move further away from equilibrium.

For markets to behave in this way of course requires the existence of certain conditions. For example, in cases where there are many buyers and many sellers of a product and it is easy for producers to increase or reduce production as in perfect competition (see pp. 58–62), we might expect to find adjustment to long-run equilibrium following this sort of pattern.

## Test your understanding

1. If an individual consumes the quantities of A and B shown below and is in equilibrium with respect to his (her) purchases, what is the marginal utility derived from A?

| Good | Price | Marginal utility |
|---|---|---|
| A | 20p | ? |
| B | 50p | 10 |

2. What is normal about a normal demand curve?
3. What factor(s) cause
   (a) a movement *along* a demand curve?
   (b) a movement *of* a demand curve?
4. A football stadium has 80,000 seats and demand for tickets for a particular game is given as:

| Price (£) | Quantity demanded |
|---|---|
| 30 | 30000 |
| 28 | 40000 |
| 26 | 50000 |
| 24 | 60000 |
| 22 | 70000 |
| 20 | 80000 |
| 18 | 90000 |

   (a) What is the equilibrium price of tickets?

(b) If the management decide for safety reasons to reduce the supply of tickets by 25 per cent what would be the new equilibrium price?

5. In a particular market $Q_d = 60 - 4p$ and $Q_s = 20 + 6p$, where $Q_d$ = quantity demanded, $Q_s$ = quantity supplied and p = price of the product. What is the equilibrium price of this product?
6. What is the relationship between three goods X, Y and Z if a rise in the price of X causes an increase in demand for Y and a reduction in demand for Z?
7. Use the following information, which relates to the market for good X, to the answer the questions below.

| Price (pence per kg) | Demand (thousand kg) | Supply (thousand kg) |
|---|---|---|
| 80 | 310 | 685 |
| 78 | 340 | 655 |
| 76 | 400 | 590 |
| 74 | 485 | 485 |
| 72 | 590 | 340 |
| 70 | 750 | 200 |

(a) What is the equilibrium price of good X?

(b) If a subsidy of 4p per kg was granted to producers of good X what would be the new equilibrium price?

(c) If, in the original situation, a tax of 6p per kg was placed on good X what would be the new equilibrium price?

# 6 Elasticity

## Price of elasticity of demand

This is usually referred to simply as elasticity of demand. It measures the responsiveness of quantity demanded to changes in price. Elasticity of demand can be measured in several ways but it is most commonly measured as:

$$\text{Price E of D} = \frac{\text{percentage change in quantity demanded}}{\text{percentage change in price}} = \frac{\Delta Q/Q\ .\ 100}{\Delta P/P\ .\ 100}$$

or

$$\text{Price E of D} = \frac{\Delta Q}{Q} \times \frac{P}{\Delta P}$$

Where the elasticity of demand is less than 1, demand is said to be *inelastic*, and where it is more than 1 demand is said to be *elastic*. The larger the value of elasticity, the more responsive is quantity demanded to changes in price.

In most cases a given demand curve does not possess a constant elasticity. In fact, the value of elasticity associated with a *given price change* varies all the way along a given demand curve. This is illustrated in Figure 6.1.

For the straight line demand curve, the gradient, $\frac{Q}{P}$ is a constant

$$= \frac{50}{2} = 25$$

$$\text{At price} = 2,\ \text{price E of D} = \frac{2}{350} \times 25 = \frac{1}{7}$$

$$\text{At price} = 4,\ \text{price E of D} = \frac{4}{300} \times 25 = \frac{1}{3}$$

So, even if the demand curve is a straight line, price elasticity of demand varies along its entire length, since the ratio $P/Q$ varies; in fact $P/Q$ rises as price rises, so that price elasticity of demand rises as we move up the demand curve. (If the demand curve is not a straight line, then $\Delta Q/\Delta P$ will usually vary *as well*!)

One point to note is that, strictly speaking, price elasticity of

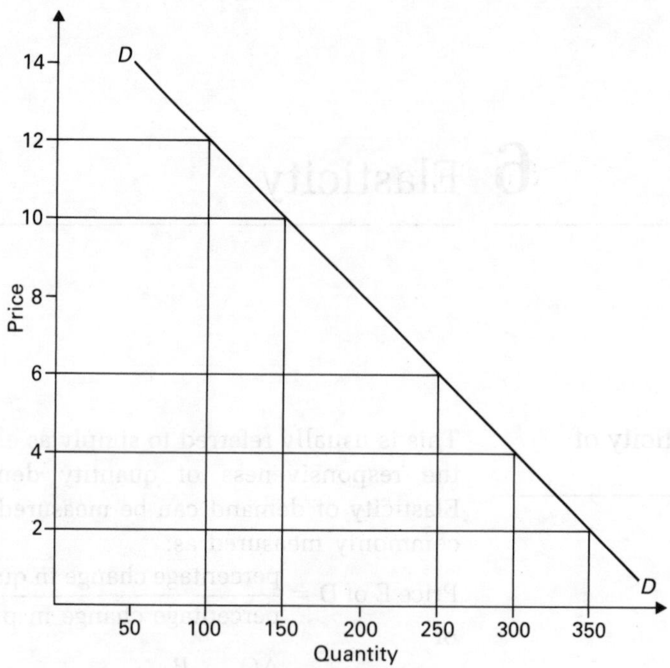


Figure 6.1 The changing value of elasticity of demand

demand is negative for all normal demand curves beause a *rise* in price leads to a *fall* in quantity demanded and vice versa. However, the negative sign is usually omitted and this convention is followed here.

## Elasticity: the limiting cases

There are three exceptions to the general rule that the value of elasticity varies along the length of a demand curve. The three exceptions are illustrated in Figure 6.2.

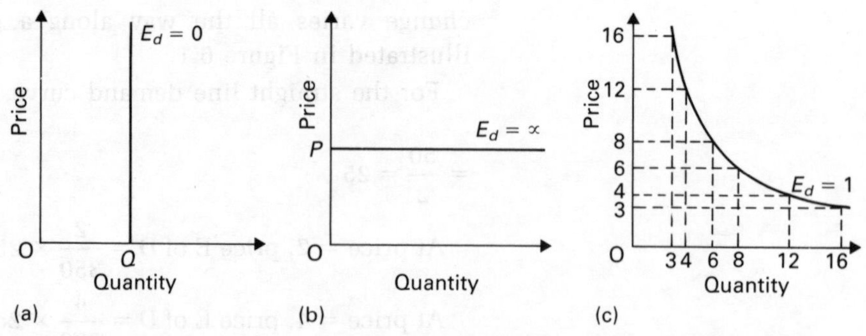


Figure 6.2 Elasticity of demand: the limiting cases

In Figure 6.2a a change in price has no effect on quantity demanded and, therefore, demand is totally inelastic. In Figure 6.2b, any increase in price leads to an infinitely large change in quantity demanded and therefore, demand is said to be infinitely elastic. In Figure 6.2c, the proportionate change in quantity demanded is exactly equal to the proportionate change in price along the entire length of the demand curve. Elasticity of demand is therefore equal to unity at all points along the entire length of the demand curve.

## Elasticity of demand and total revenue

Elasticity of demand has a crucial bearing on the way total revenue is affected by a change in price. The following relationships exist:

1. When demand is inelastic, a rise in price leads to a rise in total revenue and a fall in price leads to a fall in total revenue (see Figure 6.1).
2. When demand is elastic, a rise in price leads to a fall in total revenue and a fall in price leads to a rise in total revenue (see Figure 6.1).
3. When demand has unit elasticity a rise or fall in price has no effect on total revenue (see Figure 6.2c).

## Determinants of elasticity of demand

There are several factors which influence the value of elasticity of demand for any particular product. The most important of these are summarized below.

1. *The availability of substitutes.* This is probably the most important determinant of elasticity of demand for any particular product. When there are few close substitutes available for any particular product demand, will tend to be less elastic and therefore less responsive to changes in price. For example, demand for petrol in *total* is less elastic than demand for any *particular brand* of petrol.
2. *The proportion of income spent on the commodity.* When the cost of a commodity is a relatively small proportion of total expenditure, demand will tend to be less elastic. For example, spending on pencils accounts for a very small part of total expenditure. Consequently a rise in the price of pencils would have little impact on total expenditure, and we would therefore expect demand for pencils to be little affected by a change in their price – i.e. demand to be relatively inelastic.
3. *The number of uses the commodity has.* When a commodity has several uses, demand will tend to be less elastic. For some of these uses a change in price is likely to have little or no effect on quantity demanded. For example, electricity has many uses and this is one reason why demand for electricity tends to be inelastic.
4. *Whether the commodity is a necessity or a luxury.* It is difficult to define what is meant by the terms necessity and luxury. However, if a good is considered a necessity, demand for it will tend to be inelastic. Demand for luxuries will be more elastic.
5. *Whether the commodity is habit-forming.* Some goods, such as cigarettes, are habit-forming and in these cases demand will tend to be less elastic.
6. *Time period.* For most goods demand is less elastic in the short run than in the long run. For example, a rise in the price of

domestic gas is likely to have only a minor effect on consumption in the short run. In the longer run, economies can be made by wearing warmer clothing around the house, by better insulation, by switching to electricity for cooking and heating, etc., so that demand may then become more responsive to changes in price.

## Elasticity of supply

Just as elasticity of demand measures the responsiveness of a change in quantity demanded to a change in price, so elasticity of supply measures the responsiveness of a change in quantity supplied to a change in price. Elasticity of supply is measured in the same basic way as elasticity of demand, except, of course, we measure changes in quantity supplied.:

$$\text{i.e. Price E of S} = \frac{\%\text{ change in quantity supplied}}{\%\text{ change in price}}$$

$$\text{or Price E of S} = \frac{\Delta Q}{Q} \times \frac{P}{\Delta P}$$

Again, there are three exceptions to the general rule that elasticity of supply varies along the entire length of the supply curve. These are illustrated in Figure 6.3

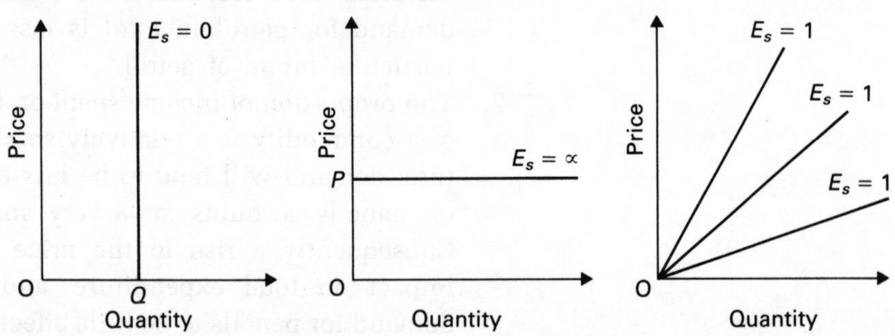


Figure 6.3 Elasticity of supply: the limiting cases

In Figure 6.3a, elasticity of supply is zero because any change in price has no effect on the quantity supplied. In Figure 6.3b, elasticity of supply is infinite because an increase in price leads to an infinitely large change in quantity supplied. In Figure 6.3c, elasticity of supply is unity because any change in price causes an equi-proportionate change in quantity supplied. (This is true of any supply curve passing through the origin.)

## Determinants of elasticity of supply

The main determinants of elasticity of supply are briefly summarised below.

### The time period

This is an important factor and in general supply is more elastic in the long run than in the short run. In fact, economists identify three time periods.

- *The momentary period* is so short that it is impossible to expand supply. Supply is completely inelastic in the momentary period as when a trawler lands it catch at the quay.

- *The short period* during which it is possible to expand supply by using more of the variable factors. For example, trawlers might stay at sea longer and take on additional crew members. However, the existence of fixed factors limits the scope for increased output. Supply is therefore relatively less elastic during the short run.
- *The long period* during which all factors are variable and supply is therefore more elastic than in either of the previous situations. Here it is possible to have more trawlers as well as additional crew members and so on.

**Factor mobility**

Although supply is more elastic in the long run, the degree of elasticity will still partly depend on factor mobility. The greater the mobility of the factors of production, the greater the elasticity of supply. For instance, a rise in the price of a good due, say, to an increase in demand, raises the producer's profits. If he can easily attract land, labour and capital from other uses by offering higher rewards (i.e. factors are mobile) then he will be more able to expand supply in response to the higher price.

**Availability of stocks**

Where a product can be stored without loss of quality or undue expense, supply will tend to be elastic, at least while stocks last. This explains why the supply of processed food will tend to be more elastic than supply of fresh food.

**Behaviour of costs as output changes**

When firms are subject to relatively small increases in average costs as output expands, supply will tend to be more elastic. However, if firms experience diminishing returns or diseconomies of scale which are severe enough, costs will rise steeply as output expands and in these circumstances supply will tend to be less elastic.

**The existence of surplus capacity**

Even if average costs do increase by small amounts as output increases supply might be relatively inelastic if firms do not have surplus, or unused, capacity. If they are operating at full capacity it will be impossible to bring about significant changes in output in the short run.

**Barriers to entry**

In certain cases it might be difficult for additional firms to enter an industry and undertake production. These barriers might take a variety of forms (see page 64) but their existence will tend to make supply less elastic than otherwise.

**Income elasticity of demand**

This measures the responsiveness of demand to changes in income.

$$\text{i.e.}\quad \text{Income E of D} = \frac{\text{\% change in quantity demanded}}{\text{\% change in income}}$$

For most goods income elasticity of demand will be positive, that is, a rise in income will lead to an increase in demand. However, there are exceptions to this rule, and for some goods a rise in income leads to a decrease in demand. Such goods are referred to as *inferior goods.*

## Cross elasticity of demand

This is a measure of the responsiveness of demand for one good to a change in the price of another:

$$\text{i.e. Cross E of D} = \frac{\text{\% change in quantity demanded of good X}}{\text{\% change in price of good Y}}$$

If the cross elasticity of demand between two goods is *positive*, the goods are *substitutes*; a rise in the price of, say, good Y, leads to an increase in the demand for good X. Moreover, the greater the positive value of cross elasticity between two goods, the greater the degree of substitutability between them.

If the cross elasticity of demand between two goods is *negative*, the goods are *complements*; a rise in the price of, say, good Y leads to a decrease in demand for good X. Again, the higher the negative value of cross elasticity between two goods, the greater the degree of complementarity between them.

## Measuring elasticities

In practice it is difficult to distinguish between a shift in demand and a movement along a demand curve, since the latter occurs when all factors which affect demand, other than price, are constant. In the real world this is an impossible condition to achieve. Consequently, when more of any commodity is sold this could imply an *increase* in demand, an *expansion* of demand, or, indeed, a combination of both. In the latter case it is extremely difficult to quantify the effect of each.

Nevertheless values for income and price elasticities of demand for foodstuffs are published in the *Annual Report of the Food Survey Committee*. Table 6.1 shows estimates of the value of income elasticity of demand and price elasticity of demand for certain foodstuffs. Of the foodstuffs listed fresh fruit has the highest income elasticity of demand at 0.66 which implies that for each 1 per cent rise in income, expenditure on fresh fruit rises by 0.66 per cent. The negative income elasticity of demand for fresh milk, bread and fresh potatoes implies that these are inferior goods although *within* each category there might be exceptions. For example, the demand for brown bread is likely to have a positive income elasticity of demand.

Table 6.2 provides estimates of cross price elasticities of demand for beef and veal, mutton and lamb, and pork. In general these statistics are consistent with conventional economic theory. The *positive* cross price elasticity of demand for beef and veal with respect to pork implies that these foods are considered to be substitutes. A 1 per cent rise in the price of beef and veal causes a 0.1 per cent increase in the demand for pork. Notice, however, the negative cross price elasticity of demand for beef and veal with respect to mutton and lamb. This implies that these foods are considered to be complements with a 1

*Table 6.1*

| Item | Income elasticity of demand 1987 | Price elasticity of demand 1982–7 |
|---|---|---|
| Liquid milk | −0.13 (0.05) | 0.13 (0.23) |
| Cheese | 0.26 (0.09) | −1.52 (0.42) |
| Carcass meat | 0.21 (0.07) | −1.17 (0.29) |
| Fresh fruit | 0.66 (0.06) | −0.53 (0.22) |
| Bread | −0.18 (0.03) | −0.25 (0.18) |
| Cakes and pastries | 0.07 (0.06) | −0.86 (0.25) |
| Beverages | −0.05 (0.10) | −0.28 (0.05) |
| Fresh potatoes | −0.43 (0.08) | −0.14 (0.03) |

*Notes:* The negative elasticity coefficient arises because for all normal goods price and quantity vary inversely. A rise in price leads to a fall in quantity demanded and vice versa. For convenience the negative coefficient is ignored in most texts.
(Figures in brackets are standard errors. They relate to inaccuracies which arise out of chance variations during the collection of samples. The extent of any inaccuracy due to this cause is rarely expected to exceed twice the standard error.)
*Source: Household Food Consumption and Expenditure 1987,* Annual Report of the Food Survey Committee, HMSO.

per cent rise in the price of beef and veal causing a 0.06 per cent rise in the consumption of mutton and lamb! No-one would seriously suggest that this was true. A more likely explanation is that the estimate is inaccurate. Gathering accurate real world data to illustrate some of the relationships known to exist can sometimes be very difficult indeed.

*Table 6.2*

| | Beef & veal | Mutton & lamb | Pork |
|---|---|---|---|
| Beef & Veal | 1.24 (0.26) | −0.06 (0.11) | 0.10 (0.10) |
| Mutton & Lamb | 0.15 (0.28) | −1.75 (0.25) | 0.03 (0.16) |
| Pork | 0.25 (0.25) | 0.03 (0.16) | −1.86 (0.22) |

*Note:* Elasticity with respect to the price of beef and veal, mutton and lamb, and pork. (Figure in brackets are standard errors.)
*Source: Household Food Consumption and Expenditure 1987,* Annual Report of the Food Survey Committee, HMSO.

## Test your understanding

1. How would knowledge of elasticity of demand be useful to:
   (a) a manager of a firm producing washing machines?
   (b) the Chancellor of the Exchequer?
2. If demand is inelastic and a firm raises the price of its product what will happen to profit? Explain your answer.
3. This question is based on the following information:

| Price of good A (£) | Quantity of good B demanded |
|---|---|
| 1 | 300 |
| 2 | 400 |

What is:

(a) the cross elasticity of good B?

(b) What is the relationship between goods A and B?

4. Is the supply of fresh vegetables likely to be more elastic or less elastic than the supply of processed vegetables? Explain your answer.

5. This question is based on the following table:

| Price (£) | Quantity demanded | Total revenue | Price elasticity of demand |
|---|---|---|---|
| 4 | 1000 | ? | 0.6 |
| 5 | 800 | ? | ? |

(a) What is the elasticity of demand when price rises from £4 to £5?

(b) How many units of good X would be demanded at a price of £3?

6. How does factor mobility influence elasticity of supply?

# 7 Market structure

The term *market structure* refers to the basic characteristic features of a market which determine the extent of competition between sellers. The extent of competition between sellers in any market depends on many factors such as the type of good sold, the number of firms in the industry, the size of firms in the industry, whether there are barriers which prevent the entry of new firms into the industry and so on. One reason why market structure is important is that the larger the number of firms in the industry and the smaller each firm, the lower the ability of an individual firm to influence the price at which their product is sold. However, as we shall see on pages 65–66, economists are interested in market structure because differences in market structure lead to differences in the allocation of resources. In this chapter we focus on monopoly and perfect competition.

## Revenue and profit

Total revenue is the firm's earnings from sales. When firms sell their products at a single price it is easy to see that total revenue is equal to price x quantity, that is, $TR = PQ$. It is also easy to see that in such cases average revenue equals price, that is $AR = TR/Q = PQ/Q = P$.

Profit is often thought of as a residual, that is, the difference between total revenue and total cost. However, economists find it useful to identify *normal profit* as the cost of the entrepreneur. It is the minimum return necessary to keep the entrepreneur in the industry in the long run, but is insufficient to attract other entrepreneurs into the industry. If profits fall below normal, the entrepreneur will leave the industry in the long run.

For analytical purposes it is usual to include an element of *normal profit* in the firm's total and its average cost of production. When firms *break even*, that is, total revenue equals total cost or average revenue equals average cost, they are earning normal profit. Anything in excess of normal profit is referred to as *supernormal profit* and anything less than normal profit is referred to as *subnormal profit* or, more commonly, simply as a loss.

## Perfect competition

A market is said to be perfectly competitive when buyers and sellers

## Assumptions

believe that individually their own behaviour has no influence on market price. The conditions which give rise to this particular market structure may be summarised as:

1. There are large numbers of both buyers and sellers in the market, each buying or selling such a small amount of the product that individually they are powerless to influence market demand or market supply.
2. Consumers are indifferent from whom they make purchases because all units of the commodity are homogeneous. In other words, they regard the product that an individual firm supplies as a perfect substitute for the product that any other firm in the same market supplies.
3. There is perfect knowledge of market conditions among buyers and sellers so that each is fully informed about the prices producers in different parts of the market are charging for their product.
4. Buyers are able to act on the information available to them and will always purchase the commodity from the seller offering the lowest price.
5. There are no long-run barriers to the entry of firms into the market, or their exit from the market.

These conditions are never fully satisfied in the real world but some markets display many of the characteristic features of perfect competition. For example, an individual farmer has little influence on the price of potatoes. (Buyers are well informed about prices, the product is homogeneous and the individual farmer produces only a small proportion of the total market supply.)

## The market and the firm

These conditions ensure that in perfectly competitive markets all firms charge an identical price for their product. Any firm attempting to charge a price above that of its competitors will face a total loss of sales. This will occur because consumers are aware of the higher price the firm is attempting to charge and, since the product is homogeneous, they will have no particular preference for this firm's product.

On the other hand, perfectly competitive firms have no incentive to lower the price of their product since they can sell their entire output at the existing market price. The firm in perfect competition is therefore a *price-taker*, that is, it accepts the market price as beyond its control.

Because of this, all firms in perfectly competitive markets perceive their own demand curves, and the demand curves of their competitors, to be perfectly elastic at the ruling market price.

Figure 7.1 shows the determination of market price in a perfectly competitive market and the individual firm's demand curve at this price. Market supply and market demand are represented by *SS* and *DD* respectively. Given these supply and demand conditions, the ruling market price is *OP*, and the firm perceives its own demand curve to be perfectly elastic at this price.

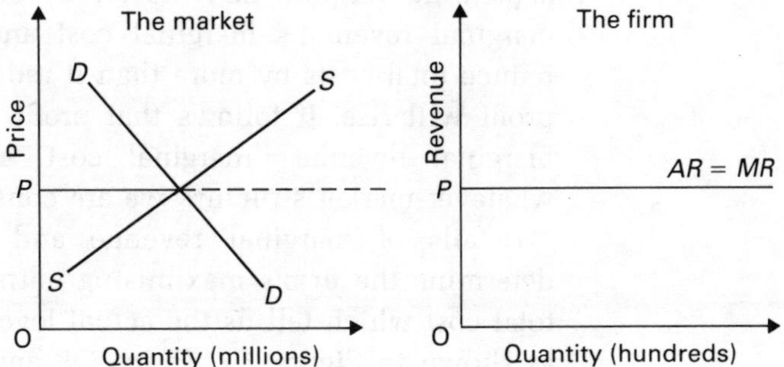


*Figure 7.1* The relationship between the market price and the firm's demand curve in perfect competition

## Average and marginal revenue

Because the firm sells its entire output at the ruling market price, each additional unit of output sold adds exactly the same amount to total revenue as each preceding unit sold. Therefore, for the firm in perfect competition, marginal revenue is constant at all levels of output and equal to market price. We shall see later that this relationship between price and marginal revenue, which is usually expressed in the form price = *AR* = *MR*, is peculiar to firms in perfectly competitive markets.

## Short-run equilibrium 1: supernormal profit

Since the firm is powerless to change the price of its product, it maximises profit by adjusting output to the point where marginal revenue equals marginal cost. Figure 7.2 shows the market equilibrium, and the short-run equilibrium position of the individual firm in perfect competition.

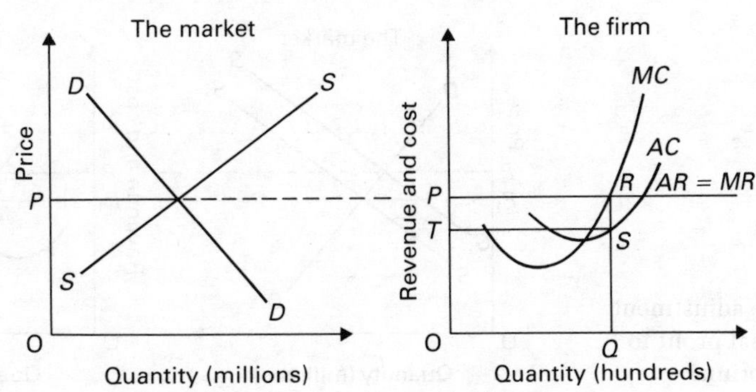


*Figure 7.2* Short-run equilibrium: supernormal profit

Given the price and costs shown in Figure 7.2, the firm's equilibrium (i.e. profit-maximising) output is OQ, because this is the output level which equates marginal revenue with marginal cost. At levels of output below OQ marginal revenue > marginal cost, so that an expansion of output adds more to total revenue than it does to total cost. In these circumstances, total profit can be increased by expanding output. Conversely, at output levels greater than OQ marginal revenue < marginal cost and a reduction in output will reduce total costs by more than it reduces total revenue so that total profit will rise. It follows that profit can only be maximised when marginal revenue = marginal cost, and this simple rule applies whatever market structure we are considering.

Details of marginal revenue and marginal cost enable us to determine the firm's maximising output, but it is total revenue and total cost which tell us the actual level of profit earned. With details as shown in Figure 7.2, (price *OP* and output OQ), total revenue = OP × OQ = *OPRQ*, while total cost = OT × OQ = *OTSQ*. Total revenue minus total cost gives total profit equal to *PRST*. Alternatively, we can say that average revenue (*OP*) minus average cost (*OT*) equals average profit (*RS*) and this multiplied by output (*OQ*) indicates that the firm is earning supernormal profit of *PRST*.

However, supernormal profit cannot continue in the long run in perfect competition because the existence of supernormal profit will attract other firms into the industry until supernormal profits are competed away. We can be certain this will happen because perfect knowledge of market conditions will ensure that firms outside the industry are aware of the level of profits earned, and the absence of long-run barriers to entry will ensure they are able to enter the industry and undertake production. As more firms enter the industry, market supply will increase and market price will fall. The adjustment from short-run equilibrium to long-run equilibrium is shown in Figure 7.3.

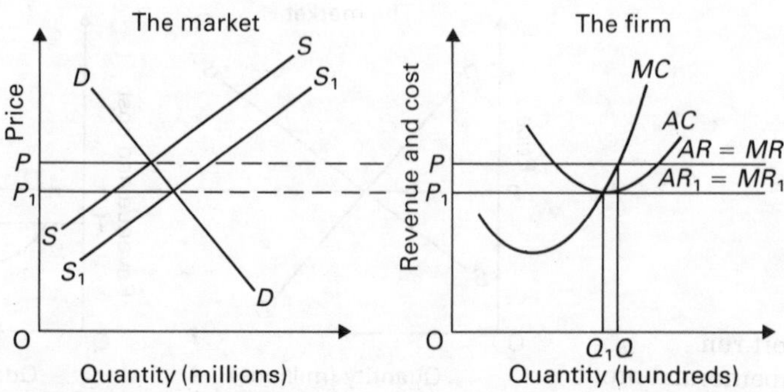


Figure 7.3 The adjustment from supernormal profit to long-run equilibrium

Market supply and market demand are initially given by *SS* and *DD* respectively, and the initial market price is O*P*. Given this price, the firm produces its equilibrium output OQ. The existence of short-run supernormal profit attracts other firms into the industry so that in the long run market supply increases to $S_1S_1$ and market price falls to $OP_1$. The individual firm is powerless to resist the reduction in market price and is forced to adjust its output so as to preserve equality between marginal revenue and marginal cost. At price $OP_1$ there is no prospect of new entrants to the industry earning anything in excess of normal profit and this is insufficient to encourage them to enter the industry. At price $OP_1$ therefore the industry is in long-run equilibrium.

## Short-run equilibrium 2: subnormal profit

For all firms, irrespective of market structure, production can only continue in the long run if *at least* normal profit is earned. However, in the short run firms might be prepared to accept a return below normal profit. In particular firms might be willing to continue producing in the short run as long as total revenue from production is at least equal to *total variable costs* of production, i.e. as long as $AR \geqslant AVC$.

In the short run firms are obliged to meet their fixed costs whether they undertake production or not. Thus, if total revenue from production is only *just sufficient* to cover the *total variable costs,* it follows that the firm is making no contribution towards covering its fixed costs. It is therefore neither better off nor worse off if it remains in the industry. If total revenue is *greater than total variable costs,* then by continuing in production, the firm makes at least some contribution towards covering the fixed costs already incurred. To cease production would leave the firm with a loss equal to its fixed costs, whereas if the firm undertakes production it will at least have a surplus over variable costs to set against its fixed costs.

On the other hand, if total revenue is *less than total variable cost,* the firm will be better off by ceasing production altogether. If it produces nothing, the firm's total loss is equal to its fixed costs. This compares with a loss equal to the deficit on variable costs *added* to the fixed costs if it undertakes production.

Because of this, it is clear that, in the short run, the minimum acceptable price if the firm is to undertake production is that price which exactly equals the minimum short-run average variable costs of production. It is for this reason that the minimum average variable cost is sometimes referred to as the 'shut-down' price. The loss situation is analysed diagrammatically in Figure 7.4.

*The minimum acceptable short-run price is OP.* This price is exactly equal to the *minimum average variable cost*, and the firm's loss is exactly equal to its fixed costs, whether it undertakes

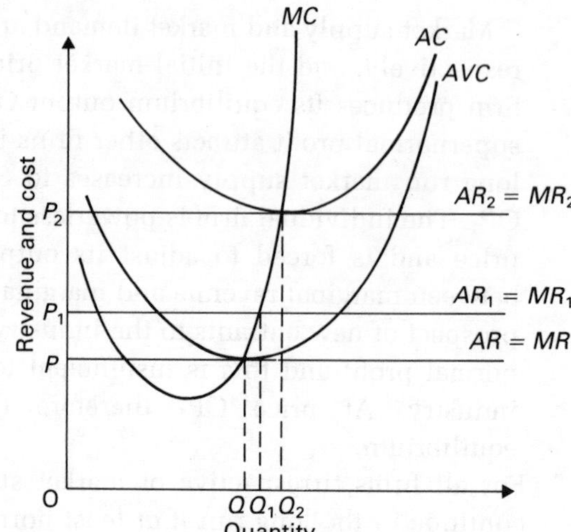


*Figure 7.4* The supply curve of the firm in perfect competition

production or not. We can see this in Figure 7.4. With price OP, the firms equilibrium output is OQ and its loss is equal to AR − AC at this level of output. But, since AR = AVC, AC − AR = AC − AVC, that is, AFC. In other words, when the price is OP, the firm's loss is exactly equal to its fixed costs.

However, such losses cannot be sustained indefinitely and in the long run some firms will be forced to leave the industry. This will shift market supply to $S_1S_1$ and raise market price to $OP_1$. Given this market price the firm's profit-maximising output is $OQ_1$ and the firm just earns normal profit, since total revenue is ($OP_1 \times OQ_1$) which equals total cost. Thus the *minimum acceptable long-run price* is that price which just equals the *minimum average total cost* of production including normal profit.

## Monopoly

A pure monopoly exists when supply of a particular good or service is in the hands of a single supplier. For convenience we usually analyse monopoly in terms of a single firm but a monopoly can also exist when a small group of firms jointly coordinate their marketing policies and so act as a single supplier. The latter situation is referred to as a cartel.

Because *market supply* is in the hands of a single supplier, a monopoly has great power to influence the price of its product. However, this does not imply that it has *total power* to fix price, since it cannot control consumer demand. In effect the monopolist has two choices:

1. to fix price and allow demand to determine supply (output),
2. to fix supply (output) and allow demand to determine price.

The inability to control market demand makes it impossible for a monopolist to simultaneously fix both price and output.

## Average and marginal revenues

Unlike the firm in perfect competition, the monopolist's average and marginal revenues will be different. This is because the monopolist faces a downward sloping demand curve and is forced to reduce price in order to expand sales. Table 7.1 is used as a basis for illustration.

*Table 7.1*

| Output/ Sales | Average Revenue | Total Revenue | Marginal Revenue |
|---|---|---|---|
| 0 | — | — | |
| | | | 20 |
| 1 | 20 | 20 | |
| | | | 18 |
| 2 | 19 | 38 | |
| | | | 16 |
| 3 | 18 | 54 | |

In order to expand sales from 1 unit to 2 units, it is necessary to reduce the price of both units. Hence price falls from £20 per unit to £19 per unit and the marginal revenue, i.e. the change in total revenue, is £18. Similarly, when price is reduced from £19 per unit to £18 per unit marginal revenue falls to £16. Hence marginal revenue will always be less than price (average revenue) under monopoly.

## The monopolist's equilibrium output

We have already seen that for all producers profits are maximised when marginal cost equals marginal revenue. Based on this principle Figure 7.5 illustrates the monopolist's equilibrium output.

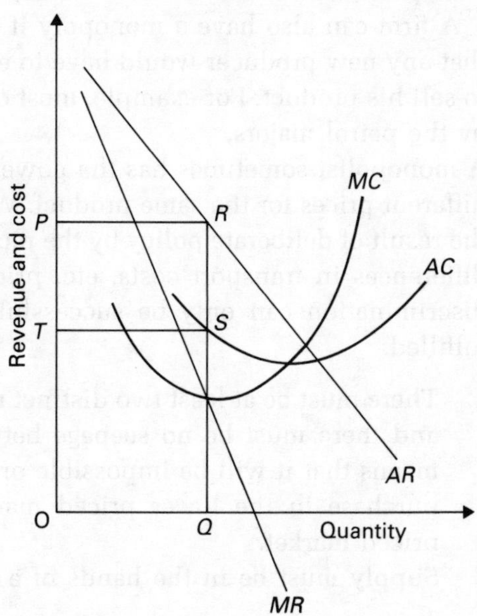


Figure 7.5 Equilibrium under monopoly

The monopolist maximises profit when price is *OP* and output *OQ* because, at this price and output combination, marginal revenue equals marginal cost. Total revenue (*OPRQ*) minus total cost (*OTSQ*) gives a profit equal to *PRST*.

It will be noted that the monopolist is earning supernormal profit, and one of the characteristic features of monopoly is that it is possible to earn this level of profit even in the long run. If supernormal profits continue in the long run this implies the existence of barriers which restrict the entry of additional firms into the industry. These barriers are therefore the very essence of monopoly power.

## Barriers to entry

### Economies of scale

Some organisations have relatively high fixed costs so that average total costs continue to fall as output expands over relatively large ranges. This is true in the production of industrial gases, tyres, motor vehicles, oil and so on. In such cases, the minimum scale of operation is likely to be relatively large. In such cases, when the market is most efficiently supplied by a single supplier a natural monopoly is said to exist.

### Legal barriers

In certain markets, legal regulations might prevent the emergence of competition. In the UK the nationalised industries have been granted the sole rights to supply particular goods or services. This represents the most complete barrier to entry since the emergence of competition is prevented by law.

### Control of factor inputs or retail outlets

Where a firm has complete control over the supply of a factor of production it may be able to exercise monopoly power over the products produced by that factor. China clay and nickel provide examples of monopoly or near monopoly control.

A firm can also have a monopoly if it controls the retail outlets so that any new producer would have to establish a distributive network to sell his product. For example, most of the filling stations are owned by the petrol majors.

## Price discrimination

A monopolist sometimes has the power to charge different customers different prices for the same product. When such price differences are the result of deliberate policy by the monopolist and are not caused by differences in transport costs, etc. *price discrimination* exists. Price discrimination can only be successful when certain conditions are fulfilled.

1. There must be at least two distinct markets for the good or service, and there must be no seepage between these two markets. This means that it will be impossible or uneconomic for consumers to purchase in the lower priced market and re-sell in the higher priced market.
2. Supply must be in the hands of a monopolist so that competing

firms are unable to enter the industry and undercut the monopolist in the higher priced markets.

3. Elasticity of demand must be different in at least two of the markets. If it were not, there could be no additional profit to the monopolist from discrimination.

At its simplest level price discrimination is illustrated in Figure 7.6.

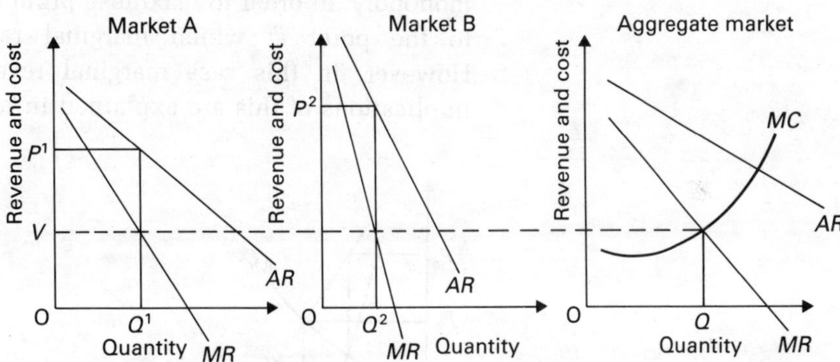


*Figure 7.6* Price discrimination
*Note:* $OQ = OQ^1 + OQ^2$

Markets A and B are separated in some way so that seepage between them is impossible. Combining the average and marginal revenues from each market yields the monopolist's *aggregate* average and marginal revenue curves. The monopolist then simply applies the profit-maximising rules established earlier and equates aggregate marginal cost with aggregate marginal revenue. This gives the profit-maximising output OQ but not the profit-maximising price. To obtain this the monopolist must equate aggregate marginal cost with marginal revenue in *each individual market*. This gives a profit-maximising price in market A of $OP_1$ and of $OP_2$ in market B, that is, a higher price in the market with the less elastic demand. The sum of the sales in both markets is equal to the total amount produced. There is *no other* distribution of output OQ between the two markets (and therefore no other market prices) which could increase total profit. For instance, selling one unit *less* in market A and one unit *more* in market B, would mean losing V units of revenue in market A and gaining *less than* V units of revenue in market B. Total revenue would have fallen which, with total costs unchanged, would reduce profit.

## Perfect competition and monopoly compared

### Resource allocation

It is sometimes alleged that the allocation of resources under perfect competition is superior to that achieved under monopoly. This is because under perfect competition price always equals marginal revenue and therefore the price consumers pay for the last unit consumed is exactly equal to its marginal cost of production. In other words the value consumers place on the last unit consumed (shown by the amount they are prepared to pay for it) exactly equals its opportunity cost (because marginal cost measures the cost of attracting resources away from alternatives). Thus, under perfect competition the amount consumers pay for the last unit produced is exactly equal to its opportunity cost of production because price equals marginal costs (see page 59). The same is not true under monopoly. In order to maximise profit the monopolist restricts output to the point at which marginal revenue equals marginal cost. However, in this case marginal revenue is *less* than price. The implications of this are explained in terms of Figure 7.7.

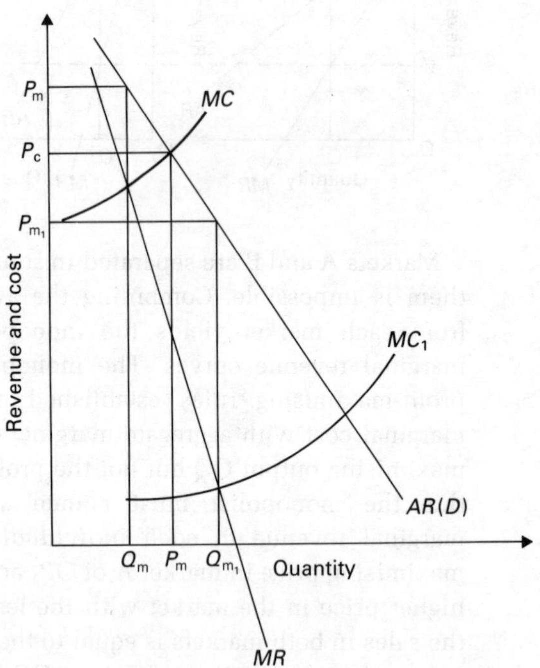


Figure 7.7 Price and output under perfect competition and monopoly

*DD* is the *market demand curve* for a product. If this was supplied under conditions of monopoly, *MR* would be the mononoplist's marginal revenue curve and *MC* the marginal cost curve. If the product was supplied under conditions of perfect competition, the *MR* curve would not exist and *MC* would be the *combined* marginal cost curve of all firms in the industry. For the present, ignore $MC_1$. Given these conditions the price and output under monoploy would be $P_m$ and $Q_m$ respectively. Price and output under perfect competition on the other hand would be $P_c$ and $Q_c$ respectively. The main point to note is that under perfect competition price exactly equals marginal cost whereas under monopoly price exceeds marginal cost.

In other words under monopoly society values additional units of the commodity more highly than it values alternatives since the price they are prepared to pay for it exceeds the cost of attracting resources away from alternatives. Because of this it is alleged that the allocation of resources under perfect competition is superior to the allocation of resources under monopoly.

### Price and output

It seems from Figure 7.7 that price is lower under perfect competition and output greater than under monopoly. However, it is possible that a monopolist will gain economies of scale that are unavailable to the small firms that undertake supply under perfect competition. If $MC$ is the industry's cost curve under perfect competition and $MC_1$ the industry's cost curve under monopoly, we find that price is lower at $P_{m1}$ and output greater at $Q_{m1}$ under monopoly than under perfect competition. Whether price is higher and output lower under monopoly than under perfect competition therefore depends on the extent to which the monopolist reaps economies of scale.

### Research and development

The absence of competition might reduce the incentive to innovate and produce efficiently. It is possible to argue that competition might encourage research and development (R & D) to a greater extent than monopoly. However, here again there is no certainty and it is possible to argue that a monopolist will be better able to finance investment in R & D and will be encouraged to do so because of the possibility of higher profits if R & D is successsful.

### Market stability

Another possibility is that markets will be more stable under monopoly than under perfect competition. In a competitive environment no *individual* firm possesses complete knowledge about the state of market demand and market supply. In these circumstances a change in demand is likely to result in an over-reaction from producers and output might fluctuate in the way predicted by the cobweb theorem before equilibrium is finally reached. However, under monopoly a single producer is more likely to possess more complete information about the state of demand and will be able to adjust market supply in an orderly manner in response to any change in market demand. The same reasoning suggests that, when a structural change in demand for a product results in a long-term reduction in demand, a monopolist is better able to carry out a programme of rationalisation. Because a monopolist has more complete information about the change in demand than a number of competing firms the monopolist is able to concentrate production in the most profitable units to bring about a long-term reduction in capacity.

### Regulating monopoly

Because of the potential disadvantages of monopoly, most countries in the developed world regulate the activities of monopolies. The type of regulation adopted might take many forms. Some of these are briefly considered below.

**Nationalisation**

Some natural monopolies have been brought into state ownership. The justification for this is that nationalised industries have less freedom to exploit their monopoly position since parliament issues White Papers which provide guidelines on pricing and investment decisions. However, recent years have seen a trend towards privatisation and denationalisation indicating that, as a means of controlling the activities of monopolies, this is no longer a viable option.

**Removing barriers to entry**

Another way of tackling the problems of monopoly is to remove the barriers which prevent the growth of competition. For example, if a domestic monopoly is protected from foreign competition by the existence of a tariff which restricts imports, the government might reduce or remove this tariff altogether.

**Taxing monopoly profits**

A different approach available to the government is to tax the profits of a monopolist. This would not protect the public from the abuses of monopoly but it would mean that, rather than there being a redistribution of income from consumers to the monopolist, there would be a redistribution from consumers to the state.

**Monopolies and Mergers Commission**

The government has set up a Monopolies and Mergers Commission to investigate the behaviour of monopolistic firms referred to it as well as to investigate the likely effects on market domination of any proposed mergers which are referred to it. The Commission has the power to obtain any information it requires from firms under investigation which is relevant to its enquiry but it has no statutory power to enforce its recommendations. Instead it can only make recommendations in its report. It is for the Secretary of State to decide whether these recommendations should be implemented. In the extreme power exists to compel monopolies to divest themselves of some of their assets, thus creating competition in the industry.

## Monopolistic competition

This market structure has features of both perfect competition and monopoly. In particular, there are no barriers to entry into the industry, but each firm produces a product which is differentiated in some way from the products of its rivals'. Such product differentiation is often achieved or reinforced by branding and advertising. Because each product is differentiated, each firm has a monopoly over the supply of its own product. It therefore faces a downward sloping demand curve for its product with respect to price. This in turn implies that its marginal revenue curve lies beneath its average revenue curve.

### Equilibrium in and the short run and the long run

As with other market structures we assume that the firm aims to maximise profit. It therefore produces that level of output at which $MC = MR$. The firm's short-run equilibrium position is shown in Figure 7.8a.

The firm is in equilibrium when it produces OQ units and charges a price of OP per unit. At this price and output combination, it earns

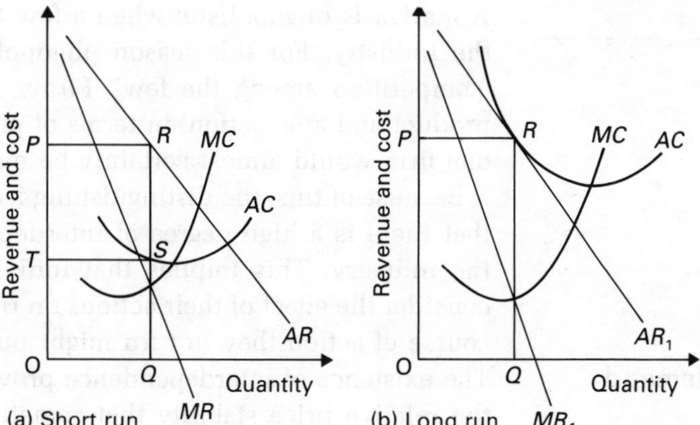


*Figure 7.8* Equilibrium under monopolistic competition

supernormal profit of *PRST*. However, this cannot represent a long-run equilibrium position because the existence of supernormal profit will attract more firms into the industry. Indeed, firms will continue to enter the industry until supernormal profits have been competed away and each firm earns only normal profit. The firm's long-run equilibrium position is shown in Figure 7.8b. The extra firms attract some, but not all, of the firm's customers. This can be shown as a leftward shift of the firm's demand curve until it touches its *AC* curve.

In the long run, total revenue = total cost = *OPRQ*. Each firm, although maximising profit (*MC* = *MR*), earns only normal profit since at output OQ price = average revenue. Consequently there is no tendency for firms to enter or leave the industry. However, this does not imply that monopolistic competition confers the same benefits on society as perfect competition. In particular, we can identify two important ways in which society is worse off.

1. In the long run, equilibrium output is not pushed to the point of maximum technical efficiency, i.e. minimum average cost. The firm in monopolistic competition therefore operates with excess capacity in the long run. This under-utilisation of capacity leads both to higher average costs than would exist if output were expanded and consequently to higher consumer prices.
2. In the long run, equilibrium output is not pushed to the point at which resources are allocated in the most efficient manner, i.e. a Pareto Optimal resource allocation. This requires price to equal marginal costs, yet here price is greater than marginal cost. This means that, if output were expanded until price = marginal cost, resource allocation could be improved, but this will not happen because the firm will make a loss.

## Oligopoly

A market is oligopolistic when a few large-scale producers dominate the industry. For this reason oligopoly is sometimes referred to as 'competition among the few'. Firms supply competing brands of a product and any 'action' in terms of price and non-price strategies by one firm would almost certainly be matched by the firm's rivals.

Because of this, the distinguishing feature of oligopolistic markets is that there is a high degree of interdependence between each firm in the industry. This implies that individual firms will be obliged to consider the effect of their actions on rival producers, and the possible course of action they in turn might pursue.

## The kinked demand curve

The existence of interdependence provides a possible explanation for the relative price stability that sometimes characterises oligopolistic markets. The suggestion is that an individual firm in oligopoly fears that, if it raises price, other firms will not follow suit. Instead, they will be content to hold their own price constant and attract consumers away from the firm which has raised the price. Because of this, the individual firm perceives demand for its product to be relatively elastic if it raises price. On the other hand, if an individual firm lowers price its competitors in the market will be compelled to match the price cut, otherwise they will lose a disproportionate amount of sales. The individual firm therefore perceives demand for its product to be relatively inelastic if it lowers price. The implications of this are illustrated in Figure 7.9.

Because the firm perceives demand to be relatively elastic if it raises price, and relatively inelastic if it reduces price, it perceives its demand curve ($DAD_1$) to be kinked at the ruling market price ($OP$). It

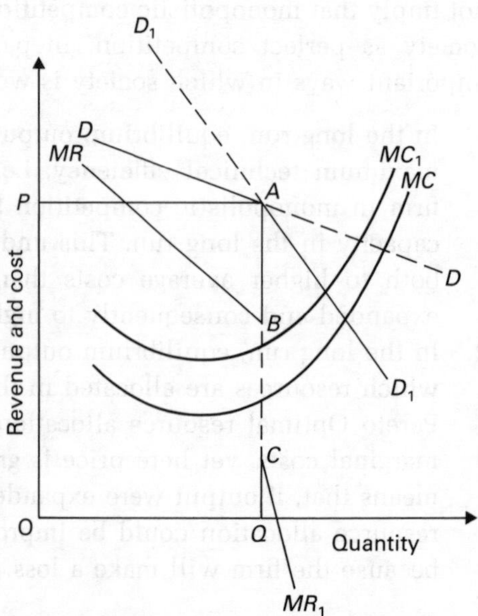


Figure 7.9
*Note:* $D_1 D_1$ = 'reaction' demand curve, with the firms price changes matched by those of its rivals
$DD$ = 'no reaction' demand curve, with price changes unmatched by those of its rivals

therefore has little incentive to alter price from OP. This can be seen from Figure 7.9 which shows that, because the firm perceives its demand curve to be kinked, it has a discontinuous marginal revenue curve. In fact, when price is OP marginal revenue is indeterminate because the firm is currently operating at a common point (A) on what is effectively two separate demand curves ($DD$ and $D_1D_1$), with associated marginal revenue curves. The region BC is therefore referred to as the region of indeterminacy. It implies that even when costs are changing, so long as marginal cost remains within the region of indeterminacy, changes in costs will have no effect on the profit-maximising price and output combination because the firm will still be producing where $MC = MR$. For example, in Figure 7.9 when marginal cost rises from $MC$ to $MC_1$ this has no effect on the price the firm charges or on the output it produces.

## Price leadership

Another possible reason for relative price stability in oligopolistic markets is that there might be an accepted price leader. Price changes are initiated by the leader and other firms in the industry simply follow suit. The role of price leader might be acquired because a firm is the largest producer in the industry, in which case we refer to 'dominant firm leadership'. Alternatively, the price leader might be the firm which most accurately perceives changes in market demand for the product. In this case we refer to 'barometric price leadership'.

Whatever the basis of leadership, its existence would explain price stability because price changes will only be initiated by a single firm. This firm would not be confronted with price cutting by other firms and therefore price would tend to be relatively stable.

## Price warfare

Whilst prices in oligopolistic markets sometimes appear relatively stable, at other times they can be highly unstable. This is particularly common when demand for the industry's product is falling, because, as sales fall, average fixed costs will rise. Individual firms are prevented from raising price because they would lose sales to competitors, and this would simply exacerbate their problems. Because of this, falling sales imply falling profits, and in these circumstances the temptation for a firm to cut its price in an attempt to prevent further loss of sales is sometimes overwhelming. However, when demand for the product is falling, an individual firm can only increase sales by attracting consumers away from rival firms. To prevent this, rival firms may well retaliate if faced with a price cut, so that profits fall still further. This may then lead to a further round of price cutting, i.e. a price war will be underway.

## Non-price competition

The existence of price wars is evidence of competition in oligopolistic markets. However, even when prices are stable, non-price competition between rival producers is often intense. This can take a variety of forms, including:

1. *Competitive advertising*. This is common in oligopolistic markets. Advertising is used to reinforce product differentiation and harden brand loyalty. It can also be used as a barrier to the entry of new firms.
2. *Promotional offers*. These are common in some oligopolistic markets such as household detergents and toothpaste. Such offers frequently take the form of veiled price reductions such as 'two for the price of one' offers or '25 per cent extra free'. In the case of petrol a common technique is to offer 'free gifts'.
3. *Extended guarantees*. This is an increasingly common technique in many of the markets for consumer durables. By offering free parts and labour guarantees for longer periods than their competitors, firms aim to increase the attractiveness of their product.
4. *Model and style changes*. Changes in models and styles can be used as a form of non-price competition. Consumers are often attracted to the latest model and even small changes in style can quickly make an existing product seem dated. Frequent changes in models and style also cuts down competition from second-hand products.

## Alternatives to profit maximisation

This chapter has stressed profit maximisation as the goal of firms. However, in practice it is doubtful whether firms pursue this goal to the exclusion of all other goals. This is especially true in modern corporations where ownership is in the hands of shareholders, but day-to-day control is exercised by salaried managers. Profit maximisation is likely to appeal to shareholders, because it will lead to higher dividends, but salaried managers might be more interested in pursuing other goals. Two alternatives are considered below.

### The sales-maximisation model

Rather than maximising profit, it has been suggested that salaried managers might attempt to maximise sales revenue subject to achieving a target rate of profit. Managers have good reason for maximising sales revenue, since it often affects their salaries and their security of tenure. In general, a higher level of sales revenue is rewarded with a higher salary.

### Behavioural models

Behavioural theories stress that firms might pursue several goals simultaneously. Each goal is set as a result of bargaining between the various groups involved, such as managers, shareholders, trade unions and so on. Where goals are in conflict with one another they must be ranked in order of importance and priority given to one rather than the other. For example, the level of output which maximises sales revenue is likely to be greater than the level of output which maximises profit. If, as a result of bargaining, profit maximisation is given priority, output will be cut back. Bargaining within the firm can clearly lead to different priorities at different times, so that behavioural models stress that no single goal can be assumed to be consistently followed by the firm.

An extension of the behavioural model is that of *satisficing*. This approach stresses that firms seek a satisfactory minimum level of achievement for various goals rather than a maximum level for any single goal. This means that many possible outcomes of price and quantity could then be regarded as situations of equilibrium for the firm.

## The costs and benefits of advertising

Whether society benefits from advertising is a contentious issue and depends in part on what we mean by advertising. In particular the distinction is sometimes made between *informative* advertising which simply provides information, and persuasive advertising which attempts to persuade potential consumers that one product is superior to other competing products.

No one would argue that informative advertising is to the benefit of the consumer. The more information consumers have at their disposal, the more rational their choices will be. In addition, since there is no attempt to persuade consumers that one product is superior to others, consumers are not provided with false information. The judgement they exercise when making choices will therefore be based on a more comprehensive understanding of the facts.

However, persuasive advertising is a different matter. Here the aim is to persuade consumers to purchase one product in preference to rival products. To do this it is necessary to highlight differences between products and if no real differences exist they must be created in the minds of consumers. This implies that advertising might provide consumers with misleading information. To the extent that this is the case the judgement of consumers will be impaired. Furthermore it is sometimes suggested that consumers will also be penalised by having to pay higher prices since advertising adds to the firm's costs of production.

Despite this there might be benefits to society. If advertising leads to an increase in demand and firms experience economies of scale as output grows, average costs of production will fall. If prices are lower as a result, the consumer benefits. Society also benefits from advertising to the extent that advertising revenue is a major source of finance for independent radio and televison as well as for provincial newspapers. In the absence of advertising revenue these could not survive.

## Test your understanding

1. What is 'perfect' about perfect competition?
2. Why are there no significant economies of scale in perfect competition?
3. The following table relates to a firm operating under conditions of perfect competition.

| Output and sales | Total cost (£) |
|---|---|
| 0 | 25 |
| 1 | 38 |
| 2 | 45 |
| 3 | 48 |
| 4 | 50 |
| 5 | 53 |
| 6 | 60 |
| 7 | 73 |
| 8 | 94 |
| 9 | 125 |
| 10 | 175 |

(a) If the current market price is £34, what is the firm's equilibrium output?

(b) What is the minimum acceptable price if the firm is to undertake production: (i) in the short run (ii) in the long run

4. How might consumers benefit from price discrimination?
5. For a firm in monopoly marginal revenue is always less than average revenue. Why is this?
6. Supply the word which correctly completes the following sentence. If other things are equal, a discriminating monopolist will charge a higher price to the group with the ______ elastic demand.
7. Which of the following is (are) always true of monopoly *and* perfect competition?
   (a) The firm produces where marginal cost equals marginal revenue.
   (b) The industry's demand curve varies inversely with price.
   (c) Marginal revenue is less than average revenue.
   (d) The firm produces where average revenue is greater than average cost.
   (e) There is an absence of competitive advertising.
   (f) The firm has no control over the price at which its product is sold.
8. Do firms in monopolistic competition operate at their optimum level in the long run?
9. What do firms in monopolistic competition have a monopoly over?
10. What is the characteristic feature of oligopoly?
11. Is the kinked demand curve a complete theory of oligopoly?

12. The diagram below shows the cost and revenue conditions of a particular firm.

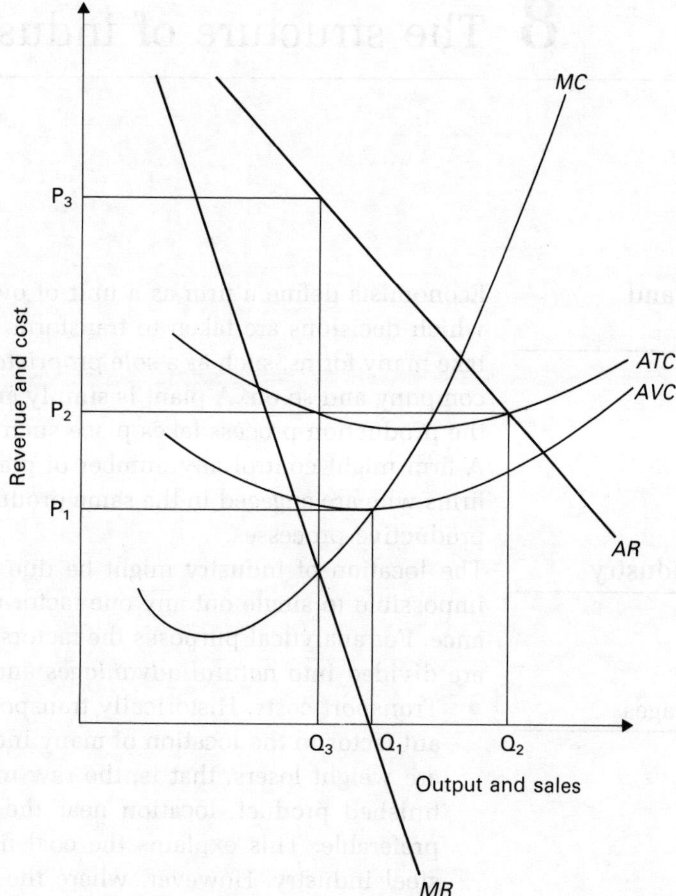


*Figure 7.10*

(a) In which type of market is this firm operating?
(b) At the equilibrium output what type of profit does the firm earn?
(c) What is the profit-maximising level of output?
(d) At what price does the firm maximise profit?
(e) At what prices does the firm break-even?
(f) What is the maximium short-run loss the firm will accept?
(g) What is the minimum short-run price the firm will accept
(h) What is the minimum long-run price the firm will accept?

# 8 The structure of industry

## Firms, plants and industries

Economists define a firm as a unit of ownership and control through which decisions are taken to transform inputs into outputs. This can take many forms, such as a *sole proprietor*, a *partnership*, a *joint-stock company* and so on. A plant is simply an *establishment* where part of the production process takes place such as a factory or a retail outlet. A firm might control any number of plants. An industry is the set of firms who are engaged in the same productive activity or use the same productive processes.

## Location of industry

The location of industry might be due to a host of factors and it is impossible to single out any one factor of over-riding general importance. For analytical purposes the factors that might influence location are divided into *natural advantages* and *acquired advantages*.

### Natural advantages

- *Transport costs*. Historically transport costs have been an important factor in the location of many industries. For industries which are weight losers, that is, the raw materials weigh more than the finished product, location near the raw material sites is clearly preferable. This explains the coal field locations of the iron and steel industry. However, where the finished product is heavy or bulky, a location near the market might be preferable. This is especially true when the value of the finished product is low in relation to the cost of transport as in the case of brewing and breadbaking.
- *Supply of labour*. An adequate supply of labour is clearly important for labour-intensive industries or for industries which require a particular type of labour. One reason why the high technology industries are attracted to the south-east of England is the availability of skilled labour, while the availability of cheap labour is an important reason for the location of many industries in Hong Kong, Taiwan and many third world countries.

### Acquired advantages

Once an industry becomes established in a particular area that area often acquires advantages that exert an influence on location. These acquired advantages are often referred to as *external economies*. These might stem from several sources.

- *Ancillary trades.* In many cases when an industry has reached a certain size in a particular area it becomes profitable for other firms who specialise in supplying the main industry to locate in the same area. In Coventry for example, there are many firms which specialise in the machinery, tools and components required by the car industry.
- *Labour.* When an industry becomes localised a pool of skilled labour is readily available to any new entrants to the industry. This is a considerable influence on the location decision because it implies lower training costs.

## Government regional policy

The government, through its regional policy, might also exert an influence on location. At present the government offers various incentives for qualifying activities which locate or expand in certain designated areas referred toa s intermediate areas and development areas.

Discretionary assistance is available in both of these areas and is mainly given in the form of a grant. To qualify for assistance a firm must initiate some activity which either creates or safeguards employment and which has an identifiable regional or national benefit. It is also necessary to demonstrate that the project is viable and that assistance is necessary for the project to go ahead. It is also necessary to demonstrate that the bulk of the finance for the project will come from the private sector.

Automatic assistance is available only to firms that locate or expand in the development areas. To qualify for assistance a project must satisfy certain criteria. In brief these are:

- The project must provide new capital assets and/or create jobs in a development area.
- The project must create new or expand existing capacity to produce goods or to provide a service.
- The project must relate to qualifying (mainly manufacturing) activities.

## Small firms

There is no uniform measure of size and therefore no single criterion against which a firm can be judged small or large. Statistically the most widely used measures are in terms of employment or turnover, that is, total revenue per year. However, capital employed is also sometimes used as a measure of size.

### Reasons for survival

Despite the advantages of economies of scale which are experienced by large firms, small firms continue to survive. There may be many reasons for this including:

Many people prefer to be self-employed and so set up their own business. However, not all people classed as self-employed would also be classed as owning a firm, for example window cleaners. Those that do own a firm often remain 'small' out of choice.

- Small firms have limited access to finance. Many rely on their own savings and that of other family members. This severely restricts growth.
- Small firms often supply small markets. This is true of small independent retailers which often serve neighbourhood communities. Some firms produce specialist goods which cannot be mass produced. In other words small firms flourish where consumers demand variety.
- Sometimes the nature of production is such that size gives no advantage. This is true of repair work and window cleaning for example.
- Firms supplying personal services are often small because the nature of the product means that growth does not confer the same advantages on producers as growth of a manufacturing firm does. This is true of hairdressing for example.
- Small firms often supply a small part of a much larger market that is of no interest to larger firms. For example, Wimpey and Barratt build housing estates but have no interest in barn conversions or house extensions. These are carried out by small jobbing builders. The two groups survive alongside each other but neither competes directly.
- Large firms often sub-contract work to smaller firms. It is often cheaper for larger firms to do so because they can accept a greater volume of work without incurring an increase in overheads. In this sense they act as agents, providing work for smaller firms and charge a fee for their services. (It is doubtful that the clients know the work is sub-contracted or they would contact the firms doing the work direct!)

In recent years the government has actively encouraged the growth of smaller firms. In particular, measures have been introduced to encourage the unemployed to set up their own businesses, and VAT regulations have been changed to ease the cash flow situation of small firms. There is also an Enterprise Allowance Scheme which pays unemployed people £40 per week for a year while they set up their own business. As a result the numbers self-employed have increased by over 40 per cent by the end of the 1980s to about 1.88m. Furthermore, the Business Expansion Scheme (BES) provides tax relief on investment by individuals in unquoted public companies, that is, those companies without a Stock Exchange quotation. There is no doubt that these measures have had a powerful impact on the growth of small firms.

## The role of small firms in the economy

Since the government has done so much to help the growth of the small firm sector it is reasonable to ask why they are considered important. One reason is that if individuals can be encouraged to set up in business rather than remain unemployed this reduces the unemployment figures but it might also improve the allocation of resources. After all, if workers are unemployed the opportunity cost of this is the output they might otherwise have produced. It is also possible that, as unemployment falls and therefore social security payments fall, the government will be able to reduce taxation. This is important because it is frequently alleged that a lower burden of taxation will increase incentives (see pages 216–217).

Another way in which small firms might promote employment is that they tend to be more labour intensive than larger firms and so have a proportionately larger effect on employment as they grow. However, there are other ways in which the growth of the small firm sector might be important to the economy. In particular they are important in providing training and it is generally argued that they can respond more flexibly to changes in market conditions because of their ability to vary output more quickly than larger firms.

## Why and how do firms grow?

There are many reasons why any individual firm might grow but the major factors are probably a desire to achieve increased profits and/or a desire to achieve greater security. Of course larger firms are not always the most profitable or the most secure, but because they often experience economies of scale they have clear advantages in both of these areas over smaller firms.

The methods by which firms grow can be classified as *internal* or *external*. Internal growth occurs when firms plough back profits into additional fixed assets and so expand their productive capacity. External growth occurs when one firm combines its existing assets with the assets of at least one other firm.

### Acquisitions and mergers

An acquisition occurs when one firm purchases another firm from its shareholders. This is often referred to as a *takeover* of one firm by another. A merger on the other hand is a voluntary agreement between two or more firms to combine their assets into a single firm. While the techniques used to achieve external growth might differ, the motives are often the same.

Firms might prefer external to internal growth for a variety of reasons. There might be specific reasons depending on the type of amalgamation or integration which takes place. These are discussed in the following section. Here we focus on some of the more general factors that might explain why firms amalgamate.

- External growth can mean the immediate transfer from one firm to another of existing brand loyalty and goodwill which takes time to build up and is not immediately available when a firm grows internally. In other words, when one firm acquires another firm it also acquires whatever consumer loyalty exists for the acquired firm's brands. The advantage of this is that if a firm grows internally it has to *persuade additional customers* to consume its products.

- External growth is sometimes used as a means of *diversifying*. Diversification is important because it increases security for a firm. A firm that produces only a single product, or a small number of related products is vulnerable to changes in demand for its product. Diversification increases the chances of long-run survival. Here again it might be considered expedient to acquire an existing firm already in the market than to attempt entry into the market as an outsider. In such cases the costs of entry can sometimes be high and when an additional producer undertakes supply it usually means an increased number of firms competing for the same sized market. This can be a dangerous strategy!
- Sometimes external growth offers the prospect of better locations. This is particularly important in retailing.
- Amalgamation might be a means of pooling expertise and sharing the costs of R & D expenditure as in the case of electronics where the R & D expenditures are particularly high. This is particularly appealing when an industry is dominated by an existing producer or where there is a threat of increased competition from abroad.
- A possible motive for an acquisition is *asset stripping*. This occurs when one firm takes over another with the intention of breaking the firm up into smaller units which are then resold. This is likely to happen when the price of a firm's equity on the stock market does not reflect the real value of its assets. One reason for this is that management of the firm is incompetent so that profits and dividends have been relatively low. If this were the only reason for asset stripping it might seem that it performed a useful role and the threat of being taken over would most likely encourage efficient management.

However, the threat of being taken over might actually encourage inefficiency because it encourages management to take a short-run perspective rather than a long-run perspective. They might therefore prefer to recommend higher dividends to shareholders rather than to plough back profits into long-run growth and projects likely to increase long-run efficiency. This is a very real possibilty. Corporate raiders are always on the look out for possible gains from asset stripping regardless of why these possible gains exist. A firm might find the value of its equity is reduced if it has embarked on an expansion programme and it might be vulnerable to the threat of a take-over before the benefits of its policies materialise.

## Horizontal integration

Horizontal integration occurs when firms in the same industry and at the same stage of the production process amalgamate. There are many motives for horizontal integration:

- Sometimes firms integrate in order to rationalise production, that is, concentrate production in the most profitable units. Such a policy, by reducing capacity in the industry, might reduce fixed costs and also result in higher prices. The combined effect might be to raise the overall profitability of firms in the industry.
- Another motive might be to take advantage of economies of scale, especially technical economies in the case of manufacturing firms. Since firms are at the same stage of production the desire to reap economies of scale is a particularly important motive for horizontal integration.
- It is possible that horizontal integration might be motivated by the desire to create a monopoly in the industry. Again, since firms are at the same stage of production, it is easy to see that horizontal integration could lead to the formation of a monopoly. For example, if a firm is able to gain control of the retail outlets or the supply of a particular input, it could effectively restrict the growth of competition and exercise monopoly power.

## Vertical integration

Vertical integration occurs when firms in the same industry but at different stages of the production process amalgamate. We can identify vertical integration backwards which occurs when firms amalgamate with other firms to bring them closer to their raw material suppliers or vertical integration forwards which brings a firm closer to its retail outlets. For example, if a newspaper publisher took over a paper mill this would be vertical integration backwards, while if a brewery took over a chain of public houses this would be vertical integration forwards. There are several possible reasons for vertical integration:

- Firms might integrate vertically for strategic reasons In the case of backward integration the aim might be to safeguard the delivery or quality of raw materials. The aim of forward integration might be to ensure that the firm has a chain of retail outlets through which its products can be distributed.
- Another possible motive for forward vertical integration is to improve and control the image of the retail outlets through which the product is distributed with the aim of increasing sales.
- Firms might gain economies of scale from either forwards or backwards integration. The increased size of the firm might make financial or managerial economies possible, for example. There might also be economies from linked processes.

There are other reasons why integration might lead to a reduction in costs. For example, when a firm acquires control of raw material supplies, inspection costs and reject rates might fall. In addition, having a reliable source of raw materials might enable firms to operate with lower stocks. Similarly if firms acquire retail outlets they might be better able to predict market demand or respond more quickly to any increase in market demand. Here again firms will be able to operate with lower stocks than previously.

## Test your understanding

1. Can a firm have more than one establishment?
2. Distinguish between a *firm*, an *establishment* and an *industry*.
3. What are the aims of the government's regional policy?
4. Why do small firms survive in the construction industry?
5. Distinguish between a merger and an aquisition.
6. Which of the following are examples of vertical integration:
   (a) a newspaper takes over a book publisher?
   (b) an abattoir takes over a chain of butchers?
   (c) a manufacturer of cars takes over a tyre company?
   (d) a mail order firm takes over a chain of retail stores?

# 9 National income accounting

## Stocks and flows

National income is a measure of the value of the output of goods and services produced by an economy over a period of time. Since national income measures production per period of time it is referred to as a *flow* concept. There is often considerable confusion between *stocks* and *flows*. A *stock* is the total accumulated quantity of any item existing at a particular time. A *flow*, on the other hand, measures the rate at which that stock is changing. When we are running a bath, for example, the quantity of water in the bath itself is the total stock of water, whereas the rate at which we are adding to that stock of water is the flow of water. Similarly, when we measure national income we are measuring the flow of output over a period of time, and this period is invariably one year.

## Nominal national income and real national income

Although national income is defined as a flow of output, it is the money value of that flow of output which is usually measured. It is not really practical to measure it as so many houses, so many cars, so many washing machines and so on, produced annually because we have no way of adding these together except in terms of their money value. Nevertheless, one reason for computing national income figures is to provide an accurate estimate of changes in the volume of output produced during one year, which can then be compared with other years. It would be misleading to simply compare the money value of output produced in two separate years because inflation will lead to a higher money value in later years irrespective of whether the volume of output has increased. In order to see what has happened to real national income when two years are compared, we must remove the effect of inflation on prices from the data. In other words, we must measure national income at constant prices. An example will illustrate how this is done:

| | National income (£m.) | Index of prices |
|---|---|---|
| Year 1 | 50,000 | 100 |
| Year 2 | 55,000 | 105 |

Between year 1 and year 2 the money value of national income has increased by 10 per cent. However, prices have increased by 5 per cent over the same period, so that the value of national income in year 2 in terms of year 1 prices is:

$$£55,000 \times \frac{100}{105} = £52,381\text{m. approx.}$$

Because we have measured national income at constant prices we can say that the volume of output or real national income, has increased by approximately 4.8 per cent compared with a rise in money national income of 10 per cent.

## Gross domestic product and gross national product

Gross Domestic Product (GDP) is the value of output produced by factors of production located within the UK. In other words, it is the sum total of all incomes earned by UK residents when producing goods and services with resources located inside the UK. However, the main official measure of total output is Gross National Product (GNP). This measures the total value of output produced, and incomes received, by UK residents from the ownership of resources, wherever these happen to be located. GNP therefore takes account of the fact that some UK residents earn incomes such as rent and profit from owning resources located abroad.

The flow of income from abroad mainly arises because foreign subsidiaries remit payments to the UK parent company. These are referred to as property income received from abroad. Similarly, foreign subsidiaries located in the UK remit payments abroad and these are referred to as property income paid abroad. The difference between these two flows of property income is referred to as net *property income from abroad*. It may be positive or negative, depending on whether there is a net inflow or net outflow of funds:

i.e. GDP + net property income from abroad = GNP.

## Gross national product and net national product

Gross National Product is the total value of incomes received by UK residents in the course of a year. It therefore includes the full value of plant and equipment produced during the course of the year (i.e. gross domestic fixed capital formation). However, over this period, existing plant and equipment will have depreciated, that is, declined in value due to wear and tear and obsolescence. In order to obtain a true measure of national income an appropriate deduction for capital depreciation must be made:

i.e. GNP − depreciation = Net National Product (NNP).

NNP is the aggregate that is most usually taken to mean national income. Despite this, GNP is the main official measure of the value of incomes received. Although net national product is conceptually the better measure, in practice it is impossible to accurately estimate the value of depreciation, that is, it is easier to measure investment gross than net. GNP is therefore more likely to give values of output and income which can be meaningfully compared over time and between countries.

## The circular flow of income

We have seen that national income is the value of output produced by a country over a particular period of time. This must be identically equal to the value of expenditures on output over the same period of time; after all, the value of output must be identically equal to expenditures on that output. Similarly spending on output must be equal to the rewards paid to the factors of production (wages, interest, rent and profit) which produced that output. This gives us the basic accounting identity:

$$\text{National income} \equiv \text{National output} \equiv \text{National expenditure}$$

which is illustrated in Figure 9.1.

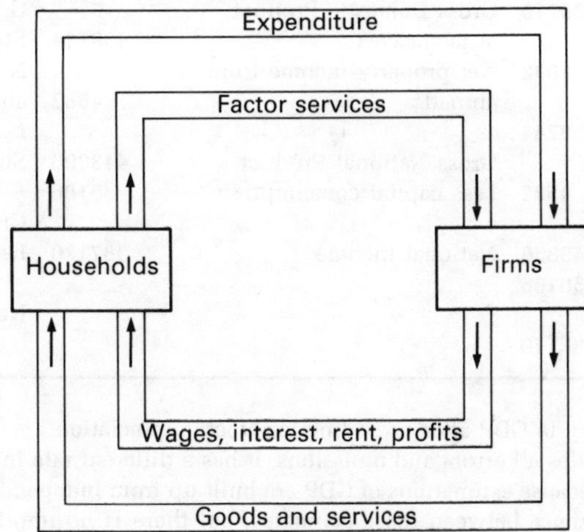


Figure 9.1 The circular flow of income

As it stands this diagram is highly unrealistic. It neglects the fact that saving and investment take place in the economy; it neglects the role of government in the economy and also the fact that in the real world international trade takes place. Nevertheless, by adjusting the circular flow to take account of these, the basic accounting identity is preserved.

## Measuring the national income

The circular flow of income illustrated in Figure 9.1 implies that there are three ways in which national income can be measured. In theory, since each measures the same aggregate, they should each give the same answer. In practice there are bound to be errors and omissions and this explains the inclusion of a *statistical discrepancy* which is an estimate (of all errors and omissions). Two further points need to be discussed. Table 9.1 shows how the national income figures for 1989 were built up.

*Table* 9.1 United Kingdom National Income in 1989 (£ million)

| Output[1] | | Income | | Expenditure | |
|---|---|---|---|---|---|
| Agriculture, forestry, fishing | 6561 | Income from employment | 284369 | Consumers' expenditure | 328453 |
| Energy & Water supply | 22619 | Income from self-employment | 53126 | General government final consumption | |
| Manufacturing | 97380 | Gross trading profits of companies | 65639 | of which: Central government | 60850 |
| Construction | 30274 | Gross trading surpluses of public corporations | 6576 | Local authorities | 38576 |
| Distribution, hotels & catering, repairs | 62133 | Gross trading surpluses of general government enterprises | 192 | Gross domestic fixed capital formation | 100472 |
| Banking, finance, insurance, business services & leasing | 86628 | Rent | 31568 | Value of physical increase in stocks & work in progress | 3102 |
| Transport and Communications | 30074 | Imputed charge for consumption of non-trading capital | 3840 | Total Domestic Expenditure at market prices | 531453 |
| Public administration, defence & compulsory social security | 29571 | *Less* stock appreciation | 7598 | Exports | 123396 |
| Ownership of dwellings | 25482 | Statistical discrepancy and income adjustment | 1032 | *Less* imports | 142527 |
| Education & health services | 42547 | Gross Domestic Product at factor cost | 438744 | Gross Domestic Product | 512322 |
| Other services | 29715 | Net property income from abroad | 4582 | Statistical discrepancy | 920 |
| Statistical discrepancy and income adjustment[2] | 1032 | Gross National Product | 443396 | Net property incomes from abroad | 4582 |
| Gross Domestic Product at factor cost | 438744 | *Less* capital consumption | 56186 | *Less* taxes on expenditure | 80136 |
| Net property income from abroad | 4582 | National Income | 387170 | Subsidies | 5668 |
| Gross National Product | 443356 | | | Gross National Product | 443356 |
| *Less* capital consumption | 56186 | | | *Less* capital consumption | 56186 |
| National Income | 387170 | | | National Income | 387170 |

[1] The contribution of each industry to GDP after providing for stock appreciation
[2] The statistical discrepancy includes all errors and omissions. It has a different rate in the expenditure estimates than in the estimates for output and income because estimations of GDP are built up from independent data on incomes expenditure. The statistical discrepancy is the difference between these estimates, but there is no implication that expenditure estimates are superior in accuracy.

Source: United Kingdom National Accounts, HMSO 1989

## The output method

A country's national income can be calculated from the output figures of all firms in the economy. However, care must be taken to ensure that all output is included in the calculation and that no output is counted twice.

### Double counting

Summing the value of output does not simply mean that we add together the value of each firm's output. To do so would give us an aggregate many times greater than national income because of *double counting*. The point is that the outputs of some firms are the inputs of other firms. For example, the output of the steel industry is partly factor input for the automobile industry and so on. Clearly, to include the total value of each industry's output in national income calculations would mean counting the value of the steel used in automobile production twice. Double counting can be avoided by summing the value added at each stage of production, or by adding together the final value of output produced. Column (a) of Table 9.1 shows how the output figures for 1989 were built up.

**Public goods and merit goods**

We have already seen in Chapter 2 that the government provides many goods and services through the non-market sector, such as education, medical care, defence and so on. Such goods and services are clearly part of the nation's output, but since they are not sold through the market sector they do not strictly have a market price. In such cases the value of the output is measured at *resource cost* or *factor cost*. In other words, the value of the service is assumed to be equivalent to the cost of the resources used to provide it. For instance, the education and health services output was valued at £42,597m. in 1989.

**Self-provided commodities**

A similar problem arises in the case of self-provided commodities, such as vegetables grown in the domestic garden, car repairs and home improvements done on a do-it-yourself basis and so on. Again, these represent output produced, but there is no market value for such output. The vast majority of self-provided commodities are omitted from the national income statistics, although an estimate of the rental value of owner-occupied dwellings is included (£25,482m. in Table 9.1).

**Exports and imports**

Not all of the nation's output is consumed domestically. Part is sold abroad as exports. Nevertheless, GDP is the value of domestically produced output and hence export earnings must be included in this figure. If exports were omitted, the value of output produced would be less than the value of incomes received from producing that output. Table 9.1 shows that in 1989 export earnings accounted for over 24 per cent of GDP.

On the other hand, a great deal of domestically produced output incorporates imported raw materials and there is a considerable amount of consumer expenditure on imported goods and services. Expenditure on imports results in a flow of factor incomes abroad. Hence the value of the import content of final output must be deducted from the output figures if GDP is to be accurately measured. Failure to do this would result in the value of total output exceeding the value of incomes received from producing that output. Table 9.1 shows that import expenditure was equivalent to almost 28 per cent of GDP in 1989.

**Net property income from abroad**

This source of income to domestic residents will not be included in the output figures of firms. We have already noted that the net inflow (+) or outflow (−) of funds must be added to GDP when calculating the value of domestically owned output, i.e. GNP. This gives a figure of £443,356m. for GNP in 1989. When we subtract depreciation of capital (capital consumption) we are left with a national income (NNP) of £387,170m.

### The income method

When calculating national product as a flow of incomes it is important to ensure that only factor rewards are included. In other words, only those incomes paid in return for some productive activity, and for which there is a corresponding output are included in national income. Of course it is the gross value of these factor rewards which must be aggregated, since this represents the value of output produced. Levying taxes on factor incomes reduces the amount factors receive, but it does not reduce the value of output produced! Income from employment (£284,369m.) and from self-emploment (£53,126m.) together make up almost 77 per cent of GNP in 1989. When calculating the aggregate value of factor incomes, adjustments might also be necessary for other reasons.

#### Transfer payments

The sum of all factor incomes is not the same as the sum of all personal incomes, since the latter includes transfer payments. These are simply transfers of income within the community, and they are not made in respect of any productive activity. Indeed, the bulk of all transfer payments within the UK are made by the government for social reasons. Examples include social security payments, pensions, child allowances and so on. Since no output is produced in respect of these payments they must not be included in the aggregate of factor incomes.

#### Undistributed surpluses

Another problem in aggregating factor incomes arises because not all factor incomes are distributed to the factors of production. Firms might retain part or all of their profits to finance future investment. Similarly, the profits of public bodies, such as nationalised industries, accrue to the government rather than to private individuals. Care must be taken to include these undistributed surpluses as factor incomes. It is therefore necessary to add the gross value of profits of companies (£65,639m.), of public corporations (£6,576m.) and of other public enterprises (£192m.), to income from employment and self-employment.

#### Stock appreciation

Care must be taken to deduct changes in the money value of stock caused by inflation. These are windfall gains, and do not represent a real increase in the value of output.

#### Net property income from abroad

When measuring either gross national product or net national product we have seen that it is necessary to add net property income from abroad to the aggregate of domestic incomes.

### The expenditure method

The final method of calculating national income is as a flow of expenditure on domestic output. However, it is only expenditure on final output which must be aggregated, otherwise there is again a danger of double counting, with intermediate expenditure such as raw materials being counted twice. Additionally, it is only expenditure on *current* output which is relevant. Secondhand goods are not part of the *current* flow of output, and factors of production have already received payment for these goods at the time they were produced. We should note, however, that any income earned by a salesman employed in the secondhand trade, or the profits of secondhand dealers, are included in the national income statistics. The service these occupations render is part of current production!

Like the output and income totals, the value of expenditure in the economy must be adjusted if it is to accurately measure national income.

**Consumers' expenditure**

At £328,453m. this is the major element in expenditure, accounting for almost 62 per cent of total domestic expenditure in 1989.

**General government final consumption**

Since only domestic expenditure on goods and services is relevant, care must be taken to deduct any expenditure on transfer payments by the government or other public authorities. Such expenditures do not contribute directly to the current flow of output and, therefore, we must only include that part of public authorities' current expenditure which is spent directly on goods and services. In 1989 public authorities' expenditure on goods and services was £99,426m., that is, almost 19 per cent of total domestic expenditure.

**Gross investment**

Expenditure on fixed capital, such as plant and machinery, must obviously be included in calculations of total expenditure. Gross Domestic Fixed Capital Formation incorporates this item and, at £100,472m. was almost 20 per cent of total domestic expenditure. What is not so obvious is that *additions to stock and work in progress* also represent investment. The factors of production which have produced this, as yet, unsold output, will still have received factor payments. To ignore additions to stock and work in progress would therefore create an imbalance between the three aggregates: output, income and expenditure. Additions to stock and work in progress are therefore treated as though they have been purchased by firms. Care must be taken then to include them in the aggregate of total expenditure. In 1989 the figure for this item came to £3,102m.

**Exports and imports**

We have already seen that it is important to include exports and exclude imports from our calculation of national income. Care must again be taken to ensure this when aggregating total expenditures.

**Net property income abroad**

As before, when moving from domestic to national income, it is important to include net property income from abroad when aggregating total expenditures.

**Taxes and subsidies**

In practice, indirect taxes (usually placed on goods and services) and subsidies might distort the accounting identity. Indirect taxes raise market prices above the amount paid out to the factors of production. Since we are interested in the value of incomes received indirect taxes must be deducted from the value of output and subsidies must be added on.

## National income and the standard of living

The most widely used statistic for measuring changes in a country's standard of living is *per capita income*. This is GNP divided by total population and provides a measure of the average amount of output available per head per year. However, simply comparing per capita income in one period with per capita income in another period can be a misleading indicator of changes in living standards for several reasons.

### Constant prices

For comparisons to be accurate it is necessary to measure changes in GNP per capita at constant prices otherwise per capita income would rise because of inflation but this would not necessarily imply that living standards had increased. Even measuring per capita income at constant prices does not provide an unambiguous measure of changes in living standards.

### Increased availability of leisure

A reduction in the size of the working week or an increase in the number of annual days holiday will have a positive effect on economic welfare even though the potential value of GNP might be adversely affected. Comparisons of economic welfare should therefore include a measure of the increased value of leisure.

### Qualitative changes in output

Another factor to consider is that over time there will be qualitative changes in the goods society consumes. Accurate comparisons of economic welfare must make some allowance for the additional satisfaction this confers on consumers.

### Non-market activities

A great deal of economic activity is unrecorded and does not appear in GNP statistics. The services of housewives are the biggest omission here though a great deal of gardening or home repairs are often done by other members of the family. It is difficult to estimate the value of these but there is no doubt that their omission reduces the reliability of GNP as a measure of economic welfare.

### Green issues

Environmental considerations are an increasingly important factor in assessing economic welfare. One consequence of modern production is air, soil and water pollution, as well as degradation of the environment. Such environmental 'costs' are unrecorded but reduce the real value of GNP below the official figures. As a consequence, the reliability of measured GNP is reduced.

It seems that GNP does not accurately measure economic welfare because it omits several important factors and inaccurately records the value of others. However, it does measure the total value of output that becomes available for consumption and this is probably the most important factor determining economic welfare.

### International comparisons

Despite the problems of measurement, GNP per capita is still the most widely used estimate of comparative living standards. Table 9.2 shows a recent comparison of international living standards in certain countries. Canada is the closest to the US in terms of GDP per head,

*Table 9.2* GDP in 1985

| Country | GDP per head(£) |
|---|---|
| USA | 9400 |
| Canada | 8500 |
| Norway | 8000 |
| Luxemburg | 7800 |
| Sweden | 7200 |
| Denmark | 7000 |
| West Germany | 6900 |
| Japan | 6600 |
| Finland | 6500 |
| France | 6500 |
| Netherlands | 6500 |
| UK | 6200 |
| Belgium | 6100 |
| Austria | 6000 |
| Italy | 5400 |
| Spain | 4400 |
| Ireland | 4000 |
| Greece | 3400 |
| Portugal | 3000 |

Source: *Economic Progress Report* No 189, March–April 1987

and Portugal the most distant, with the UK living standard on this measure about two-thirds that of the US.

However, these figures must be judged with caution and there are several problems involved in making comparisons of this nature. These are briefly summarised.

### Different methods of calculating GNP

Countries sometimes differ in the way they compute GNP. For example, unlike the UK, the Soviet Union does not include bus journeys made to or from work. The reason is that such journeys do not represent output that becomes available for consumption. They simply enable people to undertake production of goods and services for consumption by others. When GNP is computed differently, per capita income will be an unreliable guide to international living standards.

### Differences in composition of GNP

There might be substantial differences in the composition of GNP. For example, some countries spend very large amounts on defence compared with other countries. It could be argued that devoting resources to defence preserves liberty and in this way adds to the standard of living. However, it is equally true that the opportunity cost of defence expenditure is a lower output of goods for domestic consumption. In such cases international comparisons of GNP per head might give a misleading indication of *current* living standards.

There are other natural or climatic factors that might give rise to differences in the composition of output. Thus some countries devote fewer resources to the production of heat and light than is the case in countries where these are provided freely by nature. In the latter countries, resources that are not needed to provide heat and light are available for the production of other goods and services. Again, per capita income might not be very different in two countries, yet there might be marked differences in actual living standards when one country benefits relative to the other from goods provided freely by nature.

### Exports and imports

Another important factor that might reduce the credibility of per capita income as a measure of living standards is that in some countries per capita income might be relatively high in relation to domestic consumption. Many OPEC countries, for example, have relatively high per capita incomes, but these are derived mainly from *export* earnings from the sale of oil unmatched by equivalent expenditure on imports. The true standard of living for most people in these countries is therefore relatively low, since domestic income per capita is well above domestic consumption per capita. The converse is also true. It is possible for countries to raise their standard of living in the short term by importing more than they export, that is, by running a balance of payments deficit. In this case domestic consumption is raised above its usual proportion of domestic income by increasing imports relative to exports. Clearly variations between countries in the ratio of per capita income to per capita consumption can complicate the use of national income statistics in assessing standards of living.

### Distribution of income

Even if countries do have similar per capita incomes and similar per capita levels of consumption, they may still have different standards of living for the majority of their respective populations. This would happen where the distribution of income was more equal in one country than in the other. It might also happen where taxation was significantly higher for the majority of the population in one country than in the other.

### Different currencies

For purposes of international comparisons there is the problem of converting per capita incomes into a common unit of account. In practice this involves converting all per capita incomes into a single currency (usually $USA) by using *purchasing power parities*. This measures how many units of one country's currency are needed to buy exactly the same basket of goods that can be bought with a *given amount* of another country's currency. For example, the number of pounds required to buy in the UK the same goods that a given quantity of dollars buys in the USA. Any inaccuracies in converting domestic currencies to dollars using purchasing power parities will impair the reliability of comparative per capita statistics.

## Uses of national income statistics

Government's collect national income statistics for a variety of reasons. These are briefly summarised.

1. National income statistics are important in the formulation and assessment of macroeconomic policy. It is clearly important to know current levels of output and patterns of expenditure when formulating policies to combat unemployment, inflation, balance of payments deficits and so on.
2. National income statistics are used to monitor changes in real income. This is important because changes in real income have an important bearing on changes in living standards.
3. National income statistics are used to make international comparisons between the home country's economic performance with that of other countries. A *relatively* slow growth of real income is a strong indication that the economy is doing less well than it might, and often leads to a detailed scrutiny of the reasons for this 'shortfall'.
4. Per capita income statistics provide a guide to the standard of living in different countries and are used as a basis for allocating aid to third world countries.

## Personal disposable income

Despite the emphasis on national income in this chapter, for most individuals *personal disposable income* is more important. This is the flow of income that accrues to an individual or household. It consists of earned income from the sale of labour, from the ownership of assets and transfer payments less tax payments. For an individual or household, *real* personal disposable income is the main factor influencing living standards.

Personal disposable income and national income are related. If all other things remain equal as national income rises personal disposable income rises. However, the growth of national income is not the only factor influencing personal disposable income. For an individual or household it is also affected by the rate of taxation and the distribution of national income.

## Test your understanding

1. What is the difference between GNP and GDP?
2. In what circumstances will: (i) GNP > GDP (ii) GDP > GNP?
3. Which of the following are included in national income statistics?
   (a) Earnings of a member of the armed forces serving abroad.
   (b) A punter's winnings on the Grand National.
   (c) The sale of a natural resource such as coal.
   (d) Social security payments.
   (e) The payment of commission to an estate agent.
4. In a particular country over the course of a year the following changes occur: (i) imports increase by £50m., (ii) transfer

payments fall by £5m., (iii) total consumer spending increases by £80m., (iv) imports of capital equipment increase by £5m., (v) saving falls by £15m., (vi) exports increase by £40m., (vii) net property income from abroad falls by £2m., (viii) depreciation increases by £1m.

Over this period what happens to the value of:

(a) GNP?
(b) GDP?
(c) NNP?

5. If nominal national income rises by 25 per cent and over the same period inflation is at the rate of 10 per cent, what happens to real national income?
6. If nominal GNP increases and all other things remain equal, does this imply an increase in the standard of living?
7. In what circumstances will an increase in productivity *not* lead to an increase in GDP?
8. Which words correctly complete the following sentence? The main distinction between wealth and income is that wealth is a _________ whereas income is _________.
9. Why does a pension paid by the government of Great Britain not add to GNP in Great Britain, whereas a pension paid to a British national by a foreign government does?
10. What is meant by the term *real national income*?

# 10 National income determination

Conventionally, aggregate demand has been regarded as the main determinant of national income. This is an extremely important premise since it implies that aggregate demand determines aggregate supply, that is output is demand determined. Aggregate demand refers to the total of planned expenditure for the economy as a whole. Aggregate supply, on the other hand, refers to the total output of all firms in the economy. Aggregate supply is therefore the same as *real* national income, that is, the total value of output produced at constant prices. We begin by considering the components of aggregate demand.

## The components of aggregate demand

### Consumption

In the macro sense, consumption refers to the total spending of households on goods and services for their own private use. It is termed 'consumers' expenditure' in the national income accounts. Table 9.1 on page 86 shows that consumers' expenditure is by far the largest component of aggregate expenditure, comprising 60 per cent of the total. However, aggregate demand consists of spending on domestic output only. Spending on imports does not directly affect aggregate supply and therefore in computing aggregate demand we must deduct any expenditure on imports.

### Investment

Investment is the creation of any output that is not for immediate consumption. It consists of capital goods, such as factory buildings and machinery, as well as additions to the stock of raw materials, semi-finished goods or finished goods. Total investment is shown in Table 9.1 as gross domestic fixed capital formation, plus the value of the physical increase in stocks and work in progress. Investment is an important component of aggregate demand because it is highly unstable. Changes in investment are therefore an important source of changes in aggregate demand. However, for simplicity it is assumed in this chapter that investment is *autonomous* or *exogenous* that is, it is not influenced by changes in the level of national income. Investment is analysed more fully in Chapter 11.

### Government expenditure

Government expenditure has two components: spending on goods and services and transfer payments. Transfer payments are simply transfers of income within the community. They do not represent direct spending on goods and services. When spent they will add to aggregate demand but this will be reflected in consumption spending. Similarly, government spending on imports adds nothing to national income. Only government spending on real domestic output contributes directly to aggregate demand and therefore to national income.

## Exports

The sale of exports represents expenditure by foreigners on domestically produced output. Exports, *less* any imported raw material content, therefore make a direct contribution to national income.

In summary, the determinants of aggregate demand are often expressed in notation as:

$$AD = C + I + G + X - M = Y$$

where: $AD$ = aggregate demand
$C$ = consumption
$I$ = investment
$G$ = government expenditure on goods and services
$X$ = exports
$M$ = imports
$Y$ = income

## The propensity to consume and the consumption function

The relationship between consumption and disposable income is known as the propensity to consume. The *marginal propensity to consume* is the rate of change of consumption with respect to disposable income, that is $MPC = \Delta C/\Delta Yd$. The *average propensity to consume* is the proportion of total disposable income spent on consumption, that is $APC = C/Yd$.

A *consumption function* shows the different levels of consumption at different levels of income, and is usually presented in the form C = a + bY, where a and b are constants. If we initially assume a closed economy with no government sector, then any income not spent must be saved. Figure 10.1 shows a typical consumption function and the corresponding savings function.

A certain amount of consumption expenditure will always be undertaken, no matter what the level of income. Thus, a is exogenous at £1,000m., since it does not vary with income. However, as income rises this will induce a higher level of consumption spending, the extent of which will depend on the size of b, the marginal propensity to consume. In this case b is assumed to be 0.75. Figure 10.1 is based on Table 10.1.

Note that when income is less than £4,000m., consumption is greater than income. In this case consumption is financed by *dissaving*, that is, by running down savings accumulated during previous periods.

*Table 10.1*

| Income (£m.) | Consumption (£m.) | Savings (£m.) |
|---|---|---|
| 0 | 1,000 | −1,000 |
| 1,000 | 1,750 | −750 |
| 2,000 | 2,500 | −500 |
| 3,000 | 3,250 | −250 |
| 4,000 | 4,000 | 0 |
| 5,000 | 4,750 | 250 |
| 6,000 | 5,500 | 500 |
| 7,000 | 6,250 | 750 |
| 8,000 | 7,000 | 1,000 |

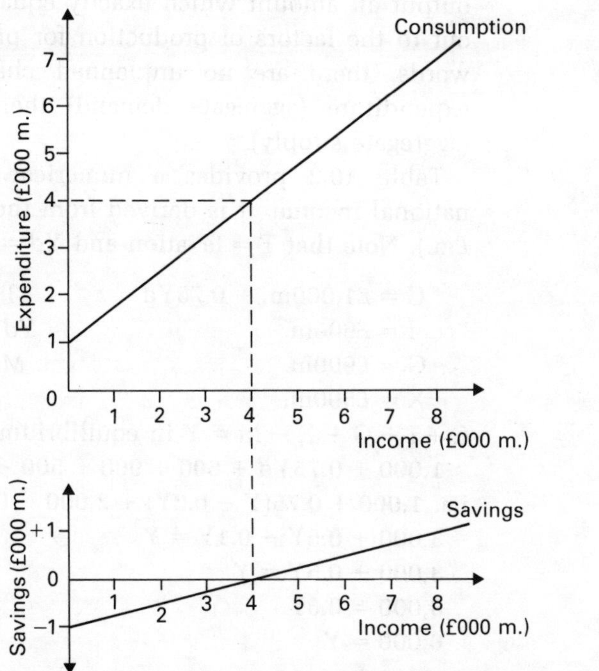


*Figure 10.1* The consumption function and the savings function

## Planned and realised values

It is important to distinguish between *planned* (or ex-ante) and *realised* (or ex-post) values. Planned expenditure in the economy is simply the aggregate spending each sector plans to undertake in the next accounting period. Realised expenditure, on the other hand, is the actual level of spending achieved by each sector over that accounting period.

Planned and realised values have particular significance in relation to investment because any excess of spending over output (or of output over spending) manifests itself in unplanned changes in stock. Since additions to stock are recorded as investment in the official statistics, it follows that any unplanned increase in stocks is referred to as unplanned investment, and that any unplanned decrease in stock is referred to as unplanned disinvestment. The importance of unplanned investment and unplanned disinvestment is that since they are unanticipated, they lead producers to revise their planned levels of output in the following period. In this way unplanned investment or unplanned disinvestment will initiate changes in national income.

## The equilibrium level of income

Equilibrium exists when there is no tendency to change. The equilibrium level of national income exists when there is no tendency for income to change. This can only occur when planned expenditure in one period exactly equals the planned output for that period. When this is the case, producers are receiving back in expenditure on their output an amount which exactly equals the amount they have paid out to the factors of production for producing that output. In other words, there are no unplanned changes in stock and planned expenditure (aggregate demand) therefore equals planned output (aggregate supply).

Table 10.2 provides a numerical example of the equilibrium national income. It is derived from the following planned values (in £m.). Note that T = taxation and Yd = disposable income.

$$C = \pounds 1{,}000\text{m.} + 0.75Yd \qquad T = 0.2Y$$
$$I = \pounds 600\text{m.} \qquad Yd = Y - T$$
$$G = \pounds 900\text{m.} \qquad M = 0.125Yd$$
$$X = \pounds 500\text{m.}$$

$C + I + G + X - M = Y$ in equilibrium

$$1{,}000 + 0.75Yd + 600 + 900 + 500 - 0.125Yd = Y$$

i.e. $1{,}000 + 0.75(Y - 0.2Y) + 2{,}000 - 0.125(Y - 0.2Y) = Y$

$$3{,}000 + 0.6Y - 0.1Y = Y$$
$$3{,}000 + 0.5Y = Y$$
$$3{,}000 = 0.5Y$$
$$6{,}000 = Y$$

*Table 10.2*

| National income (£m.) | Aggregate demand (£m.) | Unplanned change in stocks (£m.) | Tendency of change in national income |
|---|---|---|---|
| 1,000 | 3,500 | −2,500 | Increase |
| 2,000 | 4,000 | −2,000 | Increase |
| 3,000 | 4,500 | −1,500 | Increase |
| 4,000 | 5,000 | −1,000 | Increase |
| 5,000 | 5,500 | −500 | Increase |
| 6,000 | 6,000 | 0 | No change |
| 7,000 | 6,500 | 500 | Decrease |
| 8,000 | 7,000 | 1,000 | Decrease |

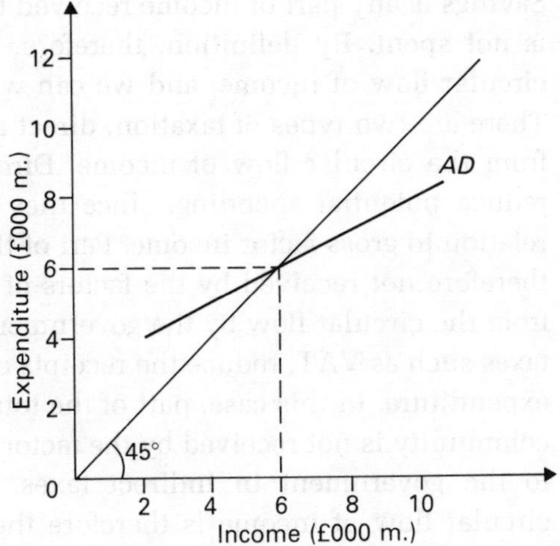


*Figure 10.2* The equilibrium level of national income

If aggregate demand were greater than £6,000m., then the value of output, *Y*, must rise. If aggregate demand were less than £6,000m., then the value of output, *Y*, must fall.

Equilibrium can also be illustrated diagramatically as in Figure 10.2. Since both axes have the same scale, the 45° line which bisects them gives the path of all points of equality between planned expenditure and planned output (national income). It therefore shows all the possible equilibrium levels of national income within the range illustrated.

It is clear that, given the aggregate demand schedule shown, £6,000m. is the equilibrium level of output (income). At levels of output below this, aggregate demand exceeds the value of national output and the tendency will be for the value of national output to rise. At levels of output (income) above this, aggregate demand is less than national output (i.e. aggregate demand is insufficient to purchase the existing level of output) and the tendency will be for the value of national output to fall. Only when Y = £6,000m. is there no tendency for national output (income) to change, because aggregate demand is just sufficient to purchase the existing level of output.

National income equilibrium can be looked at in another way, in terms of leakages and injections.

## Leakages and injections

### Leakages

A leakage is a withdrawal of potential spending from the circular flow of income. A leakage occurs when any part of the income which results from the production of domestic goods and services is not used to purchase other domestic goods and services.

We can identify three leakages from the circular flow of income: savings, taxation and import expenditure.

*Savings (S)*

Savings is any part of income received by domestic households which is not spent. By definition, therefore, savings is a leakage from the circular flow of income, and we can write $S = Yd - C$.

*Taxation (T)*

There are two types of taxation, direct and indirect. Both are leakages from the circular flow of income. Direct taxes, such as income tax, reduce potential spending, since they reduce disposable income in relation to gross factor income. Part of the value of output produced is therefore not received by the factors of production, but is withdrawn from the circular flow by the government. On the other hand, indirect taxes such as VAT, reduce the receipts of producers in relation to total expenditure. In this case, part of the total spending undertaken by the community is not received by the factors of production since it is paid to the government in indirect taxes. The total tax leak from the circular flow of income is therefore the amount paid in direct taxes plus the amount paid in indirect taxes.

*Imports (M)*

Import expenditure represents the purchase by domestic residents of output produced abroad. Imports are therefore a leakage, since part of the income received by domestic residents is not returned to the circular flow as expenditure on domestic goods and services.

Summarising, we can write that total leakages from the circular flow of income = $S + T + M$.

## Injections

An injection is an addition of spending to the circular flow of income. It consists of any expenditure on domestic goods and services which does not arise from the spending of domestic households. An injection is therefore spending other than consumption expenditure.

There are also three injections into the circular flow of income. They are investment (*I*), direct government expenditure on goods and services (*G*), and exports (*X*). Each of these was discussed earlier (see p. 89).

We can write that total injections into the circular flow of income = $I + G + X$.

## An alternative view of equilibrium

Realised injections must always equal realised leakages, but the economy can only be in equilibrium when planned injections equal planned leakages. If planned injections into the circular flow of income are greater than planned leakages from it, then national income will tend to rise. This is because planned spending will exceed national output (income), so that producers will experience unplanned disinvestment in stock and will expand output in the following period. Conversely, if planned injections are less than planned leakages, then national income will tend to fall. Planned spending will now be less than national output (income), so that there will be insufficient demand to purchase existing output. Producers will experience unplanned investment in stock and will reduce output in the following period. It follows that national income can only be in equilibrium when planned injections equal planned leakages. The equilibrium condition may therefore be stated as:

$$I + G + X = S + T + M$$

This is clearly shown in Table 10.3 which extends Table 10.2 to include the various injections and leakages discussed above. Note that planned injections are assumed to be exogenous and do not vary with income. The appropriate values (in £m.) are:

$$\begin{aligned} C &= £1{,}000\text{m.} + 0.75Yd \\ I &= £600\text{m.} \\ G &= £900\text{m.} \\ X &= £500\text{m.} \\ S &= -£1{,}000\text{m.} + 0.25Yd \\ Yd &= Y - T \\ T &= 0.2Y \\ M &= 0.125Yd \end{aligned}$$

The equilibrium level of income is £6,000m., because this is the only level of income at which planned injections equal planned leakages (see also the solution on page 102). Since planned spending exactly equals national output (income), producers will experience no unplanned investment in stock, i.e. planned investment = realised investment. There will be no incentive for producers to change output in the following period. If income is at any other level it will have a tendency to increase or to decrease. Again, equilibrium can be

*Table 10.3*

| National income Y | Aggregate demand AD | Planned savings S | Planned taxation T | Planned expenditure on imports M | Planned government expenditure G | Planned export sales X | Planned investment I | Realised investment | Tendency of change in national income |
|---|---|---|---|---|---|---|---|---|---|
| 0 | 3,000 | −1,000 | 0 | 0 | 900 | 500 | 600 | −2,400 | Increase |
| 1,000 | 3,500 | −800 | 200 | 100 | 900 | 500 | 600 | −1,900 | Increase |
| 2,000 | 4,000 | −600 | 400 | 200 | 900 | 500 | 600 | −1,400 | Increase |
| 3,000 | 4,500 | −400 | 600 | 300 | 900 | 500 | 600 | −900 | Increase |
| 4,000 | 5,000 | −200 | 800 | 400 | 900 | 500 | 600 | −400 | Increase |
| 5,000 | 5,500 | 0 | 1,000 | 500 | 900 | 500 | 600 | 100 | Increase |
| 6,000 | 6,000 | 200 | 1,200 | 600 | 900 | 500 | 600 | 600 | No change |
| 7,000 | 6,500 | 400 | 1,400 | 700 | 900 | 500 | 600 | 1,100 | Decrease |
| 8,000 | 7,000 | 600 | 1,600 | 800 | 900 | 500 | 600 | 1,600 | Decrease |

represented diagrammatically, this time using the injections and leakages approach. This can be seen in the lower part of Figure 10.3 which uses the values of Table 10.2. The upper part of the diagram reproduces Figure 10.2 in order to help us compare the two approaches.

Planned injections $(I + G + X)$ are constant at £2,000m. Planned leakages $(S + T + M)$ vary with national income. To plot the leakages curve we can add together the various values of $S$, $T$ and $M$ in Table 10.3 at each level of national income. Alternatively, we can derive the leakages function by adding together the separate functions for $S$, $T$ and $M$.

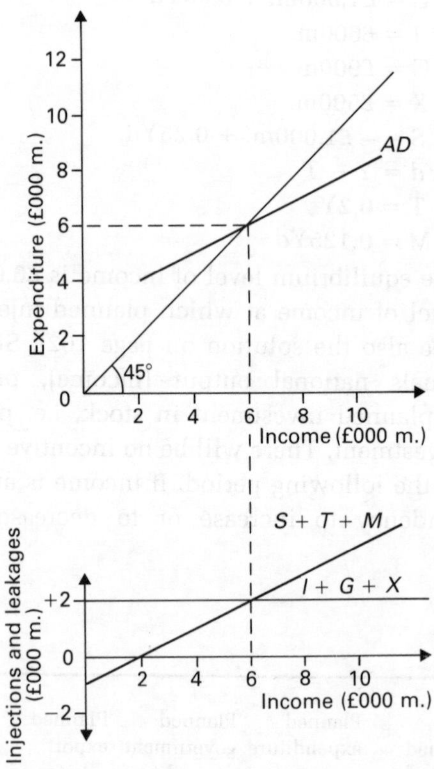


*Figure 10.3* The equilibrium level of income

## The multiplier

One of the most important features of the model of income determination is that it shows how any change in injections or leakages can lead to a more than proportional change in national income. This is known as the *multiplier* effect. It arises because an initial change in injections or leakages leads to a series of changes in national income, the cumulative effect of which exceeds the initial change which brought it about. For example, if firms increase their investment in plant and equipment, and all other things remain equal, national income will initially rise by the same amount as the increase in investment. If we assume an absence of taxation, the increased expenditure on plant and equipment will in turn be received as rewards by the factors which have produced this output. Part of this (depending on the size of the *MPC*) will be spent, generating a further increase in income, part of which will also be spent and so on. However, this process does not go on indefinitely. With each rise in income, a smaller amount will be passed on, and this will generate successively smaller changes in income.

A numerical example will help to clarify this. For simplicity we assume there is only one injection, i.e. investment, and one leakage, i.e. savings. Assume further that four-fifths of any increase in income is spent on consumption and that investment in plant and equipment rises by £100m. The letter $k$ is used to denote the multiplier.

The increase in investment initially raised income by £100m., £80m. of which is subsequently spent on consumption, so that output and income rise by a further £80m. Four-fifths of this £80m. is also spent on consumption, so that output and income rises by a further £64m., and so on. We can see that income goes on rising as a geometric progression diminishing to infinity. The first few terms of this series, together with the final value (in £m.) are set out below.

$$\Delta I = \text{£}100\text{m.}$$
$$\Delta Y = \text{£}100\text{m.} + \text{£}80\text{m.} + \text{£}64\text{m.} + \text{£}51.2\text{m.} + \ldots$$
$$\text{i.e.} \quad \Delta Y = \text{£}500\text{m.}$$
$$k = \Delta Y/\Delta I = \text{£}500\text{m.}/\text{£}100\text{m.} = 5$$

This implies that an increase in injections causes an eventual increase in income which is five times greater than the initial increase in injections.

It is equally interesting to look at what happens to savings following the increase in investment. We have seen that for each increase in income there is an increase in consumption. But since not all of the increase in income is passed on, there must also be an increase in savings. In fact, since in this discussion savings is the only leakage from the circular flow, it follows that $\Delta Y = \Delta C + \Delta S$. In other words, savings also rises as a geometric progression diminishing to infinity, and the first few terms of this series, together with the final value (in £m.) are:

$$\Delta S = \text{£}20\text{m.} + \text{£}16\text{m.} + \text{£}12.8\text{m.} + \ldots$$
$$\text{i.e.} \ \Delta S = \text{£}100\text{m.}$$

The significant point is that, following an increase in investment of £100m., income goes on rising until households wish to save a further £100m. This is because equilibrium can only exist when planned injections equal planned leakages. Following an increase in planned investment, these two items are brought into equality by an increase in income which encourages the households to revise their savings plans upwards.

### The value of the multiplier

The value of the multiplier can be obtained by using the formula:

$$k = \frac{1}{(1 - \text{common ratio})}$$

This can be applied to the example above. Thus

$$k = \frac{1}{1 - MPC} = \frac{1}{1 - 0.8} = 5$$

However, when there are other leakages from the circular flow of income, it is more usual to express the multiplier as:

$$k = \frac{1}{\text{marginal rate of leakage from gross income}}$$

In the four sector economy this can be written as:

$$k = \frac{1}{MPS + MRT + MPM}$$

Where MPS is the marginal propensity to save, MRT is the marginal rate of taxation and MPM is the marginal propensity to import. For example, using the values from which Table 10.3 was derived (i.e. $MPS = 0.25Yd$, $MRT = 0.2Y$, and $MPM = 0.125Yd$), we can calculate:

$$k = \frac{1}{0.25(0.8) + 0.2 + 0.125(0.8)}$$

$$= \frac{1}{0.5}$$

$$= 2$$

### The determinants of the multiplier

In practice the size of the multiplier might be quite small and is estimated at about 1.3–1.4 for the UK. There are many factors which influence the size of the multiplier including:

- *The distribution of income.* Since higher income groups have a higher *MPS* than lower income groups, a less equal distribution of income implies a lower value for the multiplier.
- *Taxation.* Other things being equal the higher the average rate of taxation the smaller the amount available for consumption spending and therefore the smaller the size of the multiplier. However, where taxation bears more heavily on lower income groups, this will reduce the value of the multiplier because these groups tend to have a higher *MPC*.
- *Import expenditure.* Some countries are heavily dependent on imports and have a relatively high *MPM*. In such cases the size of the multiplier will be lower than otherwise.

- *Level of employment.* When the economy is close to full employment there will be supply inelasticities or supply bottlenecks. Firms will therefore find it more difficult to recruit additional workers, to obtain additional supplies of raw materials, etc. in response to an increase in investment. This will limit any increase in output and, if the increase in investment is large enough, might generate inflation because the higher level of demand for resources would pull up their prices. Such bottlenecks will also encourage the consumption of imports. An economy which is experiencing supply inelasticities will therefore tend to have a lower value for the multiplier.
- *Levels of stock.* When firms currently have high stock levels they might choose to run down stocks rather than increase output in response to an increase in demand.
- *Expectations.* When an increase in demand is not considered to be permanent, firms might simply lengthen their waiting lists, or allow the higher level of demand to bid up the price of their products.
- *Crowding out.* The size of the multiplier will also be lower if 'crowding out' takes place. Crowding out is the term used to describe the effect of an increase in public sector investment on private sector investment. In particular it is argued that an increase in public sector investment crowds out, that is, reduces, private sector investment. Where crowding out does take place an increase in public sector investment will have a smaller multiplier effect than an increase in private sector investment.

## The balanced multiplier

The balanced budget multiplier shows the effect on income of equal changes in government expenditure and taxation. It might be expected that the net effect would be zero and that income would remain unchanged. In fact, the following example illustrates that this is not the case. Suppose there is an increase in government current expenditure of £100m., financed entirely by an increase in taxation of £100m., with $MPC = 0.8Y$ and $MPS = 0.2Y$.

The increase in government spending will lead to a diminishing series of increases in income. The first few terms and the eventual sum of this series (in £m.) are:

$$\Delta Y = £100m + £80m. + £64m. + \ldots = £500m.$$

The increase in taxation will lead to a similar series of reductions in income. However, the change in tax is not so straightforward as the change in government expenditure. Part of any increase in taxation will be financed by a reduction in the amount saved. To the extent that this is the case, the increase in one leakage from the circular flow of income (T) is in part compensated for by the reduction of another (S). In other words, the *net change* in leakages is less than the change in taxation. Thus only that part of any increase in taxation which is financed by a reduction in consumption, rather than by a reduction in savings, has any effect on income. In our example, the net increase in leakages is equal to $0.8T$, because one-fifth of the increase in taxation is financed by a cut in savings. Only that part of any increase in taxation which leads to a reduction in consumption has any effect on national income. It follows that the increase in taxation of £100m. will lead to a diminishing series of reductions in income. In this case the first few terms (in £m.) and the eventual sum of the series are:

$$\Delta Y = \frac{-\,0.8\Delta T}{1 - 0.8}$$

$$\Delta Y = -(80 + 64 + 51.2 + \ldots) = -£400\text{m.}$$

Thus the net result of an equivalent increase in $G$ and $T$ is that income rises by £100m., i.e. by the increase in government expenditure. The balanced budget multiplier therefore has a value of one.

## Equilibrium with unemployment: the deflationary gap

We have seen that with a given level of aggregate demand (i.e. given values for planned leakages and planned injections) there is only one possible equilibrium level of national income. Any other level will be unstable and the economy will be tending to move towards the equilibrium level. The main problem which Keynes was concerned with was unemployment, and it will only be by pure chance that the equilibrium level of national income will coincide with the full employment level of national income. In fact, the economy can be in equilibrium with large numbers of the workforce unemployed, and can remain in this state for some considerable period until aggregate demand increases.

In terms of our model of income determination we can say that unemployment exists when aggregate demand *falls short* of the level necessary to achieve full employment at the current price level. Keynes argued that in cases such as this the government should pursue expansionary policies to raise aggregate demand and so reduce unemployment.

In terms of Figure 10.4 we can see that with aggregate demand given by *AD*, the equilibrium level of income is *OY*. However, if $OY^f$ is the full employment level of income it is clear that BC is the deficiency of aggregate demand compared with the level necessary to generate full employment. In fact, BC is referred to as the *deflationary gap*, and a government wishing to achieve full employment must pursue policies to close the deflationary gap, such as raising the level of $G$ or reducing the level of $T$. Policies aimed at managing the level of aggregate demand so as to achieve various economic aims are discussed more fully in Chapter 20. Reducing the level of $T$ would raise disposable income, and therefore increase C at any given level of gross income.

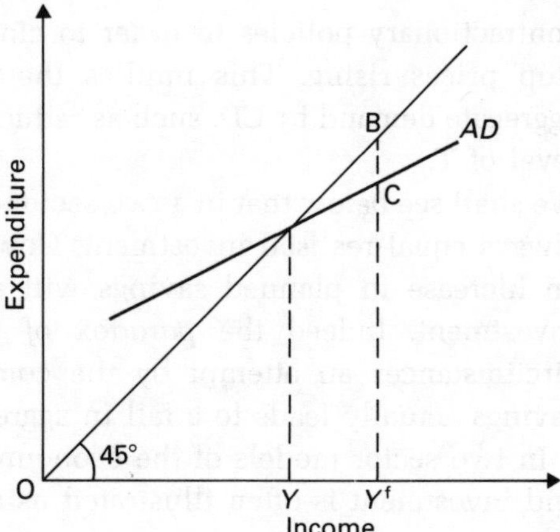


Figure 10.4 The deflationary gap

This would be shown by an upward shift of the aggregate demand function ($AD = C + I + G + X - M$).

## Overfull employment: the inflationary gap

It is possible for the level of aggregate demand to *exceed* the level necessary to achieve full employment at the current price level. In terms of Figure 10.5, $OY^f$ represents the full employment level of income. With aggregate demand equal to *AD*, the equilibrium level of income is O*Y*. However, it is impossible to achieve an equilibrium level of *real* income which is greater than the level achieved at full employment, because physical output cannot be increased beyond that achieved at full employment.

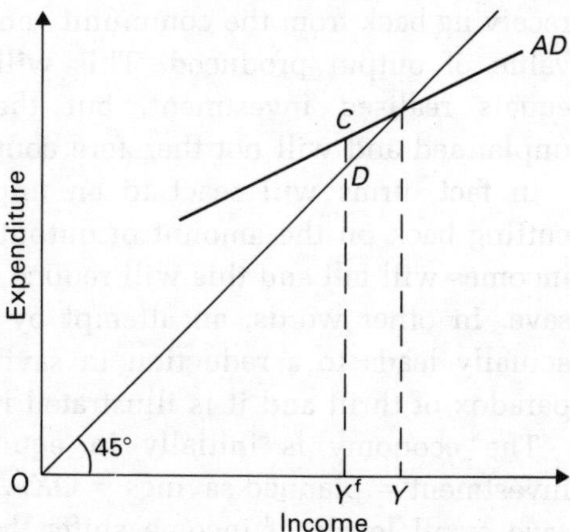


Figure 10.5 The inflationary gap

In this case OY is an unattainable level of real income. Once the economy reaches the full employment level of output, $OY^f$, any excess of aggregate demand over aggregate supply will manifest itself in rising prices. The excess of aggregate demand over the level necessary to achieve full employment, that is, *CD* in Figure 10.5, is therefore referred to as the *inflationary gap*. The government must pursue contractionary policies in order to close the inflationary gap and so stop prices rising. This implies the pursuit of policies to reduce aggregate demand by *CD*, such as reducing the level of *G* or raising the level of *T*.

## The paradox of thrift

We shall see below that in a two sector economy realised savings must always equal realised investment. However, this does not imply that an increase in planned savings will always lead to an increase in investment. Indeed the *paradox of thrift* indicates that in some circumstances an attempt by the community to increase aggregate savings actually leads to a fall in aggregate savings and investment.

In two sector models of the economy the equality between savings and investment is often illustrated using symbols:

$$Y = C + I$$
$$Y = C + S$$
$$\therefore I \equiv S$$

It seems that, on the basis of this identity, an increase in savings could indeed lead to an increase in investment. However, the identity refers to *realised* savings and *realised* investment. If *planned* savings and *planned* investment are not equal, then income will be changing so as to ensure that planned and realised savings equal planned and *realised* investment. Now, if the economy is initially in equilibrium and the community attempts to increase its savings and there is no simultaneous increase in planned investment by firms, firms will experience an unplanned increase in stocks because they will be receiving back from the community an amount which is less than the value of output produced. This will ensure that realised savings equals realised investment, but the change in investment was unplanned and will not therefore continue.

In fact, firms will react to an unplanned increase in stocks by cutting back on the amount of output they produce. As output falls incomes will fall and this will reduce the ability of the community to save. In other words, an attempt by the community to save more, actually leads to a reduction in savings. This is referred to as the paradox of thrift and it is illustrated in Figure 10.6.

The economy is initially in equilibrium at *OY* with planned investment = planned savings = OX. An increase in the propensity to save at all levels of income shifts the savings function from SS to $S_1S_1$. This causes the equilibrium level of income to fall from *OY* to $OY_1$. The equilibrium level of savings and investment is now $OX_1$, that is, the community's attempt to save more has actually resulted in a reduction in the amount saved (and a reduction in the level of investment). Note that Figure 10.4 shows autonomous and *induced*

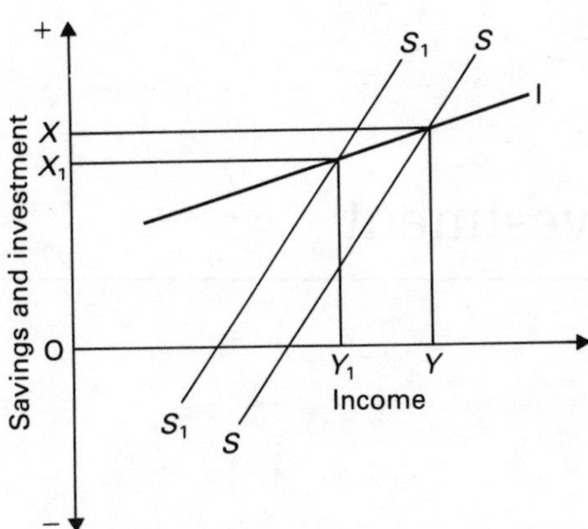


*Figure 10.6* The paradox of thrift

investment. If investment is purely autonomous, the paradox of thrift does not apply!

## Test your understanding

1. What is meant by the equilibrium level of income?
2. In an economy with no government sector and no international sector, investment is constant at £500m. and consumption is equal to £1,000m. + 0.8Y.
   (a) What is the equilibrium level of income?
   (b) What is the value of the multiplier?
   (c) What is the level of savings when the economy is in equilibrium?
3. Why must *realised* leakages always equal *realised* injections?
4. Why does a rise in *indirect* taxation lead to a fall in the value of the multiplier?
5. Is the following statement correct or incorrect? Explain your answer. 'Since for the community as a whole income must either be spent or saved, an increase in investment is only possible if there is a reduction in saving.'
6. If government policy leads to a more equal distribution of income, how will this affect the size of the multiplier?
7. If all other things remain equal, which will have the greater effect on income? Explain your answer.
   (a) An increase in government spending of £500m. on goods and services,
   (b) A reduction in taxation of £500m.?
8. If the *MPC* in a particular economy is 0.5 and the government increases transfer payments by £1,000m., by how much will income rise?

# 11 Investment

Investment is usually defined as the flow of resources devoted to maintaining and increasing the capital stock, that is those assets and skills used for future production rather than for immediate consumption. Investment therefore includes the creation of such assets as machinery, factory buildings, additional road and rail networks and so on.

In the previous chapter it was assumed that investment was autonomous. In fact this was only a simplifying assumption and there are a number of theories which attempt to explain the determinants of investment. However, there is no complete theory of investment. Instead the different theories simply highlight some of the factors which might be relevant in explaining the determinants of investment.

## Discounting to present value

In the real world an important determinant of investment is the expected net rate of return on additional capacity. This can be estimated by subtracting the estimated operating costs over the life of the asset from the expected revenue through additional sales. However, since cash today can be invested and so earn interest, it is worth more than cash in the future. Because of this, the future stream of net returns expected from the asset must be discounted to a present value (*PV*) equivalent, which can then be compared with the current cost of the asset. The most obvious discount rate to use for this purpose is the current rate of interest, since this represents the return foregone if cash is used to purchase fixed assets instead of being loaned. If the present value of this future stream of net returns is greater than the current cost of the asset (its supply price) then additional investment will be profitable. Put another way, net present value ($NPV$) = $PV$ – supply price; if $NPV$ is positive, then additional investment will be profitable.

The problem can be set out numerically. For example, assume a firm is contemplating the purchase of an additional machine with an expected life of five years and a current cost (supply price) of £10,000. Assume further that expected annual net returns (i.e. expected revenue minus expected operating costs) are £6,000, £6,000, £4,000, £2,000 and £1,000 respectively. If the machine has no scrap value after five years and the current rate of interest is 10 per cent, then the present value of the future stream of earnings from buying the machine can be set out as follows:

$$PV = \frac{£6{,}000}{(1.1)} + \frac{£6{,}000}{(1.1)^2} + \frac{£4{,}000}{(1.1)^3} + \frac{£2{,}000}{(1.1)^4} + \frac{£1{,}000}{(1.1)^5} = \frac{£19{,}000}{}$$

Thus purchasing the machine is expected to yield a return of approximately £15,405 at *current* prices. Subtracting the current cost of the machine, i.e. £10,000, still yields a positive net return of £5,405. In other words the Net Present Value (*NPV*) = *PV* − supply price = £5,405. Since *NPV* is positive, additional investment will be profitable.

## The marginal efficiency of capital

The preceding calculation is more important in explaining investment by individual firms than in explaining aggregate investment. Nevertheless, it forms the basis of the Keynesian approach to investment. The only difference is that, instead of discounting to present value, we obtain the rate at which future earnings must be discounted in order to bring their present value into equality with the current cost of the capital asset (the supply price). Keynes referred to the rate of discount which brings a stream of future earnings into equality with current capital costs as the *marginal efficiency of capital*.

If the marginal efficiency of capital (*MEC*) is greater than the current cost of borrowing funds to finance the investment, that is the rate of interest (*R*), then additional investment will be expected to yield a profit. If *MEC* = *R* then there is neither gain nor loss from the investment. If *MEC* < *R*, then the investment will be unprofitable. At any moment in time different investment projects will have a different marginal efficiency of capital, but if these are aggregated then we can obtain a marginal efficiency of capital schedule. Assuming that firms aim to maximise profit, the marginal efficiency of capital schedule will show the demand for capital at various rates of interest. This is shown in Figure 11.1. When the rate of interest is *OR* the aggregate demand for capital is *OM*.

One important feature illustrated by the diagram is that the demand for capital varies inversely with the rate of interest. There are two main reasons for this:

1. As investment increases, the return on additional investment, that is the marginal revenue productivity of capital (see page 115), is likely to fall because:

(i) Greater investment will increase the amount of goods or services available. This will tend to depress their prices, reducing the

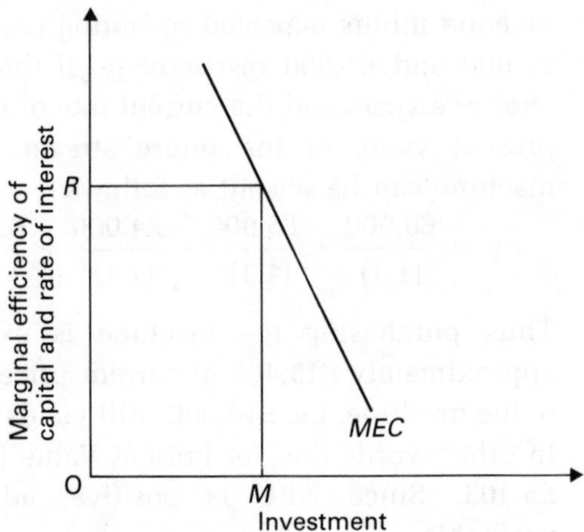


*Figure 11.1* The determination of investment

expected revenue from extra investment projects, and therefore reducing *MEC*.

(ii) As investment increases beyond some point, firms will experience diminishing returns to capital. A fall in the productivity of capital will also reduce the expected revenue from extra investment projects, and therefore reduce *MEC*.

2. Greater investment demand might pull up the cost of the capital asset (i.e. the supply price of capital), and therefore reduce *MEC*.

The combined effect of these factors will be to reduce the return on additional investment, giving a downward sloping *MEC* schedule. Thus a reduction in the rate of interest will raise the demand for capital because it will make it profitable to undertake investment projects that were unprofitable at a higher rate.

Although there is no doubt that changes in the rate of interest influence investment decisions, the relationship is unlikely to be as precise as Figure 11.1 implies. There are many reasons for this, including:

(i) A great deal of investment in the public sector is undertaken for social reasons. Economic considerations have far less influence on such investment.

(ii) In practice it is extremely difficult to estimate the marginal efficiency of capital.

(iii) The investment plans of large firms often stretch over several years and changes in the rate of interest are unlikely to persuade them to revise their plans once they have embarked upon them. Unplanned investment in stocks is unlikely to be affected by changes in the rate of interest.

(iv) In times when the government is exercising tight control over the availability of credit, it might not be possible to obtain funds for investment, even if such funds can be used profitably.

(v) Expectations can sometimes exert a powerful influence on investment. For example, if expectations about future economic conditions deteriorate, the expected revenue from any investment will fall and even a relatively low rate of interest might fail to encourage additional investment by firms. If expectations about the future improve the opposite might happen. Since expectations can change rapidly the effect of a change in the rate of interest on investment will be variable.

## The accelerator

It is also possible for changes in the level of income to exert a powerful effect on the level of investment, independently of the rate of interest. In other words, changes in the level of income might induce substantial changes in investment. This is usually referred to as the *accelerator principle*, and it is most clearly understood by reference to Table 11.1 which shows how an individual firm's investment decisions are influenced by changes in demand for its product. We assume a capital/output ratio of 2:1, that is, two units of capital are required to produce one unit of output per period, that each unit of capital has an economic life of five years and that the firm has built up its capital stock by regular additions of 2,000 units each year.

*Table 11.1*

| Year | Sales | Existing capital | Required capital | Replacement investment | Net investment | Gross investment |
|---|---|---|---|---|---|---|
| 1 | 5,000 | 10,000 | 10,000 | 2,000 | 0 | 2,000 |
| 2 | 6,000 | 10,000 | 12,000 | 2,000 | 2,000 | 4,000 |
| 3 | 7,500 | 12,000 | 15,000 | 2,000 | 3,000 | 5,000 |
| 4 | 8,000 | 15,000 | 16,000 | 2,000 | 1,000 | 3,000 |
| 5 | 7,750 | 16,000 | 15,500 | 2,000 | −500 | 1,500 |

Table 11.1 clearly shows the impact of changes in demand on investment. During year 2 sales rise by 20 per cent, but this induces a rise in gross investment (i.e. net investment + replacement investment) of 100 per cent! The proportionate change in investment is not so spectacular in year 3, with gross investment rising by only 25 per cent despite an equivalent (25 per cent) increase in sales. However, during year 4 there is a smaller proportionate increase in sales than in previous years, and this causes a decline in the absolute level of investment. A simple increase in sales is not therefore sufficient to induce an increase in investment. The level of investment will only go on rising when sales are rising at an increasing rate. The table also shows the effect of a reduction in sales on investment.

From the table we can see that $In = a\Delta Y$, where $In$ is net investment, '$a$' is the capital/output ratio (2), and $\Delta Y$ is the absolute change in sales. In practice it is unlikely that investment will vary with sales as precisely as implied in the table because:

1. Firms might meet increased demand out of stocks or might choose to lengthen waiting lists rather than increase investment.
2. Firms might consider the increase in demand is only temporary, and will not therefore raise their investment.
3. Rather than increasing investment to meet the extra demand it is more likely that firms will, initially at least, introduce overtime working and so on.
4. There are likely to be technological advances which will raise the productivity of capital and hence reduce the need for additional investment to meet increased demand for output.
5. Firms might currently have excess capacity from which they can meet any increase in demand.

Despite these qualifications there is no doubt that changes in income can exert a powerful influence on investment decisions. While the accelerator is not a precise model, it may, nevertheless, help to explain the instability of investment demand.

## Test your understanding

1. How do economists define investment?
2. How would an increase in population affect the *MEC* schedule?
3. If the volume of stocks of finished goods held by firms in an economy increases and all other things remain equal, what happens to the level of investment in this economy?
4. A company is considering purchasing a new machine for £1m. The machine has an expected life of five years and will have no scrap value at the end of that period. The expected net revenue from the machine is £1.2m. per annum. If the discount rate is 10 per cent, would purchasing the machine be expected to yield a profit?
5. If there are unemployed resources in the economy and a high degree of substitutability between capital and labour how will this affect the accelerator?
6. What is meant by the term capital/output ratio?
7. If the aggregate capital/output ratio in an economy is 2:1 and output rises by £100m., by how much will investment initially increase?

# 12 Wages and trade unions

In Chapter 8 we analysed market structure and in so doing focused on the behaviour of product markets. For convenience it was assumed that the prices of inputs were given. Here we reverse the analysis and focus on the determination of factor prices and in general it is assumed that product prices are given. Although our analysis is confined to the labour market, the classical economists extended the analysis to encompass the other factor markets of land, capital and the entrepreneur.

## The marginal productivity theory

We have seen in Chapter 3 that the marginal physical product of labour is the addition to total output from the employment of the marginal worker. The law of variable proportions predicts that marginal physical product at first rises but subsequently falls as the employment of workers increases. However, employers are not so concerned with marginal physical product as with marginal revenue product (*MRP*) and profit-maximising firms will continue to employ workers until the last person employed adds exactly the same to revenue as to costs, i.e. until *MRP* = *MC*.

This is the basic prediction of the marginal productivity theory, and it is possible to consider the implications of this in different market structures.

## Perfect competition in the factor and product markets

If we assume perfect competition in the product market, so that the firm sells its entire output at the ruling market price, and perfect competition in the labour market, so that the firm recruits workers at a constant wage rate, the profit-maximising condition is easily demonstrated.

Table 12.1 assumes a constant market price for the product of £5 per unit and a constant wage rate of £100 per worker per week.

It is clear that, after the employment of the second person and up to the employment of the ninth person, each worker adds more to revenue than to cost. After the employment of the ninth worker the situation is reversed and each additional employee adds more to costs than to revenue. It follows that profit is maximised when nine people are employed.

*Table 12.1*

| No. of workers | Total product | Marginal physical product | Marginal revenue product | Marginal cost | Total revenue product | Total cost | Profit |
|---|---|---|---|---|---|---|---|
| 1 | 12 | 12 | 60 | 100 | 60 | 100 | −40 |
| 2 | 26 | 14 | 70 | 100 | 130 | 200 | −70 |
| 3 | 50 | 24 | 120 | 100 | 250 | 300 | −50 |
| 4 | 90 | 40 | 200 | 100 | 450 | 400 | 50 |
| 5 | 140 | 50 | 250 | 100 | 700 | 500 | 200 |
| 6 | 200 | 60 | 300 | 100 | 1,000 | 600 | 400 |
| 7 | 254 | 54 | 270 | 100 | 1,270 | 700 | 570 |
| 8 | 304 | 50 | 250 | 100 | 1,520 | 800 | 720 |
| 9 | 340 | 36 | 180 | 100 | 1,700 | 900 | 800 |
| 10 | 358 | 18 | 90 | 100 | 1,790 | 1,000 | 790 |
| 11 | 374 | 16 | 80 | 100 | 1,870 | 1,100 | 770 |
| 12 | 378 | 4 | 20 | 100 | 1,890 | 1,200 | 690 |

## The individual firms demand for labour

The general relationship between *MRP*, *ARP* and the number of workers employed at a constant wage rate is set out diagrammatically in Figure 12.1 on page 117.

At a constant wage (= *MC* = *AC*) of *OW* the profit-maximising firm will employ *OM* workers, where *MRP* = *MC*. If the market wage rate increases to *OW*′, the number of workers employed will fall to *OM*′. It follows that, when there is perfect competition in the factor and product markets, the firm's demand for labour curve is that part of its *MRP* curve which lies below its *ARP* curve. At wage rates above *ARP* the firm is making a loss and will not undertake production.

## Imperfect competition in the product market

The fundamentals of the analysis are unchanged if we relax the assumption of perfect competition in the product market. There will still be a tendency for marginal revenue product at first to rise and to pull up average revenue product because of increasing returns. Subsequently the onset of diminishing returns will mean that *MRP* will fall as successive workers are employed, and this will eventually pull down the *ARP*. However, with imperfect product markets there are now two reasons why marginal revenue product declines as employment expands beyond a certain point:

1. The onset of diminishing returns
2. with imperfect product markets, firms must now reduce the price of all units in order to increase sales (see page 63).

In imperfect markets, then, marginal revenue product is determined both by marginal physical product and by the effect on market price of an increase in output. Because price will always fall in imperfect markets as output increases, the effect is to make the *MRP* curve fall

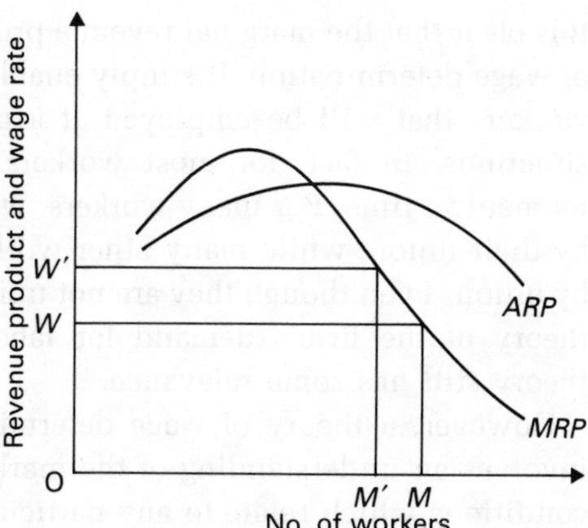


Figure 12.1 Wage rates and employment in perfect competition

more steeply than for firms in perfect competition. Nevertheless, where the firm recruits additional workers at a constant wage rate, its demand for labour is still given by its (now steeper) marginal revenue product curve.

## Imperfect competition in the factor market

When there is imperfect competition in the factor market the firm will be unable to recruit as many workers as it wishes at the ruling wage rate. Instead it will be compelled to increase wage rates in order to attract more workers. The marginal cost of employing additional workers will therefore rise as employment increases, so that the marginal cost curve will now lie above the average cost curve.

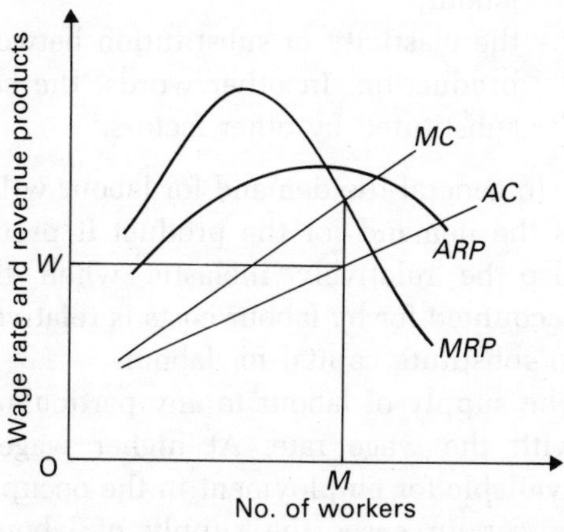


Figure 12.2 Wage rates and employment in imperfect competition

Figure 12.2 shows the equilibrium position of the firm when there is imperfect competition in the factor market. The intersection of MC with MRP determines the number of workers employed and the average cost determines the wage rate at this level of employment. In other words, because the marginal cost and average cost of employing additional workers are no longer the same, the firm's marginal revenue product curve no longer shows its demand for labour at any given wage rate.

## The industry's demand for labour

It is clear that the marginal revenue productivity theory is not a theory of wage determination. It simply enables us to identify the number of workers that will be employed at a given wage rate and in certain situations. In fact, for most workers, wage rates are fixed at any moment in time. For many workers, wages are negotiated collectively by their union, while many other workers receive the rate negotiated by unions even though they are not union members. Nevertheless, as a theory of the firm's demand for labour, the marginal productivity theory still has some relevance.

However, a theory of wage determination in competitive markets involves an understanding of the market demand and market supply conditions which relate to any particular occupation. If we know the number of workers each firm demands at any given wage rate, then we can derive the industry's demand for labour by adding together the individual firms' demand curves. Because each individual firm's demand for labour will also vary inversely with the wage rate, the industry's demand for labour will also vary inversely with the wage rate. In other words, market demand for labour will expand as the wage rate falls.

The elasticity of an industry's demand for labour will, as with any factor of production, vary directly with:

1. the elasticity of demand for the product produced by the industry,
2. the proportion of total costs of production accounted for by labour,
3. the elasticity of substitution between labour and other factors of production. In other words, the ease with which labour can be substituted by other factors.

In general the demand for labour will be less elastic, the less elastic is the demand for the product it produces. Demand for labour will also be relatively inelastic when the proportion of total costs accounted for by labour costs is relatively small or when it is not easy to substitute capital for labour.

## The supply of labour to the industry

The supply of labour to any particular occupation will vary directly with the wage rate. At higher wage rates more workers will be available for employment in the occupation and vice versa. However, in certain cases the supply of labour to an occupation might be relatively inelastic in the short run. For example, where the nature of work is highly skilled and requires considerable training, the supply of labour to the occupation will not rise substantially as wage rates increase. This is true of doctors and barristers, for example.

Nevertheless, the supply of labour to all occupations will be more elastic in the long run than in the short run. Where wages increase in particular occupations, more people will be encouraged to undertake the necessary training, so increasing the amount of labour available. In the case of unskilled labour, supply will tend to be relatively elastic in both the short run and the long run since little, if any, training is required.

## Determination of wages in a particular occupation

In competitive labour markets wage rates are determined by the forces of supply and demand for labour. In these circumstances, different wage rates between occupations will reflect differences in the respective conditions of supply and demand for labour. Figure 12.3 shows the supply and demand conditions in two hypothetical labour markets.

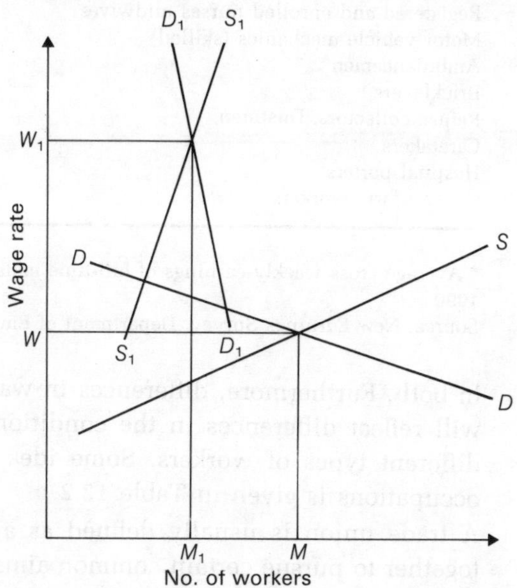


Figure 12.3 Wage determination in different labour markets

The higher wage rate in one labour market is due entirely to the fact that *at any given wage rate*, demand for labour is *greater* and supply of labour is *lower* than in the other labour market. However you should also note that, in this labour market, demand for and supply of labour are relatively inelastic compared to the labour market with the lower wage rate. The higher wage rate is therefore likely to reflect conditions in a market for skilled labour and the lower wage rate is likely to reflect conditions in a market for unskilled labour. The different elasticity conditions will be an important factor in preserving the wage differential between these labour markets.

Given a free market and a particular set of supply and demand conditions for labour, only one wage rate is sustainable: that which equates supply of labour with demand for labour. It follows that wages in a particular occupation can only change if there is a prior change in the conditions of supply, or in the conditions of demand, or

*Table 12.2*

| Occupation group | Average gross weekly earnings (£)* |
|---|---|
| Medical practitioners | 619.2 |
| Journalists | 453.2 |
| Accountants | 403.7 |
| Production and works managers, works foremen | 375.8 |
| Secondary teachers | 338.4 |
| Policemen (below sergeant) (public and private) | 335.9 |
| Coal miners (face trained) | 310.9 |
| Firemen (public and private) | 276.1 |
| Registered and enrolled nurses midwives | 244.2 |
| Motor vehicle mechanics (skilled) | 237.5 |
| Ambulancemen | 234.5 |
| Bricklayers | 228.2 |
| Refuse collectors, Dustmen | 200.2 |
| Caretakers | 184.2 |
| Hospital porters | 167.1 |
| General farm workers | 165.7 |

* Average gross weekly earnings of full-time males in selected occupations as at April 1990.
*Source: New Earnings Survey*, Department of Employment 1990.

in both. Furthermore, differences in wage rates between occupations will reflect differences in the conditions of supply and demand for different types of workers. Some idea of how wages vary between occupations is given in Table 12.2.

## The effect of a trade union

A trade union is usually defined as a group of workers who band together to pursue certain common aims, in particular wage increases for their members. A trade union can therefore influence the supply of labour to an industry depending on the extent to which the workforce are members of the union. However, their ability to obtain wage increases depends on several factors and in particular on the elasticity of demand for labour as discussed on page 118. If all other things are equal a union's ability to obtain higher wages is greater the less elastic the demand for labour. There are several areas to consider.

### Restricting supply

A union might refuse to supply workers below a particular wage rate. The implications of this are examined in Figure 12.4. Supply and demand for labour in this industry are initially represented by *SS* and *DD* respectively and the equilibrium wage rate is *OW* with *ON* workers employed. If a trade union now demands a pay rise of $WW_1$ and refuses to supply labour below $OW_1$, then the effective supply curve of labour to this industry becomes $W_1RS$. If all other things remain equal, the higher wage rate implies a reduction in the number of workers employed to $ON_1$. However, if demand for the product is rising, perhaps because of a general rise in incomes, it might be

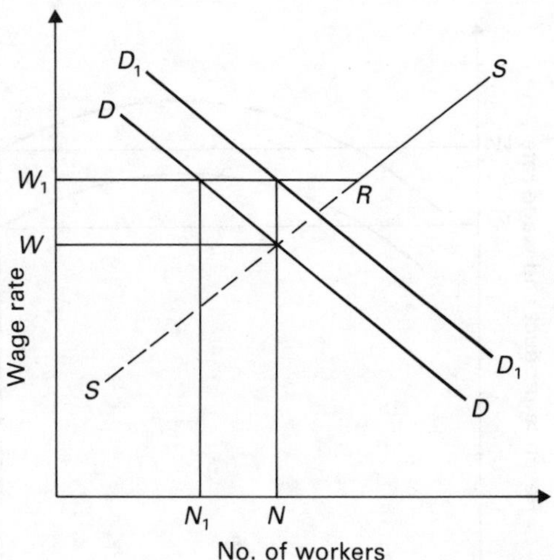


*Figure 12.4* A union negotiates a minimum wage

possible for the firm to finance the increase in wages by raising the price of the product. The effect of this will be to raise the demand for labour at each and every wage rate and in this case, when demand increases to $D_1D_1$, the result is that the higher wage rate $OW_1$ does not lead to any reduction in the number of workers employed.

In practice this is often what happens as a result of an increase in wages. Firms are able to pass on the costs of wage increases in the form of higher prices because incomes in the economy as a whole rise over time. However, when firms are unable to pass on the full effect of higher costs to consumers because demand is relatively price elastic and income inelastic, the higher wage increase might lead to some workers losing their jobs.

## Higher productivity

Another way in which a trade union might obtain a higher wage rate for its members is by increasing productivity. If all other things remain equal it is possible to increase wage rates by the same percentage as an increase in productivity without increasing average costs of produc-ion. However, because of increased productivity, the firm will have a larger output to sell, and if price remains constant this again implies an increase in demand for labour as each worker's marginal revenue product increases. Figure 12.5 illustrates that in these circumstances it is possible for a firm to pay higher wages without necessarily reducing the number of workers employed.

Initially the wage rate is *OW* and *ON* workers are employed, because profits are maximised here, that is, $MRP = MC$. If an increase in productivity shifts the *MRP* curve to $MRP_1$, it is possible to increase wages to $OW_1$ without there being any reduction in the number of workers employed. This explains why so much emphasis is attached to productivity deals when wage increases are negotiated.

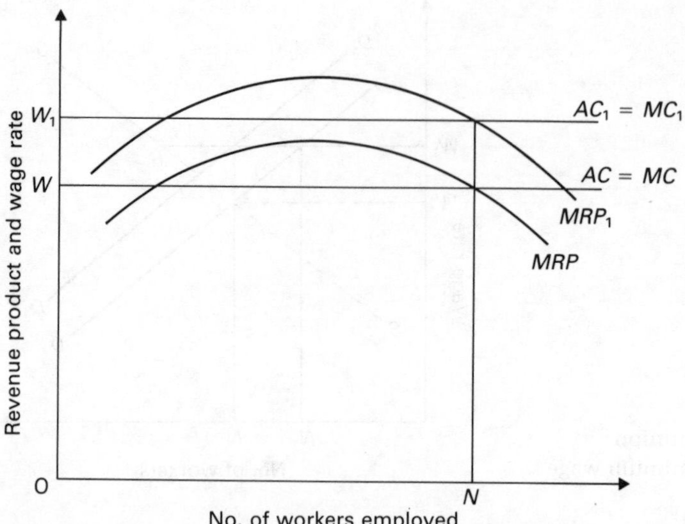


*Figure 12.5* The effect of an increase in productivity

**Profit-financed wage increases**

Even without an increase in marginal revenue productivity it might be possible for a union to obtain a substantial wage increase for its members. This would be possible if it could persuade employers to accept a cut in profits. Figure 12.6 is used to illustrate this point (and refers to a firm operating with perfect competition in the factor and product markets).

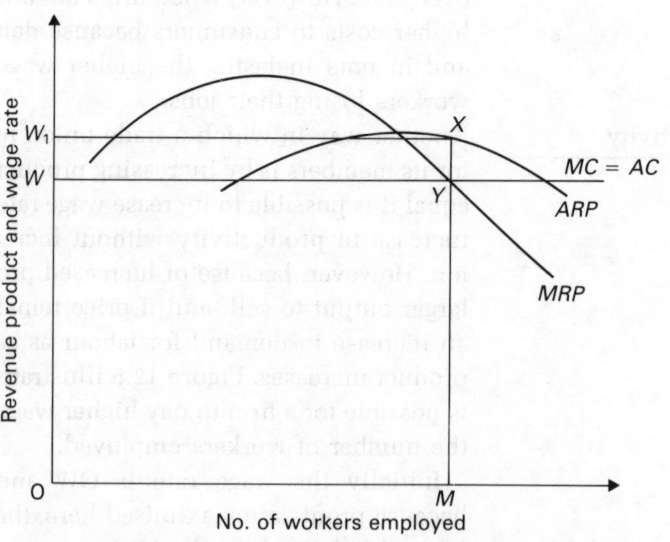


*Figure 12.6* An increase in wages financed by a cut in profits

If *ARP* and *MRP* represent the *net* returns to labour, it follows that, at the profit-maximising level of employment (OM), employers earn a surplus of XY per worker. If unions can persuade employers to accept a smaller surplus it is possible to negotiate a higher wage rate above the existing level OW, without reducing the number of workers employed. For example, employers might be willing to offer a wage of $OW_1$ rather than risk the union taking industrial action with a consequent loss of output. If the union took this course profits might be seriously affected and in these circumstances offering the higher wage rate might leave the firm earning the highest *attainable* profit.

## Reducing supply

In the long run, unions might be able to reduce the supply of labour to the industry without any of its members becoming unemployed. The most obvious way in which this can be achieved is to reduce the number of workers taken on annually. A trade union can do this by restricting the number of trainees or apprentices taken on annually, or by insisting on a reduction in the number of part-time workers. Over time as workers leave the industry through retirement and job-changing, this will bring about a reduction in the supply of workers to the industry. The affect of this is illustrated in Figure 12.7.

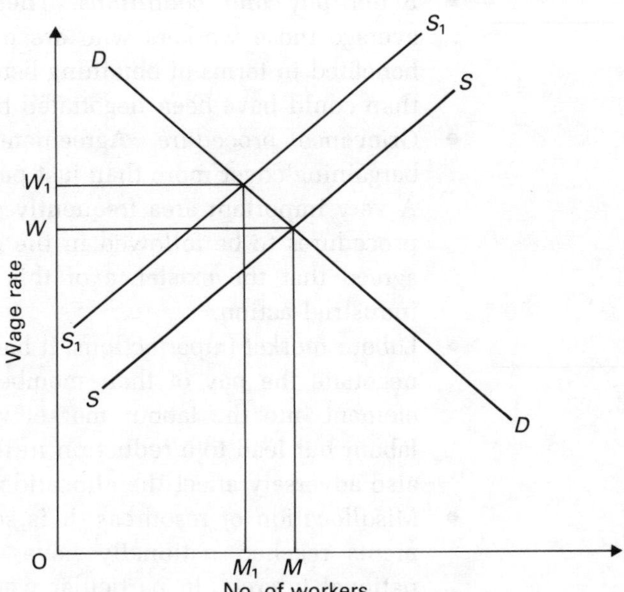


*Figure 12.7* The effect of a reduction in the supply of workers to an industry

In the long run a reduction in the number of employees taken on annually shifts the supply curve of labour from SS to $S_1S_1$. As a result, wages rise from OW to $OW_1$ and, although *employment* in the industry falls from OM to $OM_1$, higher wages have not led to union members becoming unemployed. In this sense wage increases might be self-financing because, although the wage rate has increased, the total wage bill might actually fall. In recent years wage bargaining has often been accompanied by moves to increase early retirement of workers and here again the aim is to offer a wage increase without proportionately increasing the total wage bill. Reducing the supply of labour might be particularly effective when productivity can be increased or when capital is easily substituted for labour.

## Collective bargaining

### Definition and scope

Collective bargaining is the term used to describe arrangements whereby a trade union bargains collectively on behalf of its membership about such matters as pay and conditions, rather than each person negotiating these matters individually with their employer. By bargaining collectively the aim is to strengthen the bargaining power of the workforce. In the UK a two tier system of collective bargaining is said to exist with the bargain being struck at the 'national level' and the 'local level'. Basically *minimum* pay awards and conditions are negotiated at the national level and these are supplemented at the local level so as to reflect different conditions in particular markets. Agreements in the UK normally run for twelve months, but they are not legally binding and either party can terminate them at any time.

*Advantages*

- *Better pay and conditions.* There seems little doubt that on average those workers who are members of a trade union have benefited in terms of obtaining better pay and working conditions than could have been negotiated by individual employees.
- *Grievance procedure.* Agreements reached through collective bargaining cover more than just pay and conditions of employees. A very important area frequently covered is the establishment of procedures to be followed in the event of a dispute. It is widely agreed that the existence of this has reduced the incidence of industrial action.

*Disadvantages*

- *Labour market imperfections.* It has been argued that when unions negotiate the pay of their members they introduce a monopoly element into the labour market which might raise the price of labour but lead to a reduction in the numbers employed. It might also adversely affect the allocation of resources.
- *Misallocation of resources.* It is sometimes suggested that agreements reached nationally have often had little regard to the national interest. In particular wage awards in certain industries establish minimum acceptable levels for other industries irrespective of supply and demand conditions in different labour markets. This process prevents the price mechanism from functioning efficiently in the labour market. To the extent that this has happened collective bargaining has led to inefficiency in the allocation of resources and might be a source of inflation. Similarly if bargains include agreements to maintain employment levels even after the introduction of labour-saving machinery this will create inefficiency in the allocation of resources and might again raise costs and prices.

## Minimum wage legislation

Table 12.2 indicates that there is considerable variation in wage rates earned in different occupations. Some occupations such as agricultural workers, local authority ancillaries and hotel and catering staff are frequently quoted as examples of low paid occupations. It is sometimes suggested that one way of overcoming the problem of low pay in such occupations is by the establishment of a national minimum wage. However, this is a very controversial issue, since establishing a national minimum wage might lead to other problems and it is by no means certain that it would overcome the problem of low pay. Low pay is regarded as an economic problem because it means that some people have a low standard of living. Many ideas have been put forward to deal with the problem of low pay and in particular it is often suggested that a statutory minimum wage is one of the most effective means of dealing with this problem.

## Minimum wages and unemployment

One major problem with establishing a national minimum wage is that it would almost certainly lead to unemployment in some occupations. Figure 12.8 is used as a basis for explaining how this might happen.

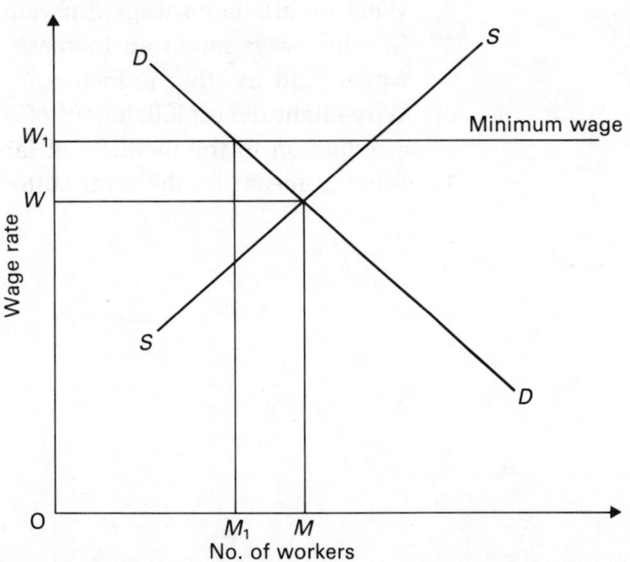


Figure 12.8 The effect of a minimum wage on numbers employed

In Figure 12.8 demand for labour is represented by *DD* and supply of labour is represented by SS. The equilibrium wage is OW and OM workers are employed. If the minimum wage is set above OW, for example at $OW_1$ those workers who receive the higher wage clearly gain when a minimum wage is established. However, by raising the price of labour, the minimum wage leads to a reduction in the number of workers employed which falls to $OM_1$. Workers who retain their jobs after the establishment of the minimum wage are therefore better off, but those who lose their jobs are likely to be worse off.

**Minimum wages and real income**

The establishment of a statutory minimum wage might lead to wage demands from trade unions in order to safeguard their established differentials. If pay awards are granted in excess of productivity, this will generate inflation and might well leave the relative position of the low paid unchanged after the establishment of a legal minimum wage. In fact the relative position of the low paid might be adversely affected as a result of such pay awards!

**Minimum wages and training**

If the minimum wage applies to all workers, this will reduce the incentive for firms to train workers, since it will represent an effective increase in training costs. This has very serious implications and could lead to major skill shortages in the future and consequently a slower growth of productivity.

## Test your understanding

1. The demand for labour is referred to as a derived demand. What does this mean?
2. If there was perfect mobility of labour would there be equality of wages between different occupations? Explain your answer.
3. Why is the demand for skilled labour likely to be less elastic than the demand for unskilled labour?
4. What functions do wage differentials perform?
5. In what ways might an increase in wages in one industry affect wages paid in other industries?
6. Why might the establishment of a national minimum wage lead to a reduction in the mobility of labour?
7. What is meant by the term collective bargaining?

# 13 Interest, rent and profit

## Interest

The previous chapter focused on the return to labour. In this chapter we are concerned with rewards to other factors of production. In the classical sense *interest* is the return to capital, *rent* is the return to land and *profit* is the return to the entrepreneur.

### Interest and its components

Interest is sometimes treated as the reward for postponing consumption but more often it is viewed as the price that has to be paid for the use of funds. In other words interest is the amount the borrower pays over and above the original amount borrowed. For convenience it is usually expressed as an annual rate so that, if one person borrows £5,000 for one year at 10 per cent, the total amount repayable in one year's time will be £5,500.

Strictly an interest payment has several components:

- A payment is necessary to persuade holders of funds to forego current consumption and so release funds for lending. After all, for most of us current consumption is preferable to future consumption. The payment of interest persuades individuals to overcome their time preference for current consumption.
- A payment is necessary to compensate for risk. There is a risk that the borrower will default on repayment of the loan when such repayment falls due. There is also the risk that inflation will reduce the real value of the amount lent so that it will buy less at the time repayment is made.
- A payment is necessary to cover the costs of administration associated with borrowing and lending.

### The rate of interest

Economists use the term 'the' rate of interest as if there was only one such rate. In fact, there are many different rates of interest, such as those charged on mortgages, bank loans, hire purchase agreements and so on. This is to be expected, and, in general, interest rates vary with the credit worthiness of the borrower and with the duration of the loan. Nevertheless, after allowance has been made for these two factors, there still remains a net or minimum rate of interest that must be paid by all borrowers.

Where interest rates in particular markets are above this minimum, after due allowance has been made for the specific circumstances of the loan and the borrower, funds will tend to move to these markets. The increase in supply will *bid down* interest rates in these markets. Conversely the shortage this creates in other markets will *bid up* interest rates in those markets. Thus, in the long run, the net rate of interest in all markets tends to equality and this provides some justification for the notion of a single rate of interest. Any reference to 'the' rate of interest therefore implies reference to a single *representative* rate of interest so that when interest rates *in general* are rising or falling this will be reflected in appropriate movements in any rate of interest which is monitored.

## Theories of the rate of interest

Economists have long been interested in what determines the rate of interest and, over the years, several theories have evolved which seek to explain how interest rates are determined. Here we concentrate on only two theories: the *loanable funds theory* and the *liquidity preference theory*.

### The loanable funds theory

This is an early theory of how interest rates are determined and, although its significance decreased after the evolution of the liquidity preference theory, it is again gathering respectability as an explanation of how interest rates are determined. The loanable funds theory focuses attention on the demand for and supply of loanable funds and the interaction of these to determine the rate of interest.

#### *Demand for loanable funds*

This theory assumes that demand for loanable funds is a derived demand and stems from the demand for capital investment by different sectors of the economy. If firms and individuals wish to invest more than they currently save, they must borrow the excess. However, if all other things are equal, the quantity of funds demanded will depend on the cost, that is, the rate of interest, because capital equipment will only be purchased if the expected *net* return from its operation is above some minimum acceptable level. The lower the rate of interest, the lower the cost of capital and, if all other things are equal, the greater the net return from any capital investment. Because of this the demand for loanable funds will be greater at lower rates of interest and vice versa, that is, the demand curve for loanable funds will be normal shaped.

In the real world of course, the demand for loanable funds is not simply determined by the demand for capital investment by firms. In particular households demand funds for the purchase of housing and many consumer durables. However, there is no doubt that demand for funds for these purposes is inversely related to changes in the rate of interest.

#### *Supply of loanable funds*

The loanable funds theory assumes that the supply of loanable funds is determined by the level of savings in the economy. For most

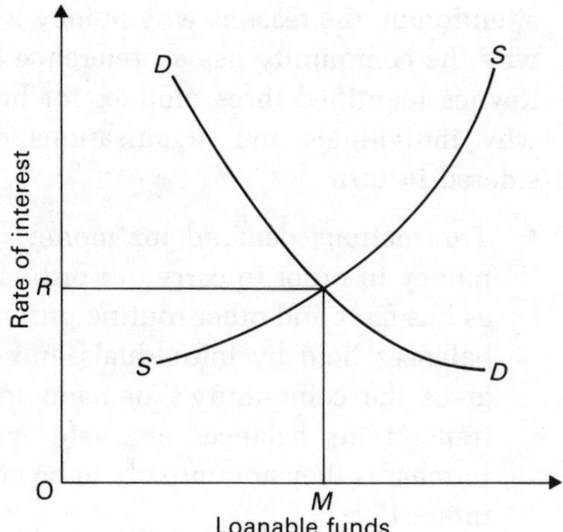


*Figure 13.1* Supply and demand for loanable funds

individuals the level of savings depends on such factors as current income, holdings of wealth and the rate of interest. If all other things are equal, a rise in the rate of interest increases the opportunity cost of current consumption because a rise in the rate of interest makes an even higher level of consumption possible in the future. Because of this it is argued that the supply of loanable funds will vary directly with the rate of interest.

*The determination of interest rates*

Figure 13.1 illustrates the determination of interest rates in terms of the loanable funds theory.

In Figure 13.1, *DD* represents the demand for loanable funds and *SS* represents the supply of loanable funds. The equilibrium rate of interest is *R* because this is the only rate at which supply of, and demand for, funds are equal. At any rate of interest above *R* there is excess supply of funds and therefore the rate of interest will fall. At any rate below *R* there is excess demand and therefore the rate of interest will rise.

Once established at *R*, the rate of interest will not change unless there is a prior change in the conditions of demand and/or a change in the conditions of supply. For example, technological advances might cause an increase in the demand for loanable funds, while a rise in income might cause an increase in the supply of loanable funds. The former would tend to pull up the rate of interest while the latter would tend to pull it down.

**The liquidity preference theory**

This theory is sometimes referred to as the 'monetary' theory of interest rates or the 'Keynesian' theory of interest rates after its originator, John Maynard Keynes. In this theory the rate of interest is determined by the demand for money to hold and the supply of money, rather than the demand for and supply of loanable funds. An important feature of the liquidity preference theory is that it focuses attention on the reasons why money is demanded, that is, the reasons why the community has a preference for liquidity.

### *Demand for money*

Keynes identified three motives for holding money, or three reasons why individuals and organisations demand money. Each is considered in turn

- *Transactions demand for money*. Everyone needs to hold some money in order to carry out ordinary, everyday transactions such as bus fares and other routine purchases. The sum of all individual balances held by individuals and institutions for such purposes gives the community's demand for transactions balances. Since transactions balances are held with the intention of financing purchases they are unlikely to be affected by changes in the rate of interest.

  One of the main determinants of the demand for transactions balances is the level of income. For most individuals and certainly for the community as a whole, as income rises expenditure increases. However, the frequency with which income is received is also an important factor determining transactions demand for money. For example, if an individual receives £140 per week and spends it at the rate of £20 per day, the average weekly holding of money, or the average weekly demand for transactions balances, is £70 and the annual level of expenditure is £7,280. On the other hand, if the same individual were paid on a four weekly cycle, income received would be £560 every four weeks. Again if expenditures were spread evenly throughout the period, the average weekly holding of money would be £280 – but the annual level of expenditure would remain constant at £7,280. In this case what is true for the individual is true for the nation. Changing the frequency with which income is received will change the community's demand for transactions balances.
- *Precautionary balances*. The demand for precautionary balances represents money balances held as a precaution against some unforeseen event such as unanticipated repair work becoming necessary on a car or a reduction in prices offering the prospect of an unanticipated bargain. Again the major determinant of precautionary balances is likely to be the level of income. An individual with an annual income of £30,000 might be expected to hold larger precautionary balances than an individual with an annual income of £5,000! Furthermore, it is normally assumed that the rate of interest has no effect on the precautionary demand for money.
- *Speculative demand for money*. The third motive identified by Keynes for holding money is the speculative motive or the asset motive. Money that is *not* required for transactions or precautionary

purposes can be held as an asset, or used to provide funds for borrowers. The problem is to identify the circumstances when an individual or institution will prefer to hold surplus balances in the form of money in preference to assets that will earn interest.

In the liquidity preference theory it is assumed that only one type of asset is available to individuals and institutions, namely securities. These are basically IOUs and we shall see on page 151 for example, that when a person makes a loan to the government they receive a government security. These IOUs will be redeemed at some stage in the future but until then the holder of a security receives interest. We therefore have to decide when a person or institution will prefer money to securities and vice versa.

For simplicity let us consider the case of a security with no fixed redemption date such as a consul which is a security, or bond, issued by the UK Government and which therefore has no risk of default. The holder of these securities receives an annual interest payment and the rate of interest is fixed in terms of the face value of the security. Thus if the nominal price, that is face value, of a security is £100 and the rate of interest is 4 per cent, the holder of this security receives £4 annually.

Although consuls carry no fixed redemption date, there is an active market in them which simply means holders of consuls can find ready buyers should they wish to sell them. However, as with all market prices, the price of consuls will vary with supply and demand so that although the holder of the security receives the same fixed payment annually, the price of the security is not fixed. To see what happens to the market rate of interest, or *yield* (r), when security prices change let us consider two examples. In the first example it is assumed that, when sold, the price of the consul is £120 and in the second example its price is £80.

Example 1 $r = \frac{£4}{£120} \times 100 = 3.33\%$

Example 2 $r = \frac{£4}{£80} \times 100 = 5\%$

Notice that, as the price of the security rises, the rate of interest falls and vice versa. This is because the annual interest payment on the security is fixed at £4 but in the first case the purchaser of the security gives up £120 to receive an annual payment of £4, but in the second case the security purchaser only parts with £80 to receive the same annual £4 interest.

This is very important because, if an investor *expects* the price of securities to rise (i.e. the rate of interest is expected to fall), he or she will prefer to hold securities rather than money because, if security prices rise, the investor makes a capital gain. On the other hand, if security prices are expected to fall (the rate of interest is expected to rise), money will be preferred to securities, thus avoiding an expected capital loss.

This is easy to understand in the case of an individual investor, but not all investors have the same expectation about security prices. At any moment in time some investors will expect there to be a rise in interest rates while others will expect a fall. However, the more interest rates rise, the more investors will come to expect the next change in interest rates to be downwards, that is, the next change in security prices will be upwards. Because of this, as interest rates rise and rise, investors will increasingly prefer to hold securities rather than money because of the expectation of making a capital gain. In fact there must be some rate of interest that is so high everyone expects the next change in interest rates to be downwards and here the speculative demand for money will be zero. The opposite is also true. As interest rates fall and fall, the more investors will come to expect the next change in interest rates to be upwards, that is, the next change in security prices to be downwards. Here money will increasingly be preferred to securities because of the expected capital loss from holding securities. Again there is some low rate of interest when everyone expects the next change in interest rates to be upwards, that is, the next change in security prices will be downwards. In this case the demand for speculative money balances will be infinite because no one will be willing to purchase securities.

*The liquidity preference curve*

Since transactions balances and precautionary balances are held with the intention of being used to make purchases as and when required they are sometimes jointly referred to as the demand for active balances. The important point about the demand for active balances is that it is not responsive to changes in the rate of interest, that is, it is interest rate inelastic. The demand for speculative balances on the other hand is sometimes referred to as the demand for idle balances since it represents money that is demanded because its face value is fixed and there is therefore no risk of capital loss.

Figure 13.2 shows that when the demand for active balances and the demand for idle balances are added together, we have the community's total demand for money or, liquidity preference, schedule.

*The supply of money*

In the liquidity preference theory this is assumed to be determined by the monetary authorities (the Treasury and the Bank of England). This implies that on a day to day basis the supply of money is not influenced by changes in the rate of interest. In the long term changes in the rate of interest exert considerable influence on the supply of money but this can be ignored because the liquidity preference theory concentrates on the determination of the rate of interest at a particular point in time when the money supply is fixed.

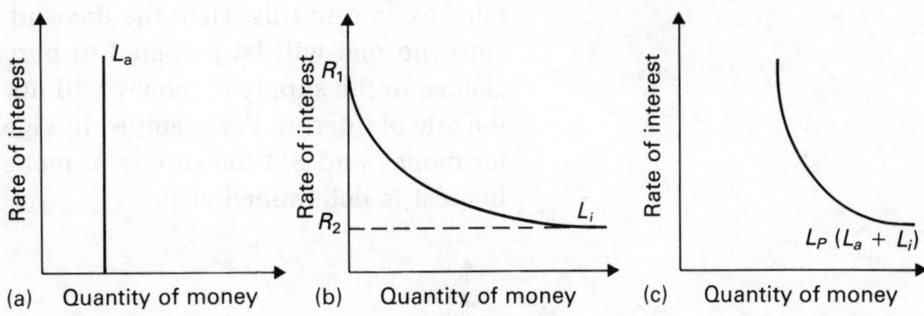


Figure 13.2 The demand for money

## *The determination of interest rates*

The interaction of supply and demand for money determines the rate of interest. In Figure 13.3 the demand for money is given by $L_P$ and the supply of money is given by *SM*. This gives an equilibrium rate of interest of *R*.

At any rate of interest above *R* supply of money exceeds demand and this will pull down the rate of interest while at any rate of interest below *R* demand for money will exceed supply and this will bid up the rate of interest. Once the rate of interest is established at *R*, it will remain at this level until there is a change in the demand for money and/or the supply of money. This implies that the authorities have two choices:

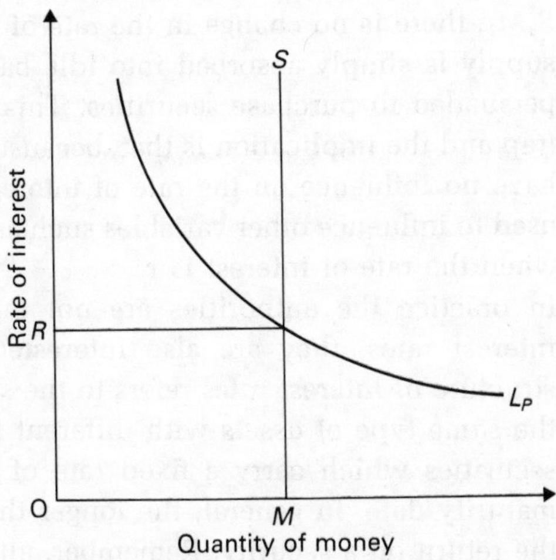


Figure 13.3 The equilibrium rate of interest
(a) Demand for active balances
(b) Demand for idle balances
(c) Total demand for money

1 They can fix the supply of money and allow interest rates to be determined by the demand for money;
2. They can fix the rate of interest and adjust the supply of money to whatever level is appropriate so as to maintain that rate of interest.

## *The liquidity trap*

We have seen that in the liquidity preference theory there is some low rate of interest when everyone expects the next change in interest rates to be upwards. Here the demand for money is infinitely elastic since no one will be prepared to purchase securities. In this case a change in the supply of money will not necessarily have any affect on the rate of interest. For example, in Figure 13.4 if $L_p$ shows the demand for money and SM the supply of money then the equilibrium rate of interest is determined at $R$.

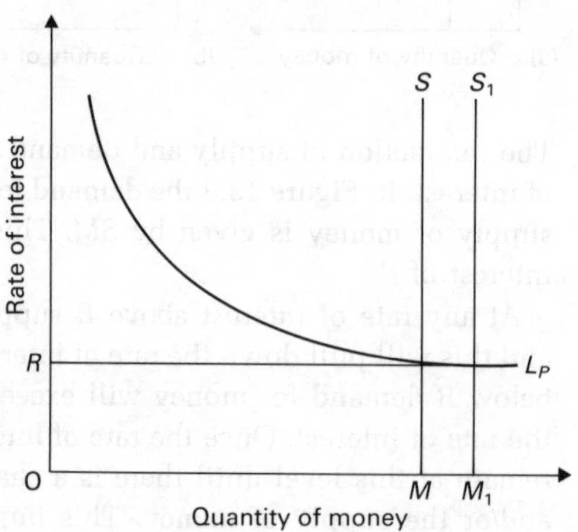


Figure 13.4 The liquidity trap

Now, if the authorities engineer an increase in the money supply to $S_1M_1$, there is no change in the rate of interest. The increased money supply is simply absorbed into idle balances because no one can be persuaded to purchase securities. This is referred to as the liquidity trap and the implication is that, because changes in the money supply have no influence on the rate of interest, monetary policy cannot be used to influence other variables such as consumption and investment when the rate of interest is $r$.

## The term structure of interest rates

In practice the authorities are not only interested in the *level* of interest rates, they are also interested in the *structure*. The *term structure of interest rates* refers to the *spread* of interest rates paid on the *same type of assets* with different times to maturity. It relates to securities which carry a fixed rate of interest and have a specified maturity date. In general, the longer the time to maturity the greater the return on a security. Remember, although the amount received is fixed as a proportion of the nominal value of a security, the rate of interest, or yield (see page 131) will vary because the market price of the security varies. Figure 13.5 shows the general relationship between the yield on a security and the length of time to maturity. This is usually referred to as the *yield curve*.

The yield curve in Figure 13.5 is referred to as a *normal* yield curve because the yield increases as the length of time to maturity increases.

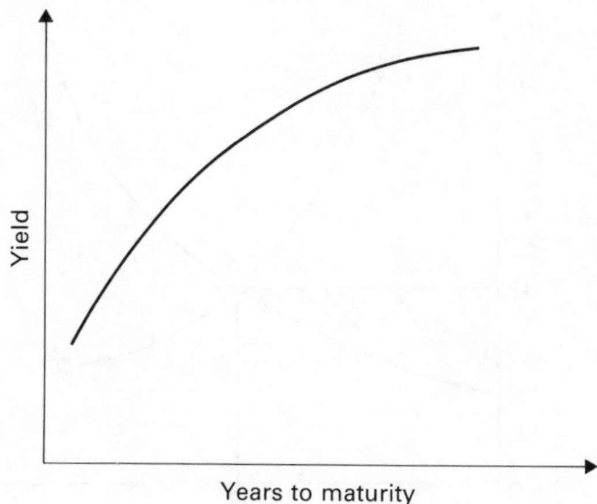


*Figure 13.5*

This is to be expected because if all other things are equal:

- the risk of default increases over time along with the risk that inflation will erode the real value of interest payments and the initial capital sum when it is repaid;
- lenders require compensation for loss of liquidity. The longer they forego current consumption, the greater the amount of compensation required.

## Rent

The classical economists argued that, as a return to land, the determination of rent could be explained by the marginal productivity theory. In other words, land would continue to be employed in any particular use until its marginal cost was equal to its marginal revenue product. It was accepted that land would continue to move between *different uses* until the ratio of its marginal revenue product/price in one use was equal to its marginal revenue product/price ratio in all other uses.

## Economic rent

In most cases a factor of production is assumed to have *transfer earnings*, that is, the minimum necessary to keep a factor of production in its present occupation. Any excess earnings above transfer earnings are referred to as economic rent. Given this definition, if *SS* and *DD* show the supply and demand conditions for labour in a particular market, it is clear that the whole of the shaded area in Figure 13.6 is economic rent.

The equilibrium wage rate in this labour market is *OW* and *OQ* workers are employed. Each worker, apart from the last one employed, earns more than his transfer earnings, that is, more than the minimum payment necessary to keep him from transferring from this occupation to an alternative occupation. The total economic rent earned by this factor of production is therefore equal to the area WRS.

It is clear that the more inelastic the supply curve of the factor, the

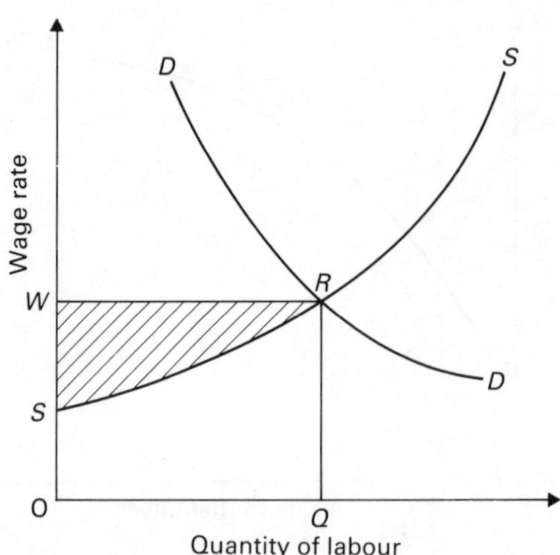


*Figure 13.6* The determination of economic rent

greater the proportion of total earnings of the factor that will constitute economic rent, and vice versa. The more inelastic *SS* in Figure 13.6, the greater will be the shaded area *WRS as a proportion* of *WRQO*, and vice versa.

## Economic rent and profit

We have seen in Chapter 7 that, if earnings fall below normal profits, in the long run the entrepreneur will leave the industry in question. In other words normal profits are the transfer earnings of the entrepreneur; any supernormal profits therefore constitute economic rent.

## Rent of ability

Some individuals possess *unique* abilities that cannot be reproduced in response to an increase in demand. From the point of view of society as a whole, the supply of such talent (e.g. film stars and entertainers) is completely inelastic. In certain cases the demand for these talents is so great that the individuals fortunate enough to possess them receive extremely high incomes. Since it is unlikely that the individuals concerned possess other unique abilities which would command similar earnings, the vast majority of their incomes from present occupations is economic rent.

## Quasi-rent

Quasi-rent, like economic rent, is a surplus above transfer earnings, but, unlike economic rent, it is only a *temporary* surplus caused by short-run inelasticity in the supply of particular factor services. Any factor of production can earn quasi-rent. For example, the supernormal profit earned in the short run in perfect competition and monopolistic competition represents quasi-rent earned by the entrepreneur. The most easily observed examples of quasi-rent occur when there are shortages of particular skills, because of an increase in demand for certain products. The earnings of workers who possess these skills rise relative to the earnings of workers in other occupations. This improved differential is often short-lived as extra recruitment increases the supply of workers to that occupation.

### Rent and prices

A common question and a source of misunderstanding for many students is the effect of rents on property prices in city centres. It is sometimes alleged that city-centre prices are higher than elsewhere because city-centre rents are higher. The basis of this allegation is that rent is a *cost* of production and that the higher this cost, the higher the final price. However, while it is true that those involved in business must cover their costs, it is *not* true that high rents cause high prices. The supply of city-centre sites is completely inelastic and it is *demand* for these sites which pulls their price up. If demand for these sites fell, there would be no reduction in the total amount supplied, so that their price would fall. In other words, the high price for city-centre sites is due to the economic rent these sites earn. Economic rent is demand determined; it does not determine prices, it is determined by price.

### Profit

In the accounting sense, profit is simply the difference between total revenue and total cost. It is therefore a composite item which includes:

1. the entrepreneur's 'wages' in return for organising the factors of production,
2. a return for organising the risks of production.

It is this return for risk-bearing that is usually regarded as profit in the economic sense.

Profit differs from other factor rewards in several ways:

1. Profit is the only factor reward that is *indeterminate* in advance of production. All other factor rewards are the subject of *contract*, but profit is simply the *residual* left after all other costs of production are met.
2. Profit is the only factor reward that *might be negative*. In fact this is not infrequent and occurs when firms make a loss from production.
3. Profit is the only factor reward *not* paid in isolation. Frequently the income of an entrepreneur contains elements of *all* other factor rewards. Sole proprietors, for example, frequently receive interest on their capital, rent on their land, wages for management, as well as true profit.

### Profit and efficiency

It is sometimes suggested that the level of profit earned by a firm, when measured as a return on capital employed, is an indicator of its efficiency. To the extent that firms of similar size sell similar products, differences in profits probably do imply differences in efficiency. Similarly, where larger firms earn a higher return on capital employed than smaller firms, this probably reflects a more efficient scale of operations.

However, there are many reasons why firms earn different levels of profit and it is not always the case that larger firms earn a higher return on capital employed than smaller firms.

1. Smaller firms might earn higher profits than larger firms because they have relatively low capital costs. For example, many sole proprietors operate from home, and this considerably reduces their fixed costs. Of course this does not necessarily mean that smaller firms are more efficient than larger firms.
2. Some firms in an industry might have lower costs and higher profits than other firms because of *external*, not *internal*, factors. For instance, they might be located in an area where skilled labour is readily available, where good transport and communication infrastructure is available, etc.
3. Relatively high profits might be due to the fact that a firm has monopoly either locally or nationally. In such cases the level of profit earned reflects an ability to exclude competition from the industry rather than efficiency in production.
4. Profits might also be bolstered by the operation of restrictive practices, such as exclusive dealing arrangements.

## Test your understanding

1. Why are interest rates always expressed as annual percentage rates?
2. Calculate the market price of a security which has no fixed redemption date but pays an annual rate of interest of 3½ per cent given that the current yield on this security is: (i) 7 per cent, (ii) 9 per cent.
3. Distinguish between active balances and idle balances.
4. What is normal about a normal yield curve?
5. What factors might cause a rise in the community's liquidity preference?
6. Distinguish between transfer earnings, economic rent and quasi-rent.
7. Outline the case for taxing economic rents. What are the problems with implementing such a tax?
8. What are the transfer earnings of the entrepreneur in the long run?

# 14 Money and banking

## Functions of money

There are four functions which money performs.

1. To act as *a medium of exchange or means of payment*. Money is unique in performing this function, since it is the only asset which is universally acceptable in exchange for goods and services. In the absence of a medium of exchange, trade could only take place if there was a double coincidence of wants; in other words, only if two people had mutually acceptable commodities to exchange. Trade of this type takes place on a basis of barter.

   Clearly, barter would restrict the growth of trade. It would also severely limit the extent to which individuals were able to specialise. By acting as a medium of exchange money therefore promotes specialisation. A person can exchange his labour for money, and then use that money to purchase the output produced by others. We have seen in Chapter 4 that specialisation greatly increases the wealth of the community. By acting as a medium of exchange money is therefore fulfilling a crucial function, enhancing trade, specialisation and wealth creation.

   The remaining functions of money stem from its use as a medium of exchange.
2. *To act as a unit of account*. By acting as a medium of exchange, money also provides a means of expressing value. The prices quoted for goods and services reflect their relative value and in this way money acts as a unit of account.
3. To act as *a store of wealth*. Because money can be exchanged immediately for goods and services, it is a convenient way of holding wealth until goods and services are required. In this sense money acts as a store of wealth.
4. To act as *a standard for deferred payment*. In the modern world, goods are often purchased on credit, with the amount to be repaid being fixed in money terms. It would be impractical to agree

repayment in terms of some other commodity; for example, it may not always be easy to predict the future availability or the future requirements for that commodity. It is therefore money which serves as a standard for deferred payments.

## Money and liquidity

We are all familiar with cash (notes and coin) as a form of money but in a modern economy like the UK cash is not the only form of money. In fact, in terms of the *value* of total transactions in the UK, *bank deposits* are much more significant than cash. In this context it is important to note that *cheques* are not money. They are simply the means of transferring ownership of a bank deposit from one person or organisation to another. A cheque that cannot be honoured against a bank deposit is not acceptable in settlement of a debt.

One important term frequently discussed in connection with money is *liquidity*. An asset is more liquid the easier it can be transformed into a means of settling a debt. Cash and bank deposits are clearly the most liquid assets of all, but other assets can be quickly transformed into the means of settling a debt and are only slightly less liquid than cash and bank deposits.

## The creation of bank deposits

We have already mentioned the importance of bank deposits as a component of the money supply but what are bank deposits and how are they created? Bank deposits come into being in one of three ways:

1. when a bank receives a deposit of cash,
2. when a bank buys a security,
3. when a bank makes a loan.

We shall look at each of these in turn, but it is important to realise that whichever way bank deposits are created, a bank must always ensure that its liabilities and assets are equal. Deposits are the liabilities of a bank, since they are bound to honour all demands for cash from individual depositors up to the full amount deposited in each individual's account. In other words, deposits are claims against a bank. The assets which banks hold, however, can take a variety of forms, but they always give the bank a claim against someone else. Notes and coin, for example, give commercial banks a claim against the central bank (the Bank of England in the UK) whereas securities and advances give the bank a claim against the borrower.

## Bank deposits and the money supply

One important aspect of bank deposit creation is its effect on the money supply. We can illustrate this by looking at each of the three ways in which bank deposits are created. The examples below record the initial impact of a £100 creation of bank deposits on the bank's assets and liabilities:

1. When a bank receives a deposit of £100 cash, the effect on its balance sheet is:

| *Liabilities* | *Assets* |
| --- | --- |
| Deposits + £100 | Notes and coin + £100 |

It is clear that a deposit of cash has no initial impact on the money supply. The same amount of money exists, it is simply held in a different form. In this example an individual has simply exchanged £100 cash for a bank deposit of £100.

2. When a bank buys a security for £100 the effect on its balance sheet is:

| *Liabilities* | *Assets* |
| --- | --- |
| Deposits + £100 | Securities + £100 |

In this case the bank's purchase of a £100 security increases the money supply by £100. This is because securities, which are not acceptable in exchange for goods and services, have been exchanged for a bank deposit which is acceptable.

3. When a bank grants a loan of £100 the effect on its balance sheet is:

| *Liabilities* | *Assets* |
| --- | --- |
| Deposits + £100 | Advances + £100 |

Again, the granting of a £100 loan increases the money supply by £100. This must be so because deposits which are immediately acceptable in exchange for goods and services, have been exchanged for a debt (an advance which is repayable at some future date).

## The multiple expansion or bank deposits

Although the purchase of securities and the granting of loans leads to an increase in the money supply, banks cannot purchase securities or grant loans indefinitely. They are obliged to pay out cash on demand to account holders up to the limit of whatever is held in each individual's account. They must therefore keep sufficient cash to meet all possible demands for it.

Nevertheless, on any particular day only a relatively small portion of the funds held by banks will be withdrawn because of the widespread use of cheques and credit cards. There may well be a very substantial outflow of funds, but there is also likely to be a very substantial inflow. Because of this, the net change in a bank's holdings of cash on any particular day is likely to be relatively small. They are therefore able to lend a substantial part of the funds deposited with them. If all banks in the system do this, and we can expect them to do so since lending is their most profitable activity, the effect will be a multiple expansion of credit following an initial deposit of cash. The following hypothetical example is used to illustrate this process.

Assume that on any particular day banks wish to maintain a ratio of 10 per cent cash to total deposits. Assume further that there is no absence of willing borrowers so that banks will lend 90 per cent of all cash deposited with them. Thus, if a bank receives a cash deposit of £1,000, it will lend £900 in the form of advances. The effect of these transactions on the bank's balance sheet is set out below.

| *Liabilities* | *Assets* |
|---|---|
| Deposits £1,000 | Cash £1,000 |
| Deposits £900 | Advances £900 |

We can assume that, having been granted loans, borrowers will spend them, with cash being withdrawn from the bank to meet these expenditures. The £900 used by borrowers to finance purchases will flow back into the banking system as someone else's deposits and will be indistinguishable from any other inflows. Thus 90 per cent of these deposits (i.e. £810) will be re-lent. Again, this will flow back into the banking system with 90 per cent of these deposits (i.e. £729) being re-lent. It is apparent that the initial deposit of £1,000 cash leads to an eventual increase in bank deposits many times greater than the initial cash deposit.

This process does not, however, go on indefinitely. In fact, the eventual increase in bank deposits is the sum of a geometric progression which reaches an upper limit as the number of terms in the progression rises. In general, the eventual increase in deposits following an initial deposit of cash is equal to:

$$\frac{1}{\text{cash ratio}} \times \text{cash reserves}$$

In this particular case we have:

$$\frac{1}{10/100} \times £1000$$

In other words, an initial cash deposit of £1,000 leads to an eventual increase in bank deposits of £10,000. Since the cash ratio is 10 per cent, this is to be expected. We are simply saying that bank deposits expand until the initial deposit of cash is just sufficient to meet day-to-day demands for cash by depositors. The size of the cash ratio, therefore, sets the upper limit on the extent to which bank deposits can be expanded following an initial deposit of cash.

It is important to realise that *individual* banks do not create credit simply by expanding their deposits by some multiple of their cash reserves. If an individual bank did this it would quickly experience a *net outflow of cash* as it was forced to *honour cheques* drawn on these deposits. In other words, there will be payments into other banks. Clearly, such a situation could not continue for long. Instead, each individual bank simply re-lends a part of whatever is deposited with it. However, the effect of this is to create a situation where the combined total level of deposits held by all banks is a *multiple* of their combined cash reserves.

## The structure of banking

### The Bank of England

The Bank of England is the central bank in the United Kingdom. It has a wide range of functions, but the following are among the most important:

1. *Monetary policy*. The Bank has responsibility for implementing the government's monetary policy (see pages 153–155).
2. *Banker to the government*. The government maintains an account with the Bank of England (the Exchequer Account) through which all tax revenues and current government expenditure are passed. It also maintains another account (the National Loans Fund) through which all government borrowing and lending are passed.
3. *Management of the foreign exchange reserves*. As agent for the Treasury the Bank manages the Exchange Equalisation Account. This account holds the country's reserves of gold and foreign currency which are used to influence the external value of sterling in line with the government's foreign exchange rate policy (see pages 191–192).
4. *Banker to the banking system*. All banks above a certain size are obliged to hold deposits at the Bank of England. In addition, the London clearing banks hold operational deposits which gives them current account facilities at the Bank of England. It is by transferring these operational deposits that interbank settlements are made at the end of each working day as the final stage of the clearing process. They also provide the banks with facilities through which they can obtain additional supplies of notes and coin when necessary.
5. *Lender of last resort*. An important function of the Bank of England is that it acts as lender of last resort to the banking system. This simply means that if the banking system is short of liquidity, the Bank of England will always be prepared to lend to it. However, it reserves the right to specify what rate of interest it will charge when lending to the banking system. We shall also see on pages 153–4 that in making finance available to the banking system the Bank of England deals only with a group of institutions known as the discount market.
6. *Note circulation*. The Bank is the sole note issuing authority in England and Wales. In this context, its responsibilities are the printing, issue and withdrawal of bank notes.

### The discount market

#### *Introduction*

The London discount market is primarily a market in short-term funds and consists of nine discount houses. Together these comprise the London Discount Market Association (LDMA). The discount houses borrow at short term, mainly from the commercial banks and use these funds to carry out their primary function, discounting (see next section) short-term instruments of credit, that is, short-term securities. Much of the borrowing is at 'call', which means that the bank can ask for repayment at any time. These funds are used by the discount houses to purchase a variety of short-term instruments such as Treasury bills, commercial bills and gilt-edged securities which are close to maturity. (The securities in which the discount market deals are discussed on pages 150–152.) Indeed, the discount houses are the principal market-makers in bills, and by borrowing from the commercial banks they provide them with a modest return on short-term loans. Currently all eligible banks are obliged to maintain at least an average of 2½ per cent of their eligible liabilities in the form of secured money with the discount market.

### *Discounting and the discount rate*

A security is discounted when it is purchased for less than its face value. The difference consists of interest which accrues from the date of purchase until the date on which the security matures, when its face value is paid by the drawee to the holder of the security. For example, if a security due to mature in ninety-one days' time with a face value of £100,000 is discounted at 10 per cent, the discount is:

$$£100{,}000 \times \frac{10}{100} \times \frac{91}{365} = £2{,}493.15$$

The seller of the bill therefore receives £97,506.85 and in this case the discount house charges a rate of interest of

$$\frac{£2{,}493.15}{£97{,}506.85} \times \frac{365}{91} \times 100 = 10.26\%.$$

The difference between interest payments made on borrowed funds and interest receipts from discounting is profit (or loss) for the discount houses.

### *Functions of the discount market*

The function of any discount house is to earn a profit from their activities. This is the reason they are in business. However, in carrying out its activities the discount market performs several important economic funtions:

The discount houses are the primary market makers in short-term securities. As market-makers they are always prepared to buy and sell (make a market) in suitable securities. The securities in which they deal are discussed more fully on pages 150–152, but are typically those with only a few months to maturity. In buying securities the discount houses are providing a source of short-term credit for those with securities to sell.

As well as buying securities the discount houses also sell securities to investors. Such investors have differing requirements in terms of the desired maturity date of securities and the amount of funds they wish to invest. The discount houses are able to arrange portfolios (groups) of securities to match the requirements of investors thereby reducing 'search costs' for the latter. For example, they purchase Treasury bills at the 'weekly auction' (see next paragraph) and, if approached, will sell these and other securities when they are closer to maturity.

The discount houses also perform an important role in financing the government's short-term borrowing. Each week the Bank of England issues Treasury bills by tender, the so-called weekly auction, and the discount houses collectively agree to 'cover the tender'. This simply means that they submit a bid for all the bills on offer, thus ensuring that the government is provided with the funds it requires. In practice the discount market only takes up a portion of the weekly issue, the remainder being allocated to those who submit the highest bids. To ensure that the discount market is always able to carry out this function, uniquely in the UK, it has direct access to the Bank of England as lender of last resort.

The discount market performs a crucial role in the implementation of the government's monetary policy. It is, in effect, the fulcrum through which the Bank of England engineers changes in short-term interest rates. The way in which the Bank does this is discussed on pages 153–154.

The discount houses borrow a large proportion of their funds from the commercial banks. Some of this money is at 'call' and repayment can be demanded almost immediately. Other funds are lent overnight. In this way the discount houses provide the commercial banks with highly liquid, yet profitable, assets.

## The clearing banks

The clearing banks are so called because they handle the exchange and settlement of cheques. One of their main functions is therefore the provision of a payments mechanism. A second important function of the clearing banks is in accepting deposits. However, we are mainly concerned with a third function, namely the provision of finance. The clearing banks are major providers of short-term finance, and their activities in the money market have an important bearing on the money supply. The eligible liabilities (ELs) of the clearing banks consist mainly of deposits, but their assets are more varied.

### *The asset side of the balance sheet*

#### *Notes and coin*

These are the bank's most liquid but least profitable asset.

#### *Balances at the Bank of England*

Of the three assets maintained at the Bank of England, only operational deposits are a liquid asset. Cash ratio deposits are not liquid, since all deposit takers with ELs in excess of £10 million are obliged to maintain such deposits at the Bank of England equal to ½ per cent of the ELs. Equally, special deposits are not liquid. More will be said about these later, but they are basically deposits 'frozen' at the Bank of England and repaid only at the Bank's discretion.

*Bills*

The banks hold a variety of bills; but these are grouped in Table 14.1 as Treasury bills, eligible bank bills, eligible local authority bills and other bills. The precise nature of these bills is discussed on page 151, and we shall see below that they are of fundamental importance in the implementation of the government's monetary policy.

*Investments*

These consist largely of the banks' holdings of gilt-edged securities, i.e. government bonds of various maturity dates. Company bonds (i.e. debentures) are also within this heading, as are holdings of equity (shares).

*Advances*

These are the banks' most profitable asset and consist of loans and overdrafts made to private customers.

*Liquidity and profitability*

A major problem facing banks and other financial intermediaries is that they must always have sufficient liquidity to meet the demands of their customers on the one hand while they must use their funds profitably on the other. The problem is that in general the most liquid assets are the least profitable. For example, advances to customers are the banks' most profitable asset but they are highly illiquid assets since they are loans which cannot be called in until the agreed redemption date. A continuing problem for all banks is therefore to achieve an acceptable balance between liquidity and profitability.

## Merchant Banks

Merchant banks perform a variety of functions in both the capital and money markets.

*Acceptance business*

This was one of the earliest activities of merchant banks. For a fee they simply add their name to bills of exchange issued by traders. In this way they guarantee payment of bills on maturity should the drawee default. Accepted bills of exchange are therefore highly marketable (liquid) securities.

*Issuing business*

One of the earliest functions of merchant banks was to raise finance for overseas trading activities but during the present century they have become more active in raising finance for the home market. In particular they now undertake the *issuing* and *underwriting* of share issues by joint stock companies and charge a fee for this service. More recently still they have combined this with financial advice, for example on the desirability of a merger.

*Wholesale banking*

Wholesale banking is a term used to describe large-scale dealing in deposits and is the most important activity of the London money markets The sums involved are not less than £¼ million and are placed for terms ranging from overnight to several months and in some cases years. The merchant banks have become active participants in the market for wholesale deposits and this is by far their

*Table 14.1*

BANKS IN THE UK: COMBINED BALANCE SHEET OF MONTHLY REPORTING INSTITUTIONS[1] AS AT 30 SEPTEMBER 1990

| LIABILITIES (£m.) | | ASSETS (£m.) | |
|---|---|---|---|
| **Sterling liabilities** | | **Sterling assets** | |
| Notes Outstanding | 1408 | Notes and Coin | 2995 |
| Deposits, of which: | | Balances with the Bank of England, of which: | |
| Sight deposits | 169341 | | |
| Time deposits | 292947 | Cash ratio deposits | |
| Certificates of deposits[2] | 52087 | Operational deposits | 1595 |
| | | Special deposits | 88 |
| Other sterling liabilities | 71147 | | — |
| | | Market loans | |
| **Other currency liabilities** | | LDMA, of which: | |
| | | Secured | 12122 |
| Deposits, of which: | | Unsecured | 102 |
| Sight and time deposits | 562192 | Other UK bank | 88420 |
| Certificates of deposit[2] | 70019 | UK bank CD's | 16371 |
| | | Building society CD's and time deposits | 2520 |
| Other foreign currency liabilities | 28130 | UK local authorities | 628 |
| | | Overseas | 28446 |
| | | Bills, of which: | |
| | | Treasury bills | 3888 |
| | | Eligible bills | 56 |
| | | Eligible bank bills | 9827 |
| | | Other bills | 574 |
| | | Advances | 367030 |
| | | Investments | 24999 |
| | | Other sterling assets | 29939 |
| | | **Other currency assets** | |
| | | Advances | 150858 |
| | | Market loans | 450214 |
| | | Bills | 3833 |
| | | Investments | 43752 |
| | | Other foreign currency assets | 9010 |
| Total liabilities | 1247269 | Total assets | 1247269 |

[1] Generally those with total balance sheet of £100m or more, or eligible liabilities of £10m or more, other than members of the LDMA

[2] and other short-term paper (short-term securities) issued.

main deposit-taking activity. In this context they are active participants in the Euro-currency markets (pages 149–150). Like all banks they earn income on the difference paid to attract funds and the amount charged when lending funds.

## Foreign Banks

The number of foreign banks operating in London has grown rapidly in recent years, from 77 in 1960 to around 450 today. In the main, foreign banks are concerned with international banking activities and are active participants in the Euro-currency markets. Indeed the bulk of their business is concerned with wholesale banking activities and, as yet, retail banking activities account for a small proportion of their activities. However, since deregulation the retail side of their activities has grown rapidly and they now compete with commercial banks for private customers; many also compete for wholesale deposits in the domestic money market.

## Non-bank financial intermediaries

All of the institutions considered thus far are referred to as *bank financial intermediaries*. However, there are other institutions which participate in the money markets which are referred to as *non-bank financial intermediaries*. The distinction between these is a legal one and is not always clear cut. Some of the more important non-bank financial intermediaries include building societies, finance houses, the National Savings Bank, insurance companies and pension funds.

## Banking regulations

In August 1981 the Bank of England introduced important new measures concerned with the activities of the monetary sector. All of the institutions described above are included in the definition of the monetary sector which currently comprises:

(a) all recognised banks and licensed deposit-takers,
(b) the National Giro Bank,
(c) the Trustree Savings Bank,
(d) the Banking Department of the Bank of England,
(e) those institutions in the Channel Islands and the Isle of Man which have opted to adhere to the new arrangements.

The regulations currently in force concerning the monetary sector are:

1. All banks and licensed deposit-takers with eligible liabilities (ELs) in excess of £10m. are required to keep non-operational deposits with the Bank of England equal to ½ per cent of total ELs. The purpose of this is to provide the Bank of England with funds and resources rather than to enable it to control the growth of ELs within the monetary sector.
2. Special deposits (see pages 154–155) are extended and now apply to all institutions within the monetary sector having ELs greater than £10m.

3. All eligible banks, that is recognised banks whose acceptances (i.e. accepted bills) are eligible for rediscount at the Bank of England, are required to hold secured call money with the LDMA. This must equal at least 2½ per cent of their ELs. They are also required to hold an amount equal to a further 2½ per cent of their ELs with other institutions in the money and gilt-edged markets (making 5 per cent in total). The purpose of this is to ensure an adequate supply of funds to enable the bill and gilt-edged markets to function efficiently. We shall see on pages 153–154 that this is necessary if the Bank's own open market operations are to be effective.
4. The previous reserve assets ratio, in which a minimum of 12½ per cent of selected liquid assets had to be kept against liabilities, was abolished in 1981. The Bank will, however, continue to monitor the liquidity ratios of the banks to ensure that they are adequate.
5. In normal circumstances the Bank will no longer publicly announce its Minimum Lending Rate (MLR), that is the rate at which it rediscounts first-class bills when acting as *lender of last resort*, but will maintain it within an unpublished band. This is to give market forces a more prominent role in determining short-term rates, which will be allowed to fluctuate within the unpublished band without the authorities intervening. This does not mean that MLR can only fluctuate within the limits initially set by the unpublished band. The authorities might vary the position of the band from time to time, and in any case have reserved the right to make public announcements about MLR in exceptional circumstances.

## The secondary or parallel money market

Alongside the primary market described above there has grown a secondary or parallel money market. This has grown rapidly since the 1960s, mainly because the secondary money market has not been subjected to the same degree of regulation by the authorities as has the primary market. Put simply, willing borrowers who have been unable to obtain funds in the primary market have turned to other institutions. These institutions have therefore grown and now compete for deposits with the primary market. The more deposits they can attract, the more loans they can create and this increases their income.

The principle markets which together make up the secondary market are described below.

### *The inter-bank market*

On any particular day certain banks will have a shortage of funds, while other banks will have a surplus. Shortages and surpluses are matched as far as possible by borrowing and lending in the interbank market. Dealings are normally in sums of £250,000 or more. Money may be lent at call, overnight, or for any period up to about five years.

However, the bulk of lending in the interbank market is for three months.

*The market for sterling certificates of deposit*

The nature of certificates of deposit (CDs) is discussed on page 151 but it is important to note here that they are a negotiable security. In other words, they can be sold on the open market at prices determined by supply and demand. The banks have benefitted particularly from the growth of a market in CDs because, by issuing such certificates (i.e. creating claims against themselves), they are able to obtain additional funds which can then be on-lent at a higher interest rate.

*The Euro-currency market*

When an exporter receives payment for goods or services in foreign currency, these can be deposited with a bank or some other licensed deposit-taker. The exporter therefore has a foreign currency deposit which will be on-lent to willing borrowers by the institution holding the deposit. It is this on-lending of foreign currency by European institutions that has given rise to the term 'Euro-currency market'.

In terms of the value of deposits held, this is the largest of the parallel money markets. Companies, banks, and even governments, borrow in the Euro-currency market, and, although funds can be borrowed for as long as five years, most borrowing is for six months or less.

## Instruments of the London money markets

The London money market mainly deals in instruments (i.e. securities) with one year or less to maturity. The main instruments traded are summarised below and any institution dealing in these instruments is therefore a participant in this market.

*Bills of exchange*

Bills of exchange are IOUs given by one person, usually a buyer of goods, to another person, usually a seller of goods. The drawee promises to pay the drawer a fixed sum of money at a specified future time. The drawer of the bill therefore gives the drawee time to sell the goods before paying for them. In the absence of this credit, buyers might not have sufficient cash to place orders and this would leave manufacturers without markets for their goods. However, bills of exchange are negotiable securities and once *accepted* (see page 146) are eligible for discounting (see page 144). This has important implications because if manufacturers granted trade credit, the reduction in their cash flow might make it impossible to finance further production without borrowing funds and incurring interest charges. In other words, by providing credit any institution discounting a bill of exchange enables production and distribution to continue uninterrupted.

*Treasury bills*

Treasury bills are issued by the Bank of England on behalf of the government and normally mature ninety-one days after issue. Like bills of exchange these are a promise to pay a fixed sum of money. The rate of interest the government pays on its short-term borrowing is therefore determined by the price at which Treasury bills can be sold at the weekly tender. The higher the bid price, the lower the rate of interest the government pays on its short-term borrowing (see page 131).

*Local authority securities*

Local authorities issue bonds which frequently mature within one year. They also issue bills which conventionally mature within ninety-one days. Like Tresaury bills these are issued by tender and, as governments have issued fewer Treasury bills, so the discount houses have acquired more local authority bills.

*Certificates of deposit*

A certificate of deposit (CD) is a document certifying that a deposit has been placed with a bank, and that the deposit is repayable with interest after a stated time. The minimum value of the deposit is usually £50,000 and CDs normally mature in twelve months or less, although they have been issued with a five-year maturity.

*Short-dated bonds*

As well as the securities discussed so far, a host of other securities are traded on the money market. As time goes by any security issued for a fixed number of years will approach its maturity date. The discount market discounts securities with five years or less to maturity, but in general it is only when securities have one year or less to maturity that they are traded on the money market.

*Euro-currency certificates of deposit*

These are similar to sterling certificates of deposit, but are given as evidence of a foreign currency deposit with a UK bank. Dollar certificates of deposit are the most important instrument traded in the Euro-currency deposit market. The most important outlet for Euro-deposits is the interbank Euro-currency market. Although banks might borrow from one another for as long as five years, most borrowing is for six months or less. Indeed, a substantial amount is typically lent overnight. As they approach maturity, certificates of deposit become more attractive to money market institutions because of their higher degree of liquidity.

*Euro-bonds*

The Euro-bond market specialises in the provision of medium-term finance. In this market banks arrange, on behalf of borrowers in the UK, to issue and to underwrite bonds. These bonds are usually taken up (i.e. purchased) by private investors who supply the appropriate amount of foreign currency. Like other securities, as Euro-bonds approach maturity they become more liquid and hence are traded on the London money markets in the same way that other short-term instruments are traded (see above – 'short-dated bonds').

## Measures of the money supply

Until now we have discussed the general area of money and liquidity without specifically defining the money supply. The measures of the money supply most commonly used in the UK at the present time are shown in Figure 14.1.

The fact that there are several measures of the money supply appears to make any reference to this concept ambiguous. However, the different measures of the money supply aim to reflect different levels of liquidity within the system. MO is a narrow measure of the money supply and provides an estimate of the level of liquidity in the economy while M2 is a measure of transactions balances. The broadest measures of money in the UK are M4, M4c and M5. These include assets which are 'near money' such as Treasury bills.

MO = Notes and coin in circulation with the public
*plus* banks' till money
*plus* banks' operational balances with the Bank of England

M2 = Notes and coin in circulation with the public
*plus* private sector non-interest-bearing sterling sight bank deposits
*plus* private sector interest-bearing retail sterling bank deposits
*plus* private sector holdings of retail building society deposits and national savings bank ordinary accounts

M4 = Notes and coin in circulation with the public
*plus* private sector sterling sight bank deposits
*plus* banks' retail deposits
*plus* building societies' shares and deposits
*plus* private sector holdings of sterling certificates of deposit

M4c = M4 *plus* private sector holdings of foreign currency deposits

M5 = M4 *plus* private sector (excluding building societies) holdings of money market instruments (bank bills, Treasury bills and local authority deposits) certificates of tax deposit and national savings instruments (excluding certificates, SAYE and other long-term deposits)

Figure 14.1 UK Monetary Aggregates
Source: *Bank of England Quarterly Bulletin*

One problem for the authorities is that having several measures of the money supply sometimes makes it difficult to assess whether monetary policy is restricting the growth of the money supply or not because the different measures of the money supply sometimes move in different directions with some aggregates rising when others are falling. (Currently the authorities take the view that narrow money is an accurate indicator of monetary conditions and, the government continues to set targets for its rate of growth.) However, the wider aggregates are also important but they are much more difficult to measure and interpret – especially during periods of rapid change in financial markets. For example, the distinction between banks and building societies is becoming increasingly blurred with building societies now providing current accounts and cheque guarantee cards for customers along with cash-point facilities and loans to meet a variety of requirements. Banks, on the other hand, have become active in the provision of mortgage finance. However, the deposits of building societies are not included in the narrower monetary aggregates.

## The mechanics of monetary policy

The term monetary policy is usually taken to include all the measures which influence the supply of money and/or the price of money (i.e. the rate of interest). In the UK, the Bank of England has overall responsibility for the implementation of monetary policy. It uses a variety of techniques.

### Open market operations

This technique involves the sale or purchase of government securities on the open market by the Bank of England. It can be used to reduce or to increase the stock of money (i.e. bank deposits) in circulation with the public.

Suppose the Bank of England wishes to reduce the money supply by open market operations. The Bank of England sells securities to the non-bank private sector, that is, to households and firms other than those engaged in banking in the private sector. These securities will be paid for by cheques drawn against deposits with the commercial banks. The Bank of England will settle these claims against banks by deducting the appropriate amount from their operational deposits. If necessary, the banks will be able to replenish their operational deposits at the Bank of England by calling in their loans to the discount market. However, there will still be a reduction in their overall level of liquidity, since loans to the discount market are liquid assets and these have now fallen in total. This reduction in liquidity will compel banks to reduce their lending, i.e. bank deposits, otherwise they risk being unable to honour all the claims that bank lending creates against them.

If the Bank of England wishes to increase the money supply by open market operations, it will purchase securities from the non-bank private sector. In this case the banks' operational deposits increase. Assuming that there are willing borrowers, then this extra liquidity can be used to increase their lending, that is, bank deposits increase.

### Interest rate policy

In practice open market operations have been used less frequently for controlling the money supply in recent years. Instead, the authorities have relied much more on money market intervention to influence interest rates, and in this way to control the growth of bank lending. A rise in interest rates might be expected to damp down the demand for bank credit, thus restricting growth of the money supply and vice versa.

The techniques of interest rate policy are complex, but under the present arrangements the clearing banks inform the Bank of England daily about the target balances for their assets they are aiming at. This information, together with the Bank's estimate of flows between the commercial banks and the public sector,* as well as seasonal patterns, etc., enables the Bank to estimate the likely shortage or surplus of funds in the money market. This estimate is announced at about 9.45 a.m., and, if necessary, a revised estimate is announced at noon.

If the Bank estimates that the market will be short of funds, it informs the discount houses that it is prepared to buy bills from them. However, it does not stipulate a price, and the discount houses must offer bills to the Bank at prices of their choosing. If the Bank of England considers that the rate of interest implied by these offers (see pages 131 and page 144 for a discussion on the relationship between security prices and the rate of interest) is consistent with the conduct of monetary policy, it will accept the offers, and the shortage of funds will be relieved. However, if the Bank considers that the rate of interest implied by these offers is too low, then it will decline to buy the bills and the discount houses will be compelled to make further offers of bills at lower prices (implying higher rates of interest). When the Bank wishes to engineer a fall in short-term rates of interest it simply increases the price at which it is prepared to buy bills from the discount houses.

The question might be asked as to how the Bank will engineer a change in short-term rates when the market is not short of funds, and so does not need to deal with the Bank. In fact, this is an unlikely occurrence, because the Bank can create shortages by increasing the weekly Treasury bill issue. Since the LDMA agree to cover the tender, this will create a shortage of funds. Alternatively, the Bank can 'fund' the national debt (see below). To engineer a fall in short-term rates the Bank simply buys securities, thus creating a surplus of funds in the money markets.

Another way in which the Bank can affect short-term rates is provided by the 1981 regulations. Under these the Bank retains the option, in exceptional circumstances, to reveal in advance the rate at which it will operate in the market for a short period ahead. It has used this option on several occasions and it has proved very effective with all institutions acting quickly to fall into line with the Bank's wishes once it has made these known. The alternative of course would be for the Bank to implement measures which would force institutions to comply with its intentions!

## Special deposits

When the Bank of England makes a call for special deposits, it requires banks and licensed deposit-takers with ELs in excess of £10m. to place funds in a special account at the Bank. Although these funds earn interest, they are effectively 'frozen', since those making the deposits do not have the right to withdraw them. The Bank of England alone decides when special deposits will be repaid. The level of special deposits is fixed as a percentage of ELs and payment is again made by a reduction in operational deposits, that is, cash reserves at

* These flows directly affect the operational deposits of the banks. For example, when tax payments are made to the Exchequer, operational deposits fall, and when the government pays for goods and services, operational deposits rise.

the Bank. A call for special deposits is the most direct means currently available to the Bank for reducing the liquidity position of banks and licensed deposit-takers and is therefore the most direct means of controlling their lending. As the stock of liquid assets falls, banks are again forced to cut their lending. Special deposits can be released when the Bank wishes to see an expansion of the money supply.

Despite this, no call has been made for special deposits since the 1970s because, as with any selective control mechanism, the result of their imposition is rapid growth of business by those organisations not subject to controls. The authorities take the view that such growth is undesirable because it represents growth of less efficient institutions, that is, institutions which only grow when other institutions are subjected to controls. This explains the emphasis on control through changes in the rate of interest. It affects all institutions indiscriminately and does not therefore encourage the growth of inefficient institutions.

### Funding

This involves the sale of more long-term debt (e.g. bonds) and the issue of less short-term debt (e.g. Treasury bills). Since Treasury bills are short-dated securities they are highly liquid assets because they can be sold easily and quickly on the money market. By issuing fewer Treasury bills the authorities can reduce the degree of liquidity in the system, and thereby restrict the ability of the banks to make loans. If a bank's holdings of Treasury bills falls and its holdings of long-term securities increases, it is likely to cut its lending for two main reasons:

1. Longer-term securities are not eligible for rediscount at the Bank of England and are therefore less liquid.
2. Although longer-term securities can be sold on the capital market, their value is less certain.

These are important considerations, since they imply that, if a bank needs to replenish its holdings of cash because of a sudden outflow of funds, it might be forced to sell its securities at unfavourable prices. Rather than risk this, banks would tend to cut their lending.

### Fiscal policy

The authorities believe that there is a close association between the amount the public sector borrows (the public sector borrowing requirement or PSBR) and the growth of M4. This relationship is discussed in detail on pages 207–209, but it is important to note here that at the present time the authorities believe that a reduction in the growth of M4 is impossible without a reduction in the size of the PSBR and for much of the 1980s made a reduction in the PSBR one of their main mechanisms for controlling the growth of the money supply.

## Test your understanding

1. What is meant by the phrase 'Money is as money does'?
2. List the following assets in order of ascending liquidity: (i) a Treasury Bill, (ii) a £5 note, (iii) a postal order.
3. For a commercial bank why are 'Investments' less liquid than 'Advances'?
4. Why is there a distinction between broad money and narrow money?
5. What is special about special deposits?
6. Why do banks compete against each other for funds and yet lend to each other in the inter-bank market?

# 15 The value of money

In itself, money has no intrinsic value. It derives value because it is acceptable in exchange for goods and services. The value of money is therefore determined by the prices of goods and services purchased with money. Clearly, if all prices in the economy rise, then a given amount of money will exchange for (or buy) fewer goods and services. In this case the value of money has fallen. Conversely, if all prices in the economy fall, the value of money has risen.

This seems simple enough, but the problem is that over any given period of time not all prices in the economy move in the same direction or by the same amount. Some prices rise and others fall. Some rise by more than others, and so on. In practice, therefore, it is difficult to measure changes in the value of money, and economists use a technique known as index numbers to estimate changes in an average of prices. Not all price changes are considered, merely those of most significance to the average person. So how do we measure changes in the value of money?

## Measuring changes in the value of money – index numbers

### Index of retail prices

Changes in the average price level are measured by index numbers and in the UK the most publicised index is the index of retail prices. This purports to measure changes in the cost of living experienced by an average household over a particular period of time. The technique is simple enough. A representative sample of the population provides a detailed record of their expenditure over a given period, usually a month, and this is used to estimate the expenditure pattern of the 'average household'. This estimate of expenditure is used to derive the items to be included in the index and the weights assigned to them; the weight being based on their relative importance. Those items which account for a larger proportion of total expenditure over the period are assigned a higher weight than items which account for a smaller proportion of total expenditure. Table 15.1 illustrates the basic principles involved in computing the index of retail prices.

In the base year (Year 1) each commodity is assigned an index

*Table 15.1*

| | Year 1 | | | | Year 2 | | | |
|---|---|---|---|---|---|---|---|---|
| Commodity | Price | Weight | Index no. | Weighted index no. | Price | Weight | Index no. | Weighted index no. |
| A | £1.00 | 4 | 100 | 400 | £1.50 | 4 | 150 | 600 |
| B | £2.00 | 2 | 100 | 200 | £2.50 | 2 | 125 | 250 |
| C | £5.00 | 3 | 100 | 300 | £6.00 | 3 | 120 | 360 |
| D | £4.00 | 1 | 100 | 100 | £6.00 | 1 | 150 | 150 |
| | Index of prices = 1000/10 = 100 | | | | Index of prices = 1360/10 = 136 | | | |

number of 100. The weighted index number of each commodity is then obtained by multiplying the index number by the weight. Adding up all the weighted index numbers and dividing by the sum of the weights, gives the value of the price index. In the example provided, the value of the price index in the base year is 100. In fact this will always be the value of the index in the base year, because each commodity is assigned a value of 100. In calculating a weighted price index in the base year we are therefore effectively multiplying 100 by the sum of the weights and then dividing the answer by the sum of the weights.

In the next period, Year 2 in Table 15.1, the index number of each commodity is simply the price of the commodity in Year 2 expressed as a percentage of its price in year 1. Thus we see that the price of commodity A in Year 2 is 150 per cent of its price in Year 1, and so on. Again, this is multiplied by the relevant weight for each commodity, and the total of all the weighted index numbers is divided by the sum of the weights to give the price index (that is, the average weighted value of all price changes) in Year 2. In this case the price index in Year 2 is 136, indicating that the average family has experienced a rise in the cost of living of 36 per cent between Year 1 and Year 2.

### Problems of interpreting changes in the RPI

Changes in the RPI are the most widely used measure of changes in the rate of inflation in the UK. However, for several reasons, changes in the RPI might not accurately measure changes in the rate of inflation. The following are some of the major reasons for this:

- A retail price index such as that illustrated in Table 15.1 measures changes in retail prices experienced by the average family. However, different families will have different patterns of consumption which might deviate substantially from that used to construct a price index. For example families with children consume different goods and services than families with no children. Similarly changes in the prices of goods and services affect people differently. For example, non-smokers are unaffected by changes in the price of tabacco and changes in the mortgage rate only affect home-buyers.

- Over time patterns of consumption change. For example, more fish is now consumed and less red meat than a decade ago. Consumption of alcohol has increased in the last decade and so on. If an index is to be accurate, the weights must be altered to reflect these changes.
- Care must also be taken to monitor changes in the institutions patronised by consumers. Here again patterns have changed with small independent retailers declining in importance and supermarkets increasing in importance. Data on prices charged in different retail outlets must reflect expenditure by consumers in these different retail outlets if an index is to be accurate.
- Over time the quality of goods changes. For example, pocket calculators are now more reliable and have a greater range of functions than models available only a few years ago. Simply monitoring price changes ignores such quality improvements.
- New goods become available and again the index must be altered to take account of these if it is to be accurate. For example, few houses had a home computer or a video in the 1970s and yet they are now quite common.

In practice, weights in the RPI and the range of goods monitored are both altered to allow for the changes mentioned above. This undoubtedly improves the accuracy of the RPI in the short term. However, it makes comparisons over long time periods imprecise.

## The tax and price index

The index of retail prices measures changes in the cost of living. But what people can buy with their earnings depends on the deductions from their pay, in particular those made in respect of income tax and national insurance contributions, as well as on the average level of prices when take home pay is spent. The tax and price index shows how the purchasing power of income is affected by changes in both direct taxes and prices.

Changes in prices, as measured by the retail price index, have a weight of about 75 per cent in the tax and price index, while changes in income tax and national insurance contributions account for the remainder. Like the retail price index, the tax and price index is a composite index reflecting the weighted experience of groups of households with different tax liabilities. The tax and price index is therefore an attempt to reflect what has happened to the purchasing power of the average household's take home pay.

## Demand-pull inflation

This occurs when there is excess demand for real output at the existing price level. In other words, aggregate **demand** exceeds aggregate supply. We have analysed this situation in terms of the inflationary gap on page 107 but the assumption there was that prices remain constant. The 45° line used to explain the Keynesian model of income determination on page 107 is effectively the aggregate supply curve of the economy. In practice, an excess of aggregate demand over aggregate supply at the existing price level, which cannot be fully accommodated by an expansion of output, will result in the price level being pulled upwards until aggregate demand and aggregate supply are brought into equality.

The process is sometimes likened to an auction. In the early stages of bidding for an item, demand usually exceeds supply, and price is pulled upwards until demand equals supply. Similarly, in the real world, if demand exceeds the limited amount of output available at the current price level, then the price level rises. However, when the economy is producing at less than full capacity, and there are substantial amounts of unemployed resources, it is likely that a rise in demand will be accommodated by an expansion of output, with little or no effect on the average price level. But as the economy approaches full employment, it becomes increasingly difficult for output to respond, and in these circumstances excess aggregate demand is at least partly manifested in higher prices. Once full employment is reached, however, any increase in aggregate demand is entirely reflected in higher prices. Because of this, *demand-pull inflation* is particularly associated with economies which are at or near full employment. The effect of increases in aggregate demand on output and the price level is illustrated in Figure 15.1.

Aggregate supply and aggregate demand are initially in equilibrium at OY with an average price level of AY/OY; that is, price equals average expenditure on output, i.e. total expenditure (total receipts of firms) divided by total output. A rise in aggregate demand to $AD_1$ results in an increase in output to the full employment level, $OY_f$, but also an increase in the price level to $BY_f/OY_f$. Any further increase in aggregate demand will simply result in higher prices, because no further expansion of output is possible.

Despite this apparently simple analysis, care must be taken to avoid confusion. As the economy approaches full employment, resources become increasingly scarce and growing competition for these will bid up their price. Firms will therefore experience rising costs. However, these cost increases are not exogenous. They are the direct result of a higher demand for final output. We shall see in the following section that an exogenous rise in costs will result in an upward shift of the entire aggregate supply curve, rather than a movement along it.

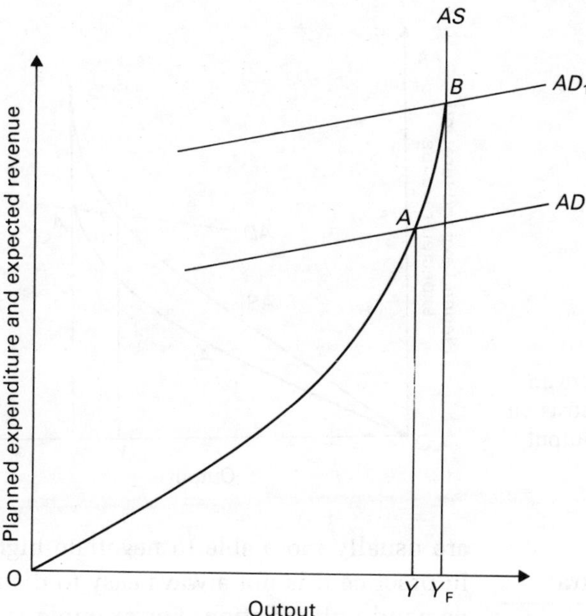


Figure 15.1 The effect of an increase in aggregate demand on real output and the price level

## Cost-push inflation

This occurs when pressure on prices results from an exogenous rise in costs. Since the share of national income paid to labour is about 70 per cent of the total of all incomes paid, wage increases in excess of productivity increases have been an important source of rising costs. Any depreciation of sterling will also have an important impact on costs in the UK (see page 201), since the UK depends heavily on imported raw materials.

An *exogenous* increase in costs, *whatever its source*, raises firms' costs at all levels of output. After an increase in costs, any given level of output will therefore only be supplied at a higher price. Although individual firms might be willing to absorb an increase in costs by cutting profits, it will be impossible for all firms to do this. Therefore the aggregate supply curve shifts upwards. With an unchanged level of aggregate demand the effect of an exogenous increase in costs on output and the price level is shown in Figure 15.2.

Aggregate supply and aggregate demand are initially in equilibrium at output $OY_f$ with the price level at $AY_f/OY_f$. Subsequently, an exogenous rise in costs shifts aggregate supply to $AS_1$ and, if all other things remain equal, equilibrium will be restored when output has fallen to OY and the price level has risen to BY/OY.

Because of the importance of wages in firms' costs, economists have coined the term *wage-push inflation* to indicate a situation when the main source of cost increases is wage increases in excess of productivity increases. Again, this is more likely to occur at higher levels of employment; as shortages of skilled labour develop, unions

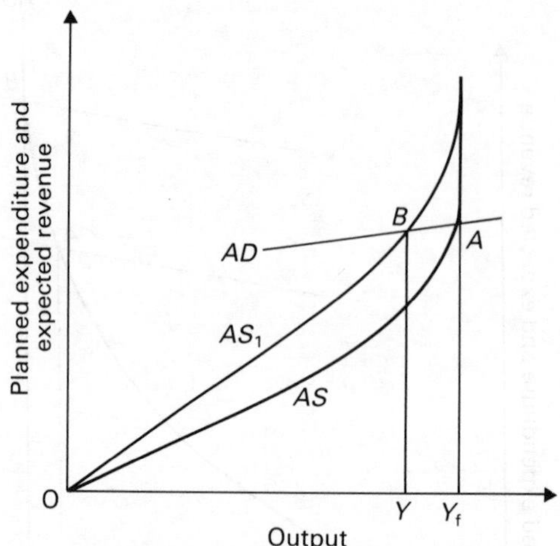


*Figure 15.2* The effect of an exogenous increase in costs on aggregate supply, real output and the price level

are usually more able to negotiate higher pay awards.

## The inflationary spiral

In practice it is not always easy to distinguish between cost-push and demand-pull inflation. For example, a rise in costs which pushes up prices will also result in higher factor incomes. At least part of these will be spent domestically and the extra demand, especially if there is a shortage of capacity, is likely to pull prices up still further. These price increases imply a fall in the real income of wage earners. It is likely that trade unions will demand compensatory pay rises, giving a still further push to inflation.

In practice, the inflationary spiral will not go on indefinitely. There are several reasons for this. The tax and benefit system acts to automatically stabilise the economy; increased expenditure on imports and a reduction in exports will raise leakages and cut injections and so on. Nevertheless, because of the potentially adverse effects of inflation, especially on the balance of payments and the allocation of resources, governments have pursued policies to actively reduce the rate of inflation rather than merely to allow the process to peter out in the fullness of time. These policies are discussed in Chapter 19.

## The causes of inflation in the UK

Table 15.2 shows the contribution made by changes in the costs of different inputs to the final price of manufacturing output. Labour costs consistently make the greatest contribution but this does not necessarily indicate that the cost-push hypothesis is correct. For example, an increase in the money supply could lead to an increase in demand for final output and encourge employers to increase wages.

## The Phillips Curve

The relationship between unemployment and inflation is generalised in the Phillips Curve. In its original form this curve indicated a negative correlation between the rate of change of wages and the level of unemployment. The impressive feature of the Phillips Curve was that the relationship it identified had been remarkably stable for a

*Table 15.2* Contributions to output* prices in manufacturing** from changes in cost components

| | Unit labour costs | Input costs | Bought-in services | Margins (residual) | Percentage change |
|---|---|---|---|---|---|
| 1980 | 9.9 | 3.7 | 5.2 | 3.4 | 15.4 |
| 1981 | 4.2 | 2.9 | 2.7 | −2.4 | 7.4 |
| 1982 | 1.3 | 2.3 | 1.1 | 2.2 | 6.9 |
| 1983 | −0.1 | 2.6 | 0.9 | 2.0 | 5.4 |
| 1984 | 0.6 | 3.0 | 0.9 | 0.6 | 3.1 |
| 1985 | 2.1 | 1.0 | 1.3 | 1.3 | 5.7 |
| 1986 | 1.6 | −3.4 | 1.0 | 4.9 | 4.1 |
| 1987 | 0.2 | 1.7 | 0.9 | 1.6 | 4.4 |
| 1988 | 0.9 | 1.6 | 1.7 | 0.6 | 4.8 |
| 1989 | 1.9 | 1.8 | 2.2 | –0.4 | 5.4 |

*Notes:* * Percentage points
** Excluding food, drink and tobacco
*Source: Bank of England Quarterly Bulletin*, August 1990

continuous period of almost a hundred years.

Soon after the original Phillips Curve was identified it was quickly discovered that there was also a significant, and stable, negative correlation between the rate of change of prices and the level of unemployment. Moreover, it was widely believed by policy makers that because the relationship had been stable for almost a hundred years, it would remain stable in the future. It therefore appeared to offer policy makers a range of policy choices. A particular level of unemployment could be traded off against a particular rate of inflation. For example, a lower level of unemployment implied a higher rate of inflation and vice versa. This inverse relationship between unemployment and the rate of inflation is shown in Figure 15.3.

However, the appeal of the Phillips Curve was not just in its apparent stability. The Phillips Curve also played a role in identifying the causes of inflation. High rates of inflation at low levels of unemployment supported both the demand-pull and cost-push explanations of inflation. At low levels of unemployment buoyant demand would pull up prices, while trade unions would be in a strong bargaining position from which they could negotiate relatively high pay awards. Buoyant demand in the economy would lower employers' resistance to pay demands since rising costs could more easily be passed on as higher prices. In contrast, at high levels of unemployment, demand in the economy would be less buoyant and the bargaining position of unions weaker.

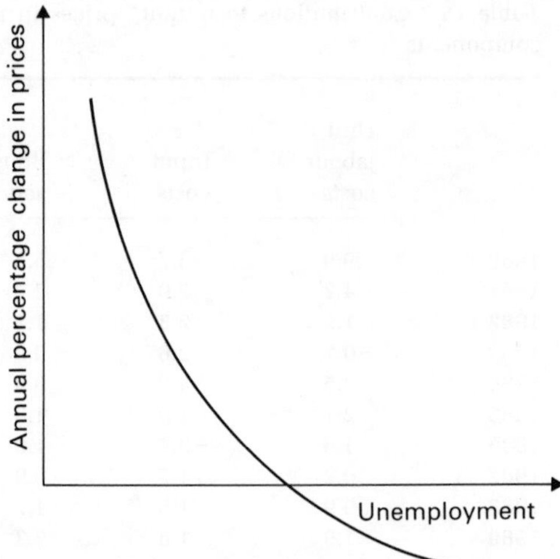


Figure 15.3 The Phillips Curve

## The breakdown of the Phillips Curve

For over a decade economic policy in the UK was implicitly based on the Phillips Curve. However, it became apparent in the late 1960s that the relationship identified by Phillips was not as stable as at first believed. Figure 15.4 shows the course of inflation and unemployment in the UK since 1969.

It is clear that a higher rate of inflation than previously is now consistent with any given level of unemployment. Various reasons have been advanced to account for this. Some economists claim that the Phillips Curve has simply moved outwards from the origin; some possible reasons for this are examined below. However, an alternative explanation is provided by the monetarists who claim that the Phillips Curve was never more than a short-run phenomenon that had no long-run validity. This view is examined in the following section.

## Causes of the breakdown of the Phillips Curve

- *Increased unemployment and welfare benefits.* One possible explanation for the breakdown of the Phillips Curve is the increasing availability of unemployment and welfare benefits. These reduce the financial pressure on the unemployed to obtain work. In this sense there is a greater willingness to accept unemployment. Taking longer to find alternative employment would cause an increase in the unemployment figures. The statistics may then show that any given level of aggregate demand and therefore rate of inflation, is associated with a greater level of unemployment than previously. This would shift the Phillips Curve rightwards and outwards, changing the inflation–unemployment relationship in the way observed in Figure 15.4. This is arguably not so much a cause for concern, as an indication that social policies designed to alleviate the financial hardships of unemployment are actually working.
- *Demographic changes.* It is likely that the demographic changes

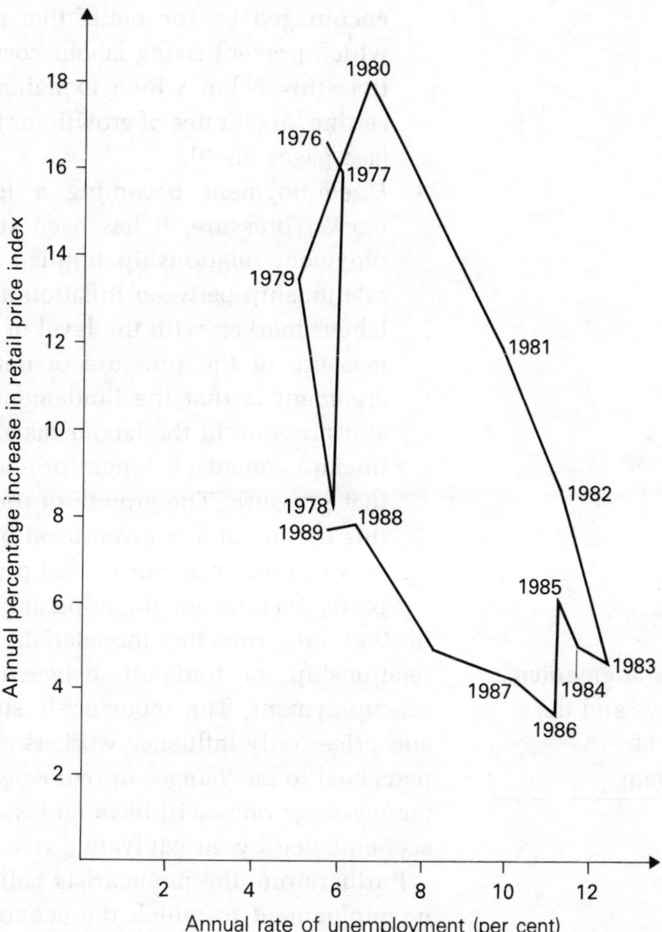


*Figure 15.4* The behaviour of unemployment and inflation in the UK 1976-

which have taken place during the post-war period have had a significant impact on the labour market, affecting the relationship between inflation and unemployment. For example, in the post-war period the female activity rate rose almost annually until about 1977, and although it has declined slightly since then, there are still currently some 10½ million women in the labour force. Labour turnover among women is considerably higher than among men. As a result, any given level of aggregate demand, and therefore rate of inflation, may again be associated with a greater level of unemployment than previously. This also would lead to a rightward and outward shift in the Phillips Curve.

- *Union militancy*. Another possible factor is that trade union militancy has increased, so that unions have felt less constrained in their wage demands by the threat of unemployment than previously; wage and price inflation would then be higher at any given level of unemployment. Union militancy may have been encouraged by the belief that governments will pursue policies which prevent rising labour costs from leading to unemployment. It is this belief which explains why some economists advocate setting target rates of growth for the money supply, as in the MTFS (see pages 28–9).

- *Unemployment becoming a less reliable indicator of labour market pressure.* It has been suggested that the inflation–unemployment relationship implied by the Phillips Curve is really a relationship between inflation and the pressure of demand in the labour market, with the level of unemployment providing a proxy measure of the pressure of demand in the labour market. The argument is that the fundamental relationship between inflation and pressure in the labour market still exists, but that the level of unemployment no longer provides an accurate proxy measure of that pressure. The growth of the black economy tends to support this notion; at any given level of offical unemployment there may now be greater labour market pressure than previously. This might partly account for the apparent breakdown of the Phillips Curve.

## The expectations-augmented Phillips Curve and the natural rate of unemployment

In the *long run* the monetarists believe that there is no stable relationship, or trade-off, between different rates of inflation and unemployment. The monetarists suggest that changes in wage rates and prices only influence workers and employers in so far as they are perceived to be changes in *real wages* or in *real prices*. Thus a rise in money wage rates will have no lasting impact on the economy if it is accompanied by an equivalent rise in prices, and vice versa.

Furthermore, the monetarists believe that there is a *natural rate of unemployment* to which the economy will tend in the long run. In fact, the natural rate of unemployment is defined as the rate that exists in the long run when the supply of, and the demand for, labour are in equilibrium. Any attempt by the authorities to reduce the level of unemployment below the natural rate will be unsuccessful in the long run, and will simply result in a higher rate of inflation. In detail, the argument is explained in terms of Figure 15.5. For simplicity it is assumed that unemployment is initially at the natural rate $U_n$, that actual and expected inflation is zero (i.e. the real wage is expected to remain constant) and that there is no change in productivity so that prices and wages change by the same proportion. $P^{e=0}$ is the short-run Phillips Curve that exists when the actual and expected rate of inflation are zero. $Pe =^{4\%}$ is the short-run Phillips Curve that exists when the actual and expected rate of inflation are 4 per cent and so on.

If the government attempts to reduce the level of unemployment to $U_1$ by an expansion of the money supply by 4 per cent, the initial result will be an increase in aggregate demand. Eventually this will pull prices up (by 4 per cent if the quantity theory, see pages 169–70,

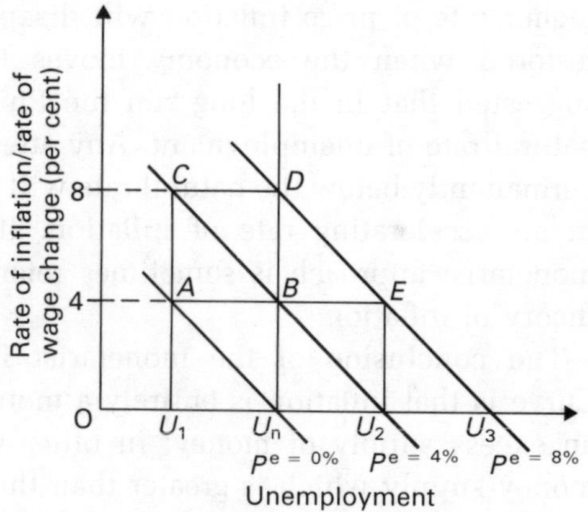


Figure 15.5 The expectations-augmented Phillips Curve

holds), and this implies a rise in the real profits of producers. They will therefore expand output, and in order to attract more workers they will raise the wage rate; to retain higher profits per unit of output, employers will raise wages by less than the increase in prices. Workers will not immediately perceive this fall in their real income, because the expected rate of inflation is zero; they will therefore interpret the higher money wage awards as an increase in real wages. The economy will therefore move to point A.

However, this does not represent a long run equilibrium situation, since it is based on *money illusion*. Once workers realise that, far from rising, their real wage has actually fallen, they will demand pay rises at least sufficient to restore their real wage. But, when wages and prices have both risen by 4 per cent, the real profits of producers will revert to their original level and they will no longer have any incentive to produce the higher level of output. They will therefore cut back production to their equilibrium level and unemployment will increase.

However, while the economy moves up the short run Phillips Curve $P^{e=0}$ it does not move back down it simply because unemployment rises. The expansion of the money supply ensures that the price level remains at the higher level. In terms of the equation of exchange (pages 169–70), since $V_y$ and $Y$ are constant, an increase in $M$ must lead to an increase in $P$. Thus equilibrium is restored when the economy moves to point B.

The expected and actual rate of inflation is now 4 per cent and the appropriate Phillips Curve is therefore $Pe = ^{4\%}$. Any further expansion of the money supply, for example, by another 4 percentage points, will initially take the economy to point C. However, the reduction in unemployment only occurs because the actual rate of inflation is different from the expected rate. Once workers realise that their expectations were incorrect, the advantage to producers from the higher rate of price inflation will disappear and equilibrium will be restored when the economy moves to D. Because of this, it is suggested that in the long run the Phillips Curve is vertical at the natural rate of unemployment. Any attempt to reduce unemployment permanently below the natural rate will simply result, in the long run, in an accelerating rate of inflation. It is for this reason that the monetarist approach is sometimes referred to as the 'accelerationist' theory of inflation.

The conclusion of the monetarist interpretation of the Phillips Curve is that inflation is entirely a monetary phenomenon caused by an excess supply of money; in other words, by an increase in the money supply which is greater than the average rise in productivity. Hence the belief that control of the money supply is all that is required to reduce inflation. For example, in terms of Figure 15.5, if the economy is at point D and the government wishes to restore average prices to the level that existed before there was any expansion of the money supply, it must reduce the money supply by 8 percentage points. If it did this all at once the economy would initially move to $U_3$, as the fall in prices that results from the lower money supply reduces real profits and leads firms to cut back output and to lay off workers. Once expectations of inflation are adjusted to the lower level (here 0 per cent) there would be lower wage settlements and real profits would be restored to their former levels. In response to this, output would rise and unemployment would fall as more workers were taken on. Equilibrium would be restored when unemployment was re-established at the natural rate, i.e. at point $U_n$.

It is of course possible to achieve the same reduction in inflation, that is from 8 per cent to zero, without such heavy unemployment. All that is required is for the government to reduce the money supply in stages until the total reduction is 8 percentage points. For example, if the government reduces the money supply by 4 percentage points the economy will move from D through point E to point B. If the money supply is then reduced by a further 4 percentage points the economy will eventually establish equilibrium at $U_n$. Again, the total reduction in the rate of inflation is 8 percentage points, but in this case it is achieved with a temporary increase in unemployment of only $U_2 - U_n$ compared with an increase of $U_3 - U_n$ when the money supply is reduced in one action by 8 percentage points.

Despite this, accepting the natural rate hypothesis does not imply that governments are powerless to influence the level of unemployment in the long run, that is, reduce the natural rate. It simply implies that unemployment cannot be permanently reduced by expanding aggregate demand. In order to reduce unemployment below the current natural rate, governments must act on those factors which determine the natural rate of unemployment, i.e. factors affecting the long-term supply of, and demand for, labour at any given real wage rate. These factors include the mobility of labour, the techniques of production, the extent of welfare benefits restrictions on competition and so on. These are usually referred to as supply-side factors and they are discussed on pages 229–236.

### The rational expectations hypothesis

The monetarist analysis presented above is based on the assumption that changes in the actual rate of inflation precede changes in the expected rate. It is, however, possible that, if governments publicly announce that the rate of growth of the money supply is to be reduced to a certain level, this will then influence expectations of inflation. In other words, to the extent that the government's target rates of growth for the money supply are publicised and are believed, then rational expectations about the future rate of inflation may be formed. If this leads to lower pay awards, inflation can be reduced without significantly affecting unemployment. Indeed, if the economy is initially at point D (the natural rate of unemployment with 8 per cent inflation) in Figure 13.5, a reduction in the money supply of 8 percentage points will, provided rational expectations lead to pay awards falling by exactly the same proportion, lead to a movement straight down the vertical Phillips Curve to point $U_n$.

## Monetarism

### Monetarism defined

At its simplest level, monetarism is a set of beliefs about the way in which changes in the money supply affect other macroeconomic variables such as the rate of inflation and nominal national income. These beliefs are based on an impressive volume of statistical information which shows a highly significant correlation between changes in the money supply and changes in the rate of inflation. However, the statistics only show an *association* between these two variables. They do not show that one is *caused* by the other. Nevertheless, the monetarists are unshakeable in their belief that changes in the money supply are the only cause of changes in the rate of inflation. While there are many varieties of monetarism, this belief is common to them all. The following discussion is an outline of the basic principles of monetarism which provide the theoretical underpinnings for this belief.

### The quantity theory of money

The basis of all monetarist thinking is the quantity theory of money. This is one of the oldest theories in economics but was refined by the American economist, Irving Fisher, earlier this century. Fisher's quantity theory of money is based on the equation of exchange and is usually expressed in the following way:

$$MV_y = PY$$

where $M$ = the total money stock
$V_y$ = income velocity of circulation or the number of times

each unit of currency is used to purchase final output in any given period of time

$P$ = average price of final output

$Y$ = the total volume of real output produced in a given period of time.

Since $P$ is the average price of final output and $Y$ is the total volume of final output, $PY$ is simply another way of expressing GNP.

It is clear that the equation of exchange is an identity or a truism. Both sides of the equation must, by definition, always be identically equal. $MV_Y$ is total spending on final output in the economy and $PY$ is total receipts from the sale of final output in the economy. By definition, total spending in one period must equal total receipts in the same period.

However, Fisher and other classical economists assumed that the economy had an in-built tendency to establish equilibrium at full employment. They therefore believed that the total volume of transactions was fixed in the short run by the amount that can be produced at full employment. Additionally, they assumed that the velocity of circulation was determined independently of changes in the money supply and changed so slowly over time that it could be treated as a constant. Accepting both these propositions leads to the conclusion that $M$ varies directly with $P$.

However, this still does not provide an adequate explanation of how the price level is determined. A further assumption frequently made by monetarist adherents to the quantity theory is that the authorities can control the money supply. Thus the basic prediction of the quantity theory becomes one in which changes in $M$ *cause* changes in $P$, and that there can be no change in $P$ *independently* of a prior change in $M$. Although, as we shall later see, the quantity theory has been reformulated, most notably by Friedman, Fisher's version remains the basis of all monetarist thinking.

## The demand for money

All monetarists accept the early quantity theory of money which focuses on the importance of changes in the money supply. However, the revival of monetarism as an economic doctrine stems largely from Friedman's re-statement of the quantity theory. This differs from the early quantity theory in that it focuses attention on the importance of the demand for money to hold.

In his re-statement Friedman suggested that the demand for money is determined by the same general factors which influence the demand for other goods and services. However, of all the factors Friedman considered, only the level of income, the price level and the expected rate of inflation, had any significant effect on the demand for money. Furthermore, Friedman claimed that the relationship between the demand for money and its determinants was highly stable over time. This is extremely important since such stability could not exist unless the velocity of circulation was also relatively stable. An increase in the demand for money to hold will reduce its velocity of circulation and vice versa. Therefore, if it can be shown that the demand for money is stable, velocity is also stable.

It is important to understand that, in arguing that velocity is stable, the monetarists are not arguing that it is constant. Instead they have always claimed that velocity changes only slowly over time and in a predictable way. In this sense it is stable from one period to the next. We shall later see that this has important implications for policy purposes.

For simplicity it is sometimes suggested that Friedman's view implies that the demand for money is a stable function of nominal national income. While not strictly correct this does not seriously misrepresent Friedman's view. In the long run the actual rate of inflation and the expected rate of inflation coincide and hence the main determinants of changes in the demand for money are changes in the actual rate of inflation (i.e. changes in the price level) and changes in real income (i.e. changes in nominal GNP). Monetarists therefore argue that, when there are changes in the supply of money, this will lead to changes in nominal GNP in order to bring the demand for money into equilibrium with the supply. Figure 15.6 is used as a basis for explanation and we can see that when $V_y$ is constant an increase in nominal income leads to a proportional increase in the demand for money. For example, when nominal income is OA, the quantity of money demanded is OB. If nominal income rises to OC, the demand for money balances rises proportionally to OD.

If the demand for money is constant at 25 per cent of GNP then $V_y$ must equal 4. If the initial level of GNP is £200m. then, assuming supply and demand for money are in equilibrium, the quantity of

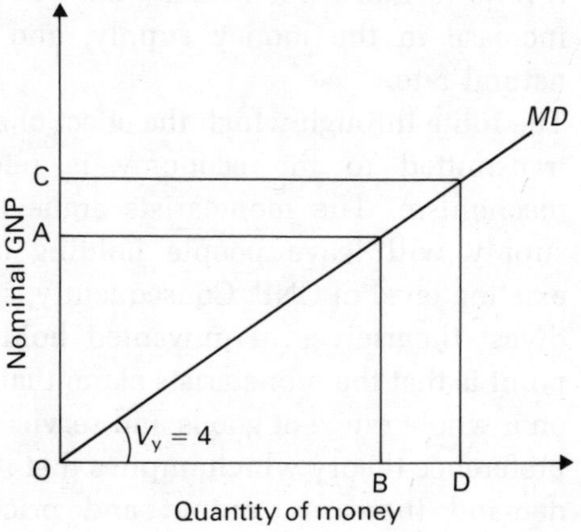


*Figure 15.6* The demand for nominal money

money demanded (and supplied) will be equal to £50m. If the money supply now increases, nominal GNP will increase and hence demand for money will also increase. For example, if the money supply increases by £10m., equilibrium can only be restored when the demand for money increases by £10m. If $V_y$ is unchanged, this implies an increase in nominal GNP of £40m. This must happen because, if the money supply increases and all other things are unchanged, people will be holding excess money balances relative to the amount they demand. The excess will be spent and will cause nominal GNP to increase until demand for money is brought into equilibrium with the increased supply of money.

However, this simple approach is ambiguous because an increase in nominal GNP can consist entirely of an increase in real income, prices unchanged, or entirely of an increase in prices, real income unchanged, or a combination of both. The monetarists claim that in the short run nominal GNP will consist of an increase in both. However, in the long run they argue that the level of real income is determined by institutional factors such as the capital stock, the mobility of labour, the rate of technological progress and so on. Such factors are not influenced by changes in the money supply. While it is possible that changes in the money supply will bring about changes in real income in the short run, such changes will only be transitory and in the long run real income will return to the level that would have existed before the increase in the money supply. Hence, an increase in the money supply above the rate of growth of real income will, in the long run, simply lead to higher prices.

This, of course, explains why, in the short run, unemployment falls below the natural rate as the money supply increases. As demand and prices rise, firms expand output and unemployment falls. Hence the economy moves up the appropriate short-run Phillips Curve. However, as expectations of inflation adjust to the higher rate, output reverts to that level which would have existed if there had been no increase in the money supply, and unemployment reverts to the natural rate.

## The transmission mechanism

The route through which the effect of a change in the money supply is transmitted to the economy is referred to as the *transmission mechanism*. The monetarists argue that an increase in the money supply will leave people holding excess money balances at the existing level of GNP. Consequently, spending will increase as people divest themselves of unwanted holdings of money. The important point is that the monetarists claim that this increased spending will be on a whole range of goods and services. (This contrasts with liquidity preference theory which implies that it will be spent on securities.) As demand increases, output and prices will rise until people are persuaded to hold the increased money supply in order to finance the increased value of their transactions. In other words, nominal GNP goes on rising until the increase in the supply of money is matched by an increase in the transactions demand for money, so that supply and demand for money are brought back into equilibrium.

## Crowding out

The term 'crowding out' refers to the extent to which an increase in public sector expenditure can only take place at the expense of private sector expenditure. The monetarists claim that in the long run crowding out occurs on a one-for-one basis. As we have seen, the monetarists argue that any increase in public expenditure that is financed by an increase in the money supply will have *no* effect on *real* GNP in the long run. However, because public expenditure is at a higher level and because aggregate expenditure (real GNP) is unchanged, then private sector expenditure must have been crowded out.

The monetarists also claim that crowding out occurs even when public sector expenditure is financed by *borrowing from the non-bank public* so that there is no change in the money supply. Their argument is that increasing borrowing by the public sector will force up interest rates because of increased competition for funds. The main impact of higher interest rates will fall on private sector investment, although there will also be some reduction in expenditure on consumer durables. Again, increased public sector expenditure crowds out private sector expenditure.

The view that an increase in public sector expenditure crowds out private sector expenditure by an equivalent amount, even when money supply is constant, can easily be explained in terms of the identity $MV_y = PY$. Since the monetarists argue that $V_y$ is constant, and since there has been no change in $M$, then $PY$, that is GNP, must also be constant. However, public sector expenditure has increased, so that private sector expenditure must have fallen by an equivalent amount within the constant GNP. In other words, an increase in public sector expenditure, even when financed by borrowing from the non-bank private sector, does not change the level of GNP, it simply changes its structure because public expenditure increases and private expenditure falls.

## The monetary rule

The monetarists therefore believe that increasing the money supply has no long-run effect on the level of *real* GNP, it simply leads to higher prices. They also believe that attempts to manage the economy by using demand management techniques increase uncertainty. This in turn makes it difficult for businesses to plan, and leads to less investment in research and development, in capacity and so on. Because of this the monetarists suggest that governments should abandon attempts to manage the level of aggregate demand, and should instead aim for a steady rate of growth of the money supply in order to achieve a particular rate of inflation. Again, their basic argument can be explained in terms of the identity $MV_y = PY$. If $Y$ grows at an average 5 per cent per annum and $V_y$ by 1 per cent per annum, then a government aiming to achieve an annual inflation rate of 2 per cent must achieve a growth of the money supply of approximately, but no more than, 10 per cent. (You can check this by substituting in $M = PY/Vy$.)

## Monetarism and Keynesianism compared

There is in fact a great deal of agreement between monetarists and Keynesians. They both accept the equation of exchange, and broadly agree on the determinants of the demand for money. However, they disagree on which factors are most significant in affecting the demand for money. This is clear in the following differences between the two schools.

### The transmission mechanism

The monetarists believe that an increase in the money supply leads to an increase in demand for all goods and services, with financial assets (securities, etc.), being just one in a range of items on which expenditure will increase. In other words, financial assets are not regarded as unique, in the sense of being close substitutes for money. An increase in the money supply will therefore lead to a direct increase in spending on goods and services, rather than just on financial assets. Nevertheless, any part of the extra money supply that is spent on securities will raise security prices, i.e. reduce interest rates. However, money demand is assumed by monetarists to vary with the level of national income and not with the rate of interest, so that little or none of the extra money supply is absorbed into idle balances as interest rates fall (i.e. demand for money is interest rate inelastic). Consequently all that the fall in interest rates will do is to encourage further consumer spending on goods and services, and of course investment expenditure.

In summary, the monetarists argue that an increase in the money supply leads to an increase in aggregate expenditure because:

1. increased holdings of money will mainly be spent on goods and services,
2. an increase in the money supply will lead to lower interest rates which encourages further consumer (and investment) spending.

In the long run, because of its effect on aggregate expenditure, an increase in the money supply has a relatively large effect on *nominal* GNP.

Keynesians, on the other hand, maintain that the demand for money is, in general, responsive to changes in the interest rate. They argue that financial assets are a close substitute for money and that an increase in the money supply will lead to increased expenditure on these. This will raise security prices, and the fall in interest rates that this implies will lead to a more than proportional increase in the demand for money as people are persuaded to hold larger idle balances. The rate of interest continues to fall until supply and demand for money are brought into equilibrium. However, because demand for money is interest rate elastic, an increase in the money supply leads to a less than proportional fall in the rate of interest.

Furthermore, the Keynesians argue that aggregate expenditure is interest rate inelastic. Any given change in interest rates therefore leads to a less than proportional change in expenditure. For example, an increase in the money supply is, via a fall in the rate of interest, mainly absorbed into idle balances and consequently has little impact on aggregate expenditure. This implies that an increase in the money supply has relatively little effect on *nominal* and *real* GNP, and explains Keynes' view that monetary policy might be ineffective in bringing about change in the economy. The opposite is true when the money supply is reduced. Because of this the Keynesians argue that monetary policy is not a very powerful tool of economic management.

In summary, the Keynesians believe that the effects of changes in the money supply are transmitted to the economy via changes in the rate of interest, but that overall there is little impact on GNP.

## The velocity of circulation

Implicit in the monetarist transmission mechanism is the belief that the velocity of circulation is unaffected by changes in the money supply. Hence a change in M leads to a proportional change in GNP. However, the Keynesians do not accept that the velocity of circulation is unaffected by changes in the money supply. For example, they argue that because an increase in the money supply has relatively little effect on GNP then, because of the identity $MV_y = \text{GNP}$, $V_y$ must fall when the money supply increases and vice versa.

For the Keynesians the extreme case occurs when the rate of interest is so low that the demand for money is infinitely elastic. This is the so-called liquidity trap (see page 134) and in these circumstances an increase in the money supply has no effect on the rate of interest at all and consequently no effect on the level of GNP. This can only occur when, for each change in the money supply, there is an exactly offsetting change in the velocity of circulation; i.e. when an increase in the money supply is completely absorbed into idle balances. It is worth noting that, because the monetarists deny that the velocity of circulation can change in response to changes in the money supply, they also deny the existence of any liquidity trap.

The available empirical evidence is inconclusive as Figure 15.7 shows.

In the short run, velocity fluctuates and appears quite unstable. In the longer run it appears to follow a clearly identifiable trend.

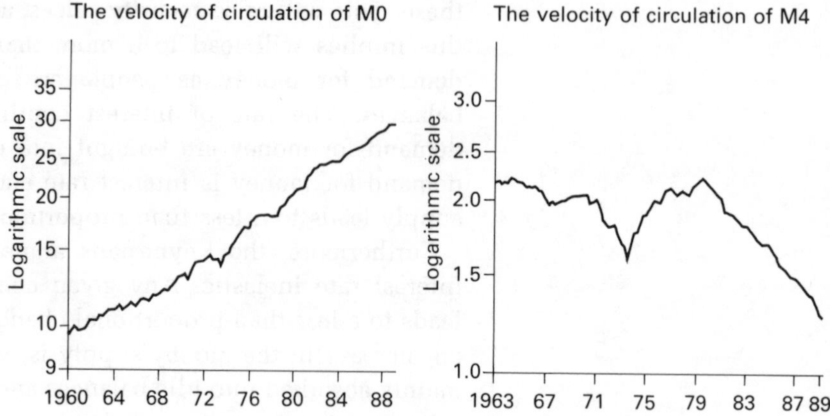

*Figure 15.7*

However, even here the evidence is ambiguous. The velocity of narrow money has followed an upward trend over the period covered, while, at least over the last decade the velocity of broad money has followed a downward trend!

### Crowding out

We have seen that the monetarists believe that crowding out takes place on a one-for-one basis. However, the Keynesians argue that this will only be true when the government increases its expenditure at a time when the economy is at full employment. At levels below this, an increase in government expenditure will draw more resources into employment, raising real GNP and real expenditure, so that private investment expenditure need not fall. One important reason why this happens, according to the Keynesians, is that the government borrows and spends funds that would otherwise have been saved. In other words, borrowing to finance government expenditure transfers funds from lower velocity users to higher velocity users. The resulting increase in aggregate demand then results in an increase in aggregate supply.

### The multiplier

The monetarists believe that the value of the multiplier is relatively low. For example, if crowding out takes place on a one-for-one basis, then increased government expenditure financed by borrowing from the non-bank private sector has a zero multiplier effect. The Keynesians, on the other hand, argue that the multiplier will have a relatively high value. The empirical evidence that is available tends to support the view that the multiplier has a relatively low value.

### Stability of the economy

The Keynesians believe that aggregate demand, and therefore employment, is subject to sharp fluctuations, so that the government has an important role to play in stabilising aggregate demand. In contrast to this the monetarists believe that the economy is inherently stable, at least in the long run, with aggregate demand and employment not being subject to sharp fluctuations. Because of this the monetarists claim that stabilisation policy is not only unnecessary, but may actually have a destabilising effect on the economy, causing greater short-run fluctuations in GNP than would otherwise have occurred. Where increased government expenditure leads to an increase in the money supply, it will result in higher prices which will further increase uncertainty.

## Changes in the money supply and changes in the price level

The monetarist argument is that a change in the price level can only be caused by a change in the money supply, and that a change in the money supply is all that is required to cause a change in the price level. The Keynesian position is that a change in the velocity of circulation can cause changes in the price level which are independent of changes in the money supply. Nevertheless, the Keynesians agree that changes in the money supply are correlated significantly with changes in the price level. However, they do not accept that this implies causation. They argue that the money supply is determined endogenously and simply responds passively to changes in the demand for money and therefore to changes in the price level.

Table 15.2 on page 163 shows the contribution made by changes in the costs of different inputs to the final price of manufacturing output. Labour costs consistently make the greatest contribution but this does not necessarily indicate that the cost-push hypothesis is correct. For example, an increase in the money supply could lead to an increase in demand for final output and encourage employers to increase wages.

## Test your understanding

1. If the price level rises why does the value of money fall?
2. The following index numbers of retail prices have a value in the base year of 100.
   What is the current value of the index of retail prices?

| Good | Weight | Index no. |
|---|---|---|
| A | 2 | 125 |
| B | 1 | 140 |
| C | 3 | 150 |
| D | 4 | 80 |

3. In practice why is it sometimes difficult to distinguish between demand-pull and cost-push inflation?
4. What is the difference between the equation of exchange and the quantity theory of money?
5. How will each of the following affect the demand for money? Assume all other things remain equal in each case.
   (a) A fall in national income.
   (b) A fall in the rate of interest.
   (c) A rise in the money supply.
6. What is natural about the natural rate of unemployment?

7. How will each of the following affect the natural rate of unemployment?
   (a) Increased mobility of labour.
   (b) A reduction in social security benefit.
   (c) An increase in the rate of inflation.
8. What is meant by the term 'crowding out' and why is it important?
9. Through what mechanisms do a) Keynesians and b) monetarists argue that an increase in the money supply will affect other economic variables such as nominal income?

# 16 International trade and protection

International trade arises for many reasons, but the most obvious one is that different countries have different factor endowments, and the international mobility of these factors is severely limited. International trade therefore makes available to consumers in one country, products which are only produced in other countries.

However, the fact is that the vast majority of goods and services which countries buy from abroad they could produce for themselves domestically. The main reason they are imported is that they can be produced with greater relative efficiency by foreign firms than by domestic firms. It is therefore important to understand the circumstances in which specialisation and trade can be mutually beneficial.

For simplicity our analysis of international trade is limited to the simple case when two countries produce the same two goods. However, the conclusions can be generalised and applied to a world consisting of many countries producing many commodities.

## Absolute advantage

A country is said to have an absolute advantage in the production of a commodity when it is more efficient than other countries at producing that commodity. In other words, when it can produce more of a commodity than other countries using the same amount of resources. When two countries each have an absolute advantage in different commodities, total world output can be increased when each country specialises in the production of those commodities in which it has an absolute advantage. This is easily demonstrated in terms of Table 16.1. For simplicity it is assumed that each country has $X$ resources and that initially each devotes half of its resources to the production of each good.

It is clear that total world output is greater when each country specialises in the production of that good where it has an absolute advantage. However, whether each country *gains* from specialisation and trade is not yet clear since no mention has been made of the rate at which goods can be exchanged for one another, that is, the *terms of trade*. In fact, for trade to be mutually beneficial the terms of trade

*Table 16.1*

| | Before specialisation | |
|---|---|---|
| | Number of cars | Tonnes of wheat |
| | that can be produced from *X* resources | that can be produced from *X* resources |
| Country A | 100 | 500 |
| Country B | 200 | 400 |
| Total output | 300 | 900 |
| | **After specialisation** | |
| | Number of cars produced | Tonnes of wheat produced |
| Country A | — | 1000 |
| Country B | 400 | — |
| Total output | 400 | 1000 |

must lie somewhere between the *domestic opportunity cost ratios*. In our example these are 1:5 in country A and 1:2 in country B. The importance of the domestic opportunity cost ratios is now clear. For example, if goods can be exchanged in the ratio 1:3 this implies that country A can obtain a car from country B for only 3 tonnes of wheat whereas each car produced domestically 'costs' 5 tonnes of wheat. For country B each car traded buys 3 tonnes of wheat, whereas each car given up domestically makes possible the production of only 2 tonnes of wheat.

## Comparative advantage

Even when a country has an absolute advantage in the production of *both* commodities, trade can still be mutually beneficial so long as each country has a *comparative advantage*. Table 16.2 is used as a basis for explanation.

Country A has an absolute advantage in the production of both wheat and cars since, with a given amount of resources, it can produce more of both goods than country B.

*Table 16.2*

| | Tonnes of wheat that can be produced from *X* resources | Number of cars that can be produced from *X* resources |
|---|---|---|
| Country A | 40 | 10 |
| Country B | 20 | 8 |

However, if we examine the domestic opportunity cost ratios, it is clear that each country has a *relative*, or *comparative*, advantage in the production of one commodity. In country A the domestic opportunity cost ratio is such that 4 tonnes of wheat must be given up for each car produced. However, in country B the domestic opportunity cost ratio is such that only 2½ tonnes of wheat must be given up for each car produced. A country has a comparative advantage in that product for which it has a lower domestic opportunity cost ratio than its competitor. Country B, therefore, has a comparative advantage in the production of cars since, for each car that is produced, less wheat is sacrificed in B than in A.

The same reasoning shows that country A has a comparative advantage in the production of wheat. For each tonne of wheat produced country A must sacrifice 0.25 cars, whereas in country B each tonne of wheat produced 'costs' more, i.e. 0.4 cars.

It is easy to show that, if both countries specialise in the production of the good in which they have a comparative advantage, the combined output of both goods will be greater than when each country produces both goods. However, specialisation and trade can only be mutually beneficial if the terms of trade, that is, the rate at which one good exchanges for another, lie somewhere between the respective domestic opportunity cost ratios. This is easily demonstrated. For example, if the terms of trade are that one car exchanges for 3 tonnes of wheat, this reduces the cost of cars in terms of wheat for country A, and reduces the cost of wheat in terms of cars for country B. Hence any given amount of one good foregone gives both countries more of the other goods after trade than is possible from domestic production.

## Assumptions

In discussing the possibility of trade in terms of absolute and comparative advantage several assumptions have been made. Some have been explicitly mentioned, but others have not. These are important because the absence of such conditions in the real world will considerably reduce the possible gains from trade. The main assumptions on which our discussion of absolute and comparative advantage is based are set out below.

### Perfect factor mobility

We have assumed that countries can shift resources from the production of one good to the production of another good. In practice there is likely to be a certain amount of factor immobility which will prevent this, especially in the short run.

### Constant costs

In assuming constant costs we are discounting the possibility of lower unit costs as output expands, for instance because of economies of scale or higher unit costs as output expands, because of diseconomies of scale. In practice, this is unlikely to be the case and it is much more realistic to suppose that a country may only have a comparative advantage in the production of a particular commodity up to a certain level of output. If production expands beyond this point, then rising costs will reduce or even remove altogether the country's comparative advantage.

**Technical change**

Changes in technology bring about changes in productive efficiency. Because of this, a country might have a comparative advantage in the production of a particular commodity at one point in time, but this might be lost to another more technologically advanced country at a different point in time.

**Barriers to trade**

Countries do not always trade freely with each other. The existence of restrictions on trade clearly limits the scope for specialisation between countries.

**Divergence between real values and money values**

It has been assumed that the money prices of goods accurately reflect their domestic opportunity costs. For example, where the domestic opportunity cost ratio was four tonnes of wheat for one car, we have implicitly assumed that the price the consumer pays for a car is four times the price paid for a tonne of wheat. In a world of perfect competition where price is equated with marginal cost, this will be the case; but in the real world, where prices are distorted by imperfect competition in factor and product markets, as well as by taxes and subsidies, it is unlikely to be the case. Since consumption and production decisions are based on money values rather than real values, if money prices are out of line with real costs, it may no longer be possible for countries to gain from trade by specialising in the production of those commodities in which they have a real (comparative cost) advantage.

**The terms of trade**

The terms of trade are the rate at which one nation's output exchanges against another nation's output. In the previous examples we assumed only two countries, each trading a single product. However, in the real world, where many countries trade many different commodities, it is not so easy to estimate the terms of trade. In practice, the prices of commodities traded are measured by an index of prices. The terms of trade index is the ratio of an index of export prices to an index of import prices. Thus the terms of trade index can be calculated as:

$$\frac{\text{Index of export prices}}{\text{Index of import prices}} \times 100$$

**Index of import prices**

In the base year the value of the terms of trade index will be 100, i.e. 100/100 × 100. Changes in the terms of trade are measured by changes in the value of this index.

**Favourable and unfavourable movements in the terms of trade**

A movement in the terms of trade is said to be *favourable* whenever export prices rise relative to import prices; in other words, whenever the terms of trade index rises. Care must be taken here because this does not necessarily imply that the terms of trade index has a value greater than 100! If the terms of trade index in one year is greater than its value the previous year, then there has been a favourable movement in the terms of trade. Conversely, a movement in the terms of trade is said to be *unfavourable* whenever the terms of trade index falls.

Favourable movements in the terms of trade are so called because they imply a 'favourable' change in the opportunity cost of imports in terms of exports. For example, if export prices rise while import prices remain constant, a given volume of exports will exchange for a greater volume of imports. In other words, a favourable movement in the terms of trade makes possible an increase in real income. Because of this, the price effects of an increase in the terms of trade are said to be favourable when export prices rise faster than import prices (or when export prices fall more slowly than import prices). Unfavourable movements in the terms of trade occur when the opposite is true.

Great care must be taken over interpreting a favourable or unfavourable movement in the terms of trade. It is the *price changes* which are favourable or unfavourable. The overall effect on revenue from exports or expenditure on imports of a favourable movement in the terms of trade might actually be disadvantageous, and vice versa. This is because changes in revenue and expenditure consist of price and volume changes. A favourable movement in prices might have an adverse effect on the volume of exports sold, or on the volume of imports bought. For example, where demand for exports is elastic, a rise in the price of exports will lead to a reduction in revenue from export sales because there will be a more than proportionate reduction in the volume of exports sold (see pages 198–9). In this case, the so-called favourable movement in the terms of trade might actually cause a balance of payments problem!

## Types of restriction on trade

Despite the potential gains from trade, countries sometimes adopt measures to restrict international trade. There are various types of restriction including the following:

### Tariffs

These are simply taxes placed on import commodities. Where a tariff is levied on a commodity its price is increased in the domestic economy. Tariffs may be *specific*, i.e. lump sum, in nature, or *ad valorem*, i.e. proportional to the value of the article. They can be applied individually to particular products or across the board.

### Quotas

These are a volume restriction on imports. Specific limits are placed on the quantity of particular products that can be imported. Again they can be applied selectively or across the board.

### Subsidies

By subsidising exported commodities their competitiveness can be increased in foreign markets. Subsidising domestic products lowers their price and hence reduces competition from imports.

### Exchange controls

By restricting the supply of foreign currency to particular purchases, governments are able to exercise a great deal of control over which commodities are imported, and in what quantities.

## The new protectionism

The new protectionism encompasses a variety of restrictions some of which are difficult to identify as a restriction on trade. Some common non-tariff barriers used as protective measures in recent years include:

- *Voluntary export restraints (VERs).* These are agreements between two countries such that one country agrees to limit exports of particular goods to another country for a specific period of time. One example of this is the Japanese agreement to limit the export of cars to the UK.
- *Government contracts.* It is possible that governments deliberately place contracts with domestic producers as a means of restricting imports.
- *Customs procedures.* In some countries customs procedures are deliberately excessive. The most often quoted example is that of France which insisted that imports of video equipment must pass through an office in Poitiers, many miles from the ports of entry. With a staff of only eight this undoubtedly resulted in a delay of several weeks in the import of video recorders.
- *Health and safety standards.* Strict standards can be imposed on imports such as restrictions on the ingredients of foods or the exhaust emission levels from cars to protect domestic industry.

## Motives for protection

There are several arguments for protection but at the present time most economists consider these arguments to be quite weak.

### To aid economic recovery

It has been argued that, if domestic industry is protected, demand will switch from imports to domestic goods and services and this will raise output and employment in the domestic economy. This, in particular, is the view of the Cambridge Economic Policy Group. However, protection imposes higher prices on consumers, might encourage inefficiency in protected firms, and could lead other countries to retaliate which would damage exports, thus offsetting any gains in terms of output and employment. Exports might also fall if protection in the UK leads to a reduction in incomes abroad (because imports into the UK fall) leaving foreigners with less ability to purchase British output.

### To remove a balance of payments deficit

Here again it is suggested that widespread protection can remove a balance-of-payments deficit. The argument is similar to that outlined above but the point is that protection does not remove the cause of the deficit which is lack of competitiveness. Often this might be lack of non-price competitiveness in areas such as quality, reliability, delivery, design, inefficient marketing and so on.

### To reduce structural unemployment

In this case protection is directed to a single industry. It has the same possible effects as that previously outlined with respect to protecting industries to aid economic recovery. However, in this case it is less likely to reduce incomes abroad because protection is only granted to a single industry, but more likely to encourage inefficiency in that industry.

**To protect an infant industry**

It is sometimes suggested that in the early stages of growth, infant industries require protection from foreign competition. However, it is almost impossible to identify potentially successful infant industries and bearing the risks of financing infant industries is the function of the entrepreneur. Entrepreneurs will finance infant industries when they believe they will be successful in the long run. If they are not prepared to do this the prospects of success must be thought poor.

**Strategic reasons**

Another possible motive for protection is that it is considered desirable to produce certain essential goods, such as food and energy, domestically rather than become dependent on another country for their supply. In these circumstances supply might be withheld to exert political pressure. Strategic factors are one reason for the CAP operated by the EC.

## Test your understanding

1. Distinguish between absolute advantage and comparative advantage.
2. Why do countries trade?
3. What factors might limit the scope for specialisation?
4. Using equal amounts of resources two countries, X and Y, have the following production possibilities:

| | Good A | Good B |
|---|---|---|
| Country X | 2 | 5 |
| Country Y | 4 | 10 |

   Can trade be mutually beneficial in these circumstances? Explain your answer.
5. Why are the terms of trade measured as an index?
6. What might cause a favourable movement in the terms of trade?
7. Distinguish between a tariff and a quota.
8. Who gains and who loses when a government imposes a tariff on imports of a particular good?

# 17 The balance of payments and exchange rates

## The balance of payments

A country's balance of payments is simply an annual record of its financial dealings with the rest of the world. In practice, all transactions which make up the balance of payments are either *autonomous transactions* or *accommodating transactions.* Autonomous transactions are those which take place for their own sake. They reflect voluntary decisions to buy, sell, lend or borrow. Accommodating transactions, on the other hand, are those which are necessary because the net value of all autonomous transactions yields either a deficit in the balance of payments (outflows > inflows) or a surplus (inflows > outflows).

In the UK all international transactions are recorded in the current account of the balance of payments and/or the capital account (now referred to as *Transactions in UK assets and liabilities*) of the balance of payments. The accounts are constructed on the principle of *double entry bookkeeping* thus ensuring that the accounts always balance in *accounting terms.* One entry shows the *original transaction*, the other shows the *way in which it was financed.* For example, the purchase of cars from Japan would be recorded as a visible import in the current account. It would also be recorded in the capital account perhaps as a loan from an overseas bank if this was how the deal was financed.

### The current account

This account records dealings in visible trade, that is exports and imports of goods, and invisible trade which consists mainly of trade in services. As Table 17.1 on page 188 shows the visible balance (−£14,936m.) when added to the invisible balance (£5,621m) gives the current balance (−£14,936m.).

### The capital account (changes in UK external assets and liabilities)

This section of the balance of payments account records capital movements between the UK and the rest of the world. Such capital movements are undertaken by governments, firms and private individuals, and may be short term or long term. Capital outflows are given a *negative* sign in the accounts, and capital inflows a *positive* sign.

- *Short-term capital flows.* These arise mainly because of the purchase and sale of short-term instruments by foreign nationals and because of movements of bank deposits as payment for transactions in the current account. For example, when people abroad deposit cash into current accounts in London or purchase Treasury bills, commercial bills of exchange or local authority bills, this is referred to as short-term investment in the UK. Short-term capital flows are therefore purely monetary flows, since they do not involve the creation of *physical* assets. Because of this they are highly liquid and are sometimes referred to as *hot money* since they can be moved from one country to another country very rapidly.
- *Long-term capital flows.* These consist of *direct investment*, which is the creation of real physical assets such as factory buildings, *portfolio investment*, which is purely financial transactions such as the purchase or sale of equity in joint stock companies and *other external assets (liabilities) of central government*, which includes such items as subscriptions to international organisations, for example contributions to the EC budget or overseas aid.

One important point to note is that *changes in the official reserves* arise because any deficit or surplus on the current account is not completely offset by other transactions in the capital account. A negative entry indicates that the authorities have used part of the reserves to bring the balance-of-payments into balance and vice versa. However, it is important to note that the change in the reserves is not *necessarily* identical to the balance-of-payments deficit or surplus, because the authorities sometimes borrow from abroad to finance a deficit.

### The balancing item

The balance-of-payments account records the effect on foreign currency earnings and expenditure of millions of transactions. In calculations of this magnitude there are bound to be errors and omissions; the balancing item records the collective value of these. Its value is known because the Bank of England's records show the net result of all foreign currency transactions. A positive value, as in Table 17.1, indicates that there has been unrecorded net exports and a negative figure that there has been unrecorded net imports.

### Balance in the balance of payments

Because the balance-of-payments always balances, this does not imply that it never gives cause for concern. When discussing deficits or surpluses in the balance-of-payments, attention focuses on the current account because it is this account which records *autonomous transactions*. *Accommodating transactions* in the capital account simply ensure that the deficit is financed or the surplus disposed of. Balance in the accounts is achieved by *accommodating transactions* and, in the case of deficit countries at least, there is a limit on the

*Table 17.1*

| | | | | |
|---|---|---|---|---|
| Current Account | | | | |
| *Visible trade* | | | | |
| Exports | 80157 | | | |
| Imports | −100714 | | | |
| Visible Balance | | | | −20557 |
| *Invisible trade* | | | | |
| Sea transport | 3544 | −4501 | −957 | |
| Civil aviation | 3192 | 4125 | −933 | |
| Travel | 6085 | 8127 | −2042 | |
| Financial and other services | 14156 | −4960 | 9196 | |
| General government | 518 | −2354 | −1836 | |
| Interest profits and dividends | 55564 | −49793 | 5572 | |
| Transfers | 2117 | 5383 | −3576 | |
| Invisible balance | | | 5621 | |
| *Current balance* | | | | −14936 |
| *Capital Account (Transactions in UK assets and liabilities)* | | | | |

*Table 17.1* continued

| | | | |
|---|---|---|---|
| *Transactions in assets* | | | |
| Direct investment overseas | −15110 | | |
| Portfolio investment overseas | −10308 | | |
| Loans to overseas residents by UK banks | −19261 | | |
| Other private lending and deposits overseas | −2328 | | |
| Changes in official reserves | −2761 | | |
| Other external assets of central government | −894 | | |
| | | −50662 | |
| *Transactions in liabilities* | | | |
| Direct investment in UK | 7804 | | |
| Portfolio investment in UK | 3597 | | |
| Loans to UK residents from overseas banks | 33856 | | |
| Other private lending and deposits from overseas | 5561 | | |
| Other external liabilities of central government | 902 | | |
| | | 51720 | |
| Net transactions | | | 1058 |
| Balancing item | | | 13878 |

*Source:* HMSO

ability of the authorities to sustain these. For instance, a deficit leads to an outflow of foreign currency reserves which are limited in value, or borrowings from abroad which are also limited by foreign perceptions of credit-worthiness, etc. Clearly, balance of payments deficits cannot be sustained indefinitely and sooner or later the authorities will be compelled to take action if deficits continue (see pp. 198–202).

## The rate of exchange

Exchange rates are the rates at which one country's currency can be exchanged for other currencies in the foreign exchange market. There are various kinds of exchange rate systems, but for simplicity economists identify two broad types: floating exchange rates and fixed exchange rates. The determination of exchange rates in each of these is considered in turn, but first we must clarify what is often a source of confusion over the use of terminology.

In markets where exchange rates *float*, an increase in the external value of a currency is referred to as *appreciation* and a decrease in the external value of a currency is referred to as *depreciation*. In markets where exchange rates are fixed, when the authorities raise the external value of the currency to a higher fixed parity we refer to *revaluation*. A change to a lower fixed parity is referred to as *devaluation*.

## Floating exchange rates

Where exchange rates are allowed to float freely, the value of one currency in terms of others is determined by the operation of market forces. In other words, the exchange rate for a currency is determined by the interaction of demand for, and supply of, that currency in the market for foreign exchange.

### Demand

Demand for foreign currency arises out of the desire to purchase another country's exports or to invest abroad. For example, the demand for sterling in the foreign exchange market arises partly from the desire of foreigners to purchase UK goods and services, or to invest in the UK. Like all normal demand curves the demand for sterling varies inversely with its price. The reason for this is simple. Consider the external value of sterling in relation to American dollars; at a rate of exchange of £1 = $2, it is clear that a £100 export from the UK costs an American importer $200. If the rate of exchange *falls* to £1 = $1.80, the *same* £100 export now costs an American importer only $180. At the lower price more British exports will be demanded. Consequently, as the rate of exchange falls, there will be a rise in the quantity of sterling demanded on the foreign exchange market to pay for these exports.

### Supply

Similarly, the supply of sterling on the foreign exchange market arises from the demand by UK importers for goods and services produced abroad, or from the desire to invest abroad. For example, in order to buy American exports, UK importers will require dollars. These can be obtained through the foreign exchange market where sterling is exchanged for dollars. Hence, the supply of sterling on the foreign exchange market is derived from the demand for imports into the UK, and from the need to purchase foreign currencies to finance UK investment overseas.

The supply curve for sterling (or any other currency) on the foreign exchange market will also be normal-shaped, with the supply of sterling varying directly with its international price. For example, if the current rate of exchange is £1 = $1.50, a $300 American export will cost an importer in the UK £200. However, if the rate of exchange *increased* to £1 = $1.60, the same good costing $300 in America would now have a price in the UK of £187.5. In other words, as the rate of exchange rises, the price of imports falls. At the lower domestic price we can assume that more imports will be demanded. It follows that as the rate of exchange increases there will be a rise in the quantity of sterling supplied to the foreign exchange market.

In a free market, exchange rates will be determined by the interaction of demand for, and supply of, the currency. The rate established will be the equilibrium rate and there can be no deviation from this unless the *conditions* of demand or supply change. Figure 17.1 illustrates how the exchange rate for sterling against dollars is determined.

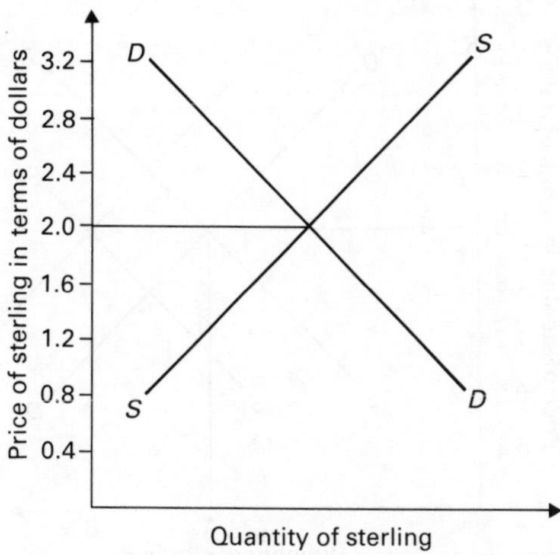


*Figure 17.1* The equilibrium rate of exchange

Figure 17.1 shows that with demand and supply conditions given by *DD* and *SS* the equilibrium exchange rate is £1 = $2. At any rate of exchange below this there will be a shortage of sterling and its exchange value will rise. At any rate above this there will be a surplus of sterling and its exchange value will fall.

The factors which cause changes in floating rates are many and varied. Changes in a country's current balance are clearly important, since sales of exports and purchases of imports are major factors affecting the demand for, and supply of, different currencies on the foreign exchange market. Changes in interest rates are also important, as these are likely to cause changes in short-term capital flows and therefore in the demand/supply schedules. Rumours of expected changes in exchange rates are also likely to influence short-term capital flows. For instance, capital gains can be made by moving funds into a currency before it appreciates against other currencies, and then back into the original currency after appreciation. Capital losses can be avoided by moving funds out of a currency *before* it depreciates, and then back into it after depreciation.

## Fixed exchange rates

It is possible for governments to fix the external value of their currency in relation to other currencies. A fixed exchange rate is maintained by intervention through central banks in the foreign exchange market. Such intervention is designed to offset changes in the conditions of supply or demand in the foreign exchange market which would otherwise cause fluctuations in exchange rates. The way in which exchange rate stability is maintained by intervention is explained using Figure 17.2.

Assume that the rate of exchange between sterling and the dollar is fixed at £1 = $2 and that supply and demand conditions for sterling are initially represented by *SS* and *DD* respectively. If the UK demand

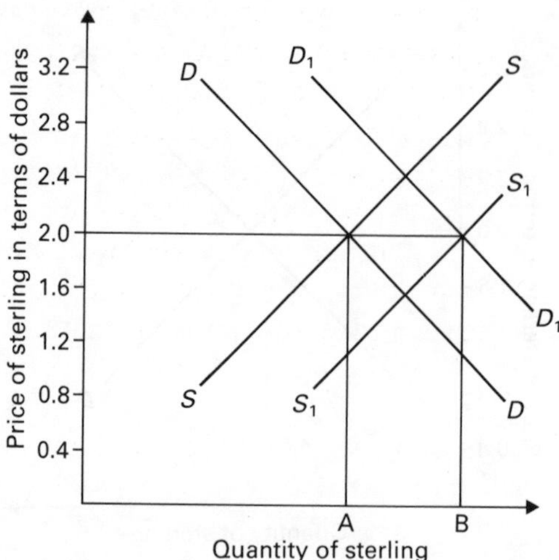


Figure 17.2 Maintaining a fixed exchange rate

for imports now increases, there will be an *increase in the supply of sterling* on the foreign exchange market shown by the shift in the supply to $S_1S_1$. This will cause downward pressure on the sterling exchange rate and in a free market its value would fall to £1 = $1.60. However, because the authorities are committed to maintaining the exchange rate for sterling at £1 = $2, they will be forced to buy the excess supply of sterling (AB) that exists at this exchange rate, using dollars from the foreign exchange reserves. The increased demand for sterling is shown by an outward movement of the demand curve to $D_1D_1$ which exactly offsets the increase in supply and prevents any movement in exchange rates.

Whatever the cause of pressure on fixed exchange rates, the authorities must take action which exactly offsets changes in the conditions of supply or demand in the foreign exchange market if fixed parity values between different currencies are to be maintained. (You should check your understanding of this by considering what action the authorities would take to neutralise the effect of an increase in demand for sterling on the foreign exchange market.)

## Fixed and floating exchange rates compared

### Advantages of floating exchange rates

1. *Automatic adjustment to balance of payments disequilibrium.* The main advantage of floating exchange rates is undoubtedly that it provides an *automatic* mechanism for the maintenance of balance-of-payments equilibrium. Thus, if demand for imports by the UK is rising relative to the rest of the world's demand for UK exports, there will be an excess supply of sterling on the foreign exchange market. This will cause the sterling exchange rate to *depreciate*, reducing the price of exports in foreign markets and raising the price of imports in the domestic market. As exports become cheaper foreigners will buy more of them, and as imports

become more expensive fewer will be bought by domestic residents. It is therefore argued that currency depreciation will prevent the emergence of deficits on the balance-of-payments, and that currency appreciation will eliminate any emerging surplus. In practice, movements in exchange rates do not always eliminate deficits and surpluses as simply as implied here, and this aspect of exchange rates is examined more fully on pages 198–202.

2. *Greater freedom to pursue domestic goals.* Because floating exchange rates make the balance of payments self-correcting, it is sometimes argued that governments are free to pursue whatever policies they wish in the domestic economy. Specifically, governments are more free to pursue policies designed to achieve full employment and economic growth. Under fixed exchange rates, a 'dash for growth' may result in an increase in imports – a balance-of-payments crisis – and therefore a deflation of domestic demand to curb imports. This is the familiar 'stop-go' cycle. The argument for floating exchange rates is that the exchange rate will *automatically* fall to eliminate any emerging deficit and to reduce the need for any deflation of domestic demand. Again, this is something of an over-simplification, but there is general agreement that floating exchange rates give governments greater freedom of action in the domestic economy.
3. *Economies in the use of foreign exchange reserves.* Suppose there is pressure on the pound under a fixed exchange rate system, as was the case in Figure 17.2. In this case, the Bank of England would have to intervene to buy sterling with its gold and foreign exchange rate reserves in order to maintain the par value at £1 = $2. Under a floating system the Bank of England can simply let the pound depreciate to £1 = $1.60, and will not have to purchase the excess supply of sterling A-B. As a result the Bank of England need not maintain gold and foreign exchange reserves to as high a level under a floating system as under a fixed system.
4. *Less speculative activity.* The suggestion here is that a speculative movement of funds out of a currency could actually result in a loss under a floating system; unlike the fixed exchange rate system where no losses are incurred. With a fixed exchange rate system the pressure builds up in one direction; for example, a country with a balance-of-payments deficit can hardly revalue its currency All it can do is retain its present par value or devalue. In the *first case* the speculator does not lose should he have moved his money out of the currency; in the *second case*, he makes a speculative gain. Suppose a speculator has £100m. and that the initial rate of exchange is £1 = $2. If the UK has a balance-of-payments deficit he may move out of sterling as he fears *devaluation*. He now has

$200m. *If* the UK *does devalue* to, say, £1 = $1, then he can return to sterling *after* the devaluation and receive £200m., i.e. a capital *gain* of £100m. If he is wrong and sterling resists devaluation, he can return to sterling and receive £100m., i.e. no loss, except for transactions costs (brokerage fees, etc.)

The situation is different under a floating rate system because the possibility of a capital gain exists. It is argued that this encourages speculative activity and might destabilise exchange rates. If speculative pressure builds up in one direction it might bring about the changes speculators expect (self-fulfilling expectations). With a floating rate system the pound can therefore depreciate, or appreciate because of speculative activity.

These arguments constitute a powerful case for floating exchange rates. However, there are disadvantages and these are discussed below.

## Disadvantages

1. *Increased uncertainty*. It is sometimes suggested that floating rates increase *uncertainty* in international trade. The possibility of changes in the external value of different currencies might deter long-term international investment or might make firms reluctant to negotiate long-run trade contracts with different countries. There is much greater certainty when foreign exchange rates are fixed.
2. *Increased speculative activity*. We have seen that an argument in favour of a floating system is that it allegedly deters speculative activity as there are now possibilities of *losses*. But there are also greater opportunities for *gains*, given the greater number of changes taking place in exchange rates. This might encourage speculative activity under floating exchange rates.
3. *Increased volatility of exchange rates*. Frequent short-run changes in exchange rates can have serious repercussions in the domestic economy. Where exchange rates float, flows of capital into a currency, attracted by higher short-term interest rates, can cause some currencies to appreciate; while flows of capital out of a currency can cause it to depreciate. When a country's currency appreciates, its exports become less competitive in world markets, and industries which produce import substitutes find it more difficult to compete in the domestic economy because imports become relatively cheaper. Conversely, when a country's currency depreciates, export and import-competing industries boom. Where appreciation or depreciation is caused by a fundamental change in the pattern of world consumption or changes in a country's comparative advantage, these changes in exchange rates might be necessary and desirable. However, where exchange rates float,

fluctuations can be caused by speculative flows in response to changes in short-term interest rates. Because of factor immobility such currency changes can lead to a serious misallocation of resources and cause unemployment. Where rates of exchange are fixed, intervention by the authorities in the foreign exchange market will avoid short-run fluctuations. Fundamental changes in supply or demand conditions for particular currencies can be accommodated by a change from one fixed parity to a lower or higher fixed parity as appropriate.

### Dirty floating or managed flexibility

Although fixed exchange rates were maintained between most of the world's major currencies for over 25 years after the Second World War, for most of the period since 1972 rates of exchange have been allowed to float. However, this does not necessarily imply that floating rates of exchange are superior to fixed rates, since there has been no commitment to allow exchange rates to float freely. The system that now exists with respect to the dollar is effectively a compromise between fixed and floating rates. The authorities often intervene to neutralise short-run pressure on exchange rates, but market forces now play a more important role in the determination of exchange rates. This exchange rate system is usually referred to as *managed flexibility*, although, because the authorities do not always make it clear that they are using the reserves to support a currency's external value, the system is sometimes referred to as *dirty floating*.

### The European Monetary System (EMS)

There are two main strands to the EMS: the ERM and the ECU. The ERM is the exchange rate mechanism whereby participating countries agree to maintain exchange rates *vis-à-vis* other participating countries within 2¼ per cent (6 per cent in the case of Italy and the UK at present) of the agreed rate. The ECU is the European Currency Unit. The value of the ECU is determined by a weighted average basket of EC member currencies. As well as there being an agreed rate between all participating currencies in relation to each other, each currency has an agreed value against the ECU with the same 2¼ per cent margin of fluctuation. The purpose of this is to generate a *divergence indicator* equal to 75 per cent of the agreed value of any currency against the ECU. There is a presumption that the authorities of any country whose currency deviates by *more than 75 per cent* of its *agreed value against the ECU*, and therefore approaches the 2¼ per cent limit, will intervene to halt the divergence.

### Why the UK joined the ERM

There are many reasons why the UK joined the ERM in October 1990. Here we summarise the main points.

- *Exchange rate stability*. One major advantage of ERM membership is that it would provide a means of achieving a more stable exchange rate. This would remove an element of uncertainty from international trade and would prevent sterling rising or falling rapidly in response to changes in the price of oil for example. A rapid appreciation of sterling can handicap exporters and a rapid fall might be inflationary.

- *Lower interest rates.* Another possibility is that membership of the ERM will permit lower interest rates. It is argued that relative interest rates in the UK have been higher than they otherwise might have been because of the need to compensate holders of sterling for accepting the risk of depreciation due to the weak current account. Full membership of the EMS removes the risk of depreciation and therefore removes the need to offer an interest rate premium.
- *Lower inflation.* It is argued that inflation in Britain will fall and converge with the lower rate of inflation in other ERM countries because a fixed rate of exchange can only be maintained if countries have similar rates of inflation. If these differ markedly, a country with a higher rate of inflation will experience a balance-of-payments deficit and an outflow of reserves. This cannot continue indefinitely and ultimately inflation will have to be reduced. Given the commitment of EMS members to achieving low rates of inflation as a full member Britain will be compelled to adopt policies which would also achieve a low rate of inflation.

## Effective exchange rates

Throughout this chapter we have ignored any ambiguity over our definition of exchange rate changes. Indeed, there is no ambiguity when exchange rates are fixed, because when one country changes the external value of its currency it does so by an equivalent amount against the currencies of all its trading partners. For example, when sterling was devalued by 14.3 per cent in November 1967, this was the rate of devaluation against *all* currencies. However, when exchange rates float it is possible for a currency to be appreciating against some currencies and depreciating against others. Alternatively, it might depreciate against some currencies by a greater amount than against other currencies and so on. A more sophisticated measure of the exchange rate is then necessary in order to assess whether a particular currency is appreciating or depreciating.

One way would be to take a straightforward average of the way one currency has moved against all other currencies. However, this would be unsatisfactory because some exchange rate changes are more important for a country than others. A second possibility would be to construct a 'trade weighted index'. Such an index for the UK, for example, would show the value of sterling measured against an average of all other currencies weighted according to their importance as a trading partner. Here again this is not entirely satisfactory because it takes no account of the fact that the UK does not only trade bilaterally with its partners, but also competes against them in world markets. It is necessary to take this fact into account when measuring the importance of exchange rate movements for a country's balance-of-payments.

There is no universally accepted measure of the *effective exchange rate* for a currency, but the method used at the moment takes both factors mentioned above into consideration. Thus, in the case of the effective exchange rate for sterling, the weight attached to the US dollar and to the Japanese yen are both greater than the share of UK exports to, or imports from, these countries. This is because both of these countries are important competitors for the UK in many world markets.

In summary, we can say that, at present, effective exchange rates are designed to answer the following question: 'What uniform percentage change in the sterling exchange rate against every other currency would have had the same effect on the UK's trade balances as the set of changes that have actually taken place?'

## The real exchange rate

The real exchange rate is an index which takes account of differences in international rates of inflation on the competitiveness of exports and imports. For example, if sterling appreciates against the US dollar by 5 per cent, this does not necessarily imply that UK goods will be 5 per cent more expensive relative to USA goods. This will only be the case if the rate of inflation in the UK and the USA are equal. In this case a 5 per cent appreciation in the *nominal sterling exchange rate* also implies a 5 per cent appreciation in the *real sterling exchange rate*. However, if there are different rates of inflation in the UK and the USA, changes in the nominal exchange rate will be different from changes in the real exchange rate. The real exchange rate is usually expressed as:

$$e^r = eP^*/P$$

Where $e^r$ is the real exchange rate, $e$ is the effective exchange rate, $P^*$ is an index of foreign prices and $P$ is an index of the domestic price level. We can now see what happens to the real exchange rate if there is inflation in the UK of 10 per cent, inflation in other countries of 4 per cent and a 2 per cent depreciation of sterling. If we assume the effective exchange rate depreciates from 100 to 90, the result of these changes is ($90 \times 110/104 = 95.19$) a depreciation in the real effective exchange rate of about 4.81 per cent.

When the value of the real exchange rate falls (either because of a relatively lower domestic rate of inflation, a relatively higher rate of inflation abroad or because of a rise in the effective exchange rate), British goods become more competitive and vice versa.

## Exchange rate changes and balance of payments adjustment

Whether changes in the exchange rate succeed in removing a balance-of-payments deficit or surplus depends on many factors. We concentrate here on those factors which determine whether a downward movement in the exchange rate, that is devaluation or depreciation, will succeed in removing a balance-of-payments deficit. For simplicity, the use of the term depreciation in this section will refer to either. Whether revaluation or appreciation will succeed in removing a balance-of-payments surplus depends on the opposite set of factors.

Depreciation exerts its most powerful impact on the current account of the balance-of-payments. Before we formally consider the circumstances in which it will remove a balance-of-payments deficit, therefore, it is important to be clear about the way in which depreciation affects the prices of exports and imports. When a currency depreciates it reduces the *foreign price of exports*. For example, if sterling depreciates against the dollar from £1 = $1.20 to £1 = $1.10, then the price of a car exported to America which costs £10,000 in the UK falls from $12.000 before depreciation to $11,000 after depreciation. The sterling price of the car is unchanged: depreciation *reduces the foreign* price.

The situation is exactly the opposite for imports. Depreciation raises the *domestic price of imports*. Again, if sterling depreciates from £1 = $1.20 to £1 = $1.10, the price of a good imported by the UK which costs $2,400 in America rises from £2,000 to £2,181.8. The dollar price of the good is unchanged: depreciation *raises the domestic* price.

There are two broad approaches to balance-of-payments adjustment: the *elasticities approach* and the *absorption approach*. Each is considered in turn.

## The elasticities approach

This approach stresses the effect of *relative* price changes on the balance-of-payments. It implies that whether depreciation will remove a balance-of-payments deficit or not depends primarily on the price elasticities of demand for exports and for imports, since it is this above all else that determines the *net change* in the flow of funds to the current account following depreciation. If demand for *exports* is elastic (i.e. greater than one), depreciation will lead to a rise in *foreign currency earnings* because the proportionate increase in quantity sold will be greater than the proportionate reduction in price. However, the *foreign price of imports* is unchanged so that any reduction in the quantity bought will lead to a reduction in *foreign currency expenditure*. In other words, if elasticity of demand for imports is greater than zero, foreign currency expenditure on imports will fall following depreciation.

The importance of these elasticities of demand are generalised in the *Marshall-Lerner* condition. This implies that depreciation will lead to an improvement in the balance of payments if the sum of the price elasticities of demand for exports and imports exceeds unity.

The following example clarifies this. For simplicity the balance of payments is presented in foreign currency values.

Assume sterling depreciates against the dollar by 10 per cent from £1 = $1.20 to £1 = $1.08. Thus export prices (which are denominated in foreign currency) fall in the ratio 0.12/1.20, that is, a fall of 10 per cent. Import prices (which are denominated in sterling), on the other hand, rise in the ratio 0.12/1.08, that is, a rise of 11.1 per cent*. If the elasticity of demand for exports is 1.6 and the elasticity of demand for imports is 1.5, the effect on the balance of payments of this depreciation is easily demonstrated.

*Initial balance of payments position*

| Exports ($M) | Imports ($M) |
|---|---|
| 2,000 | 2,100 |

Sterling depreciates by 10 per cent

| | |
|---|---|
| Elasticity of demand = | Elasticity of demand = |
| $1.6 = \dfrac{\%\ \Delta Qx}{\%\ \Delta Px}$ | $1.5 = \dfrac{\%\ \Delta Qm}{\%\ \Delta Pm}$ |
| therefore $\%\ \Delta Qx = 16\%$ | therefore $\%\ \Delta Qm = 16.5\%$ |

*After depreciation*

| Exports ($M) | Imports** ($M) |
|---|---|
| 2145.6 | 1750.35 |

However, over time, demand for exports and imports is much more elastic. Patterns of consumption and investment flows change in response to the price changes brought about by depreciation. Because of this, depreciation only leads to an improvement in the balance of payments in the long run. The initial deterioration and subsequent improvement in the balance of payments is usually referred to as the 'J curve' effect. The adverse initial impact on the balance of payments is often thought to average around eighteen months or so. The general effect is illustrated in Figure 17.3 on page 200.

* This is easily verified. A good costing $1.20 in America costs a UK importer £1 before depreciation and £1.11 after depreciation, an increase of 11.1 per cent.

** The relationship between total revenue (expenditure) and elasticity of demand was discussed in Chapter 5. Care must be taken when measuring the change in import expenditure, however, because the foreign price of imports is unchanged. This implies that a 16.65 per cent reduction in quantity demanded will lead to a 16.65 per cent reduction in foreign currency expenditure on imports. It is a good idea to work out several examples of your own to satisfy yourself of the importance of the Marshall–Lerner condition.

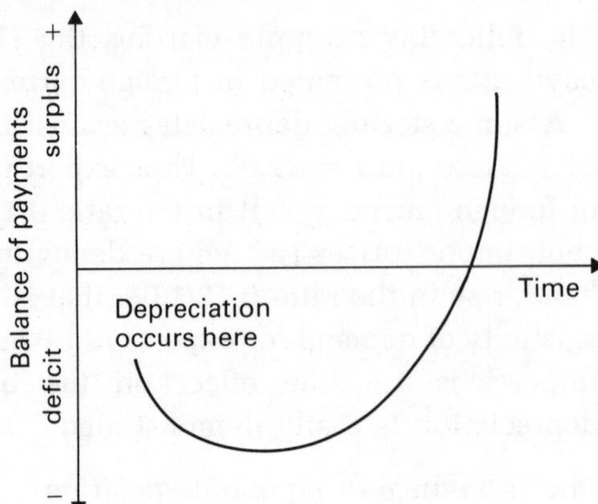


*Figure 17.3* The effect of depreciation on the balance of payments

It seems that, so long as the elasticity conditions are favourable, depreciation will lead to an improvement in the balance-of-payments position. However, elasticity conditions are unlikely to be favourable in the short run. It takes time for people to adjust their patterns of consumption and change their investment plans. The result is that depreciation *initially* leads to an increased balance-of-payments deficit. Foreign currency spending on imports is largely unchanged, because much the same quantity of imports are consumed at an unchanged foreign price. On the other hand, foreign currency earnings fall because much the same volume of exports are sold at a lower foreign price. Hence, the balance of payments *initially* deteriorates after depreciation.

However, over time, demand for exports and imports is much more elastic. Patterns of consumption and investment flows change in response to the price changes brought about by depreciation. Because of this, depreciation only leads to an improvement in the balance of payments in the long run. The *initial* deterioration and subsequent improvement in the balance of payments is usually referred to as the 'J curve' effect. The adverse initial impact on the balance of payments is often thought to average around eighteen months or so. The general effect is illustrated in Figure 17.3

## The absorption approach

This analysis of balance of payments adjustment is based on the income accounting identity:

$Y = C + I + G + X - M$, which can be rewritten as

$Y - (C + I + G) = X - M$

i.e. $Y - A = X - M$, where $A$ = domestic absorption

This implies that the balance of payments of a country is equal to domestic income minus domestic expenditure (or absorption). A deficit on the balance of payments will exist when the country absorbs more goods and services than it produces, that is when $(C + I + G) > Y$.

It follows from this that depreciation or devaluation can only succeed if it increases domestic output (income) relative to absorption, or reduces absorption relative to domestic output (income). The absorption approach therefore places much more emphasis on the level of domestic demand as the main determinant of the balance-of-payments position rather than on relative price levels.

The absorption approach shows that when there is full employment in the economy it is impossible to raise domestic output (income) and therefore it is necessary to deflate the domestic economy in order to reduce absorption and to release resources for export production. However, elasticities are still important. Simply depressing domestic demand does not guarantee that the resources released will be transferred into export production, though it is usually effective in reducing demand for imports.

## General problems of adjustment

Despite the general predictions of these two approaches to the balance of payments adjustment, there are other factors which have an important influence on the effect of depreciation. Essentially both approaches are *static*. In the real world there are other dynamic factors to consider. These include the following.

### Income effects

If depreciation succeeds in reducing the flow of imports, it will bring about a reduction in the national income of those countries whose exports, which are the counterpart of these imports, have fallen. As income in these countries falls, their own ability to import from the depreciating country will fall. This will have a particularly significant effect where demand for imports in these countries is *income elastic*. Additionally, it is possible that falling national income will tend to reduce the pressure on prices and make exports from these countries more competitive. This will be particularly important where demand for their exports is *price elastic*. Because of these income (and price) effects in the foreign country even if export revenues rise for the domestic country after depreciation, they might subsequently fall. Similarly, any reduction in domestic imports might be subsequently reversed. To the extent that income (and price) effects operate in this way, depreciation will not necessarily be successful in the long run.

### Domestic inflation

A potentially serious problem following depreciation is domestic inflation, especially where imports consist of raw materials. Rising import costs can quickly erode any price advantages conferred by depreciation, resulting in a continuing deficit on the balance of payments.

### Price adjustments

Just as inflation can wipe out the gains from depreciation, administered price changes can have the same effect. In the export market, instead of offering lower foreign prices following depreciation, there is some evidence that firms raise domestic prices and in so doing rctain foreign prices at the pre-depreciation level. For example, following depreciation of sterling from £1 = $1.20 to £1 = $1.08, a product costing £10,000 in the domestic market would cost a foreign importer $12,000 before depreciation and (all other things remaining equal) $10,800 after depreciation. However, if the domestic price was increased from £10,000 to £11,111, depreciation would have an imperceptible impact on the foreign price.

Exporters might have many reasons for wishing to maintain price stability. It avoids the threat of retaliation by foreign firms and the possibility of a damaging price war. Where a multi-national corporation has subsidiaries in many countries it might wish to avoid competition between these by administering price changes to offset those brought about by depreciation. Probably most important of all, however, is that by raising domestic prices (and keeping the foreign price constant) firms are able to increase profits. The same volume of goods and services are sold but at a higher price. For whatever reason, to the extent that prices are adjusted in the way described above, the effect will be to mitigate the gains from depreciation.

## Policies to deal with a balance of payments deficit

Broadly, there are three courses open to *deficit* countries: *depreciation* of the currency, *deflation* of the domestic economy, or some form of *direct restriction on imports*. In practice, countries are unlikely to adopt only one of these to the exclusion of the others and might even adopt a combination of all three.

- *Depreciation*. This involves lowering the exchange rate with the aim of increasing receipts from abroad and reducing expenditure on imports. The success of this policy in removing a deficit therefore depends on the elasticities of demand for exports and imports. However, it also depends on whether rising import prices lead to a higher domestic rate of inflation. If this happens, the relative advantage conferred by depreciation will quickly be eroded.
- *Deflation*. Deflating the level of aggregate demand works in two ways. First, as demand and output fall, the ability to buy imports falls. Secondly, and in the longer term, deflation reduces the domestic rate of inflation, and so increases the competitiveness of exports. The attraction of this policy is that, if it is severe enough, deflation will always remove a balance-of-payments deficit. The disadvantage is that it works by depressing domestic income, which lowers living standards and increases unemployment. Moreover, deflation does not offer a permanent means of removing a balance-of-payments deficit – unless the level of demand is permanently depressed. As soon as demand is expanded the deficit will reappear.
- *Restricting imports*. Restrictions on imports can take several

forms: tariffs, quotas, subsidies on domestic products, and so on – although none of these is an option available to the UK because of its membership of the EEC. Such measures will probably be successful in the short run but have considerable disadvantages. They might provoke retaliation, lead to higher prices and encourage inefficiency overall, resulting in a less efficient allocation of resources.

## Test your understanding

1. What is the difference between
   (i) the balance of trade and the terms of trade?
   (ii) the visible balance and the invisible balance?
2. What does the balancing item balance?
3. How do the authorities maintain the par value of a fixed exchange rate?
4. If the exchange rate is fixed does this imply that the price of X and M are fixed?
5. Why does the balance of payments always balance?
6. What is the difference between a clean float or a dirty float?
7. Why is the level of reserves a country holds when exchange rates are fixed related to the policies it is prepared to adopt to deal with a balance of payments deficit?
8. What is meant by the term 'hot money'?
9. How does a rise in domestic interest rates affect
   (i) the current account?
   (ii) the capital account?
10. If the sum of the elasticities of demand for exports and imports is less than one and the exchange rate depreciates, what happens to the current account?

# 18 Public finance

## Reasons for the growth of public expenditure

Public finance is about government expenditure and revenue. Current government expenditure is discussed on page 205. However, during the twentieth century the *growth* of public expenditure has been due to certain specific factors.

- *World wars.* The war-time expenditure of both world wars led to a permanent increase in the size of the national debt (see pages 210–211). In other words, the UK government financed part of its war-time expenditure by borrowing. It has been estimated that 28 per cent of the amount required to finance the First World War, and 50 per cent of the amount required to finance the Second World War was borrowed. Such borrowings have not been repaid and have substantially increased annual expenditure on debt interest payments.
- *Growth of the welfare state.* Expenditure on the welfare state, especially in post-war years, has been an extremely important factor in the overall growth of public spending. Since the 1940s the state has provided a comprehensive package of health care and education. There has also been a relatively large growth in transfer payments such as social security benefits. These have grown partly because of the desire to establish minimum levels of disposable income and partly because of the desire to stabilise levels of disposable income in the event of a wage earner becoming unemployed.
- *Economic management.* In post-war years governments have varied their level of expenditure in pursuit of certain economic aims. For example, increased spending has been used to combat unemployment. As government expenditure rises, aggregate demand rises and unemployment falls. This is the traditional Keynesian remedy for unemployment as described in Chapter 10, and its implications are discussed more fully in Chapter 19. It is sufficient to note here that governments have increased expenditure in order to boost aggregate demand.

- *Inflation.* Despite the factors mentioned above, the main reason for the growth of public expenditure in recent years has been the relatively high rates of inflation that persisted from the late 1960s until the early 1980s.

## Extent of government spending

Every year, usually in January, the government publishes its expenditure plan for the coming years. Table 18.1 shows how public expenditure on different economic activities has changed in recent years.

*Table 18.1*

| | 1979–80 £ million | 1984–85 £ million | 1989–90 £ million | 1991–92 £ million |
|---|---|---|---|---|
| Defence | 9,226 | 17,201 | 19,200 | 22,100 |
| Overseas aid | 802 | 1,091 | 1,355 | 1,540 |
| Other overseas services | 1,305 | 1,684 | 1,815 | 2,580 |
| Agriculture, fisheries, food and forestry | 1,038 | 2,412 | 2,412 | 2,810 |
| Trade, industry, energy and employment | 2,892 | 8,976 | 6,852 | 6,690 |
| Education and science | 9,350 | 16,981 | 22,483 | 25,270 |
| Arts and libraries | | 818 | 1,136 | 1,240 |
| Transport | 2,972 | 5,547 | 5,931 | 6,970 |
| Housing | 4,699 | 4,396 | 3,236 | 3,500 |
| Other environmental services | 2,873 | 4,950 | 5,690 | 6,080 |
| Law, order and protective services | 2,586 | 6,090 | 8,606 | 10,190 |
| Health and personal social services | 8,899 | 19,615 | 26,940 | 30,230 |
| Social security | 19,400 | 39,299 | 49,141 | 60,500 |
| Miscellaneous | 1,982 | 2,971 | 4,343 | 5,100 |

*Source: Economic Progress Report*, No 143, March 1982, Public Expenditure Plans 1989–90 to 1991–1992, HMSO

## The Budget

The Budget is an occasion when the Chancellor presents an account of government expenditure and revenue for the ending financial year and presents his estimates of revenue for the coming financial year to Parliament. The estimates of expenditure for the coming financial year are presented to Parliament earlier in the year, usually in January. Table 18.1 provides a summary of the proportion of revenue raised from the different sources and the proportion spent on different categories.

However, the Budget is not simply a financial statement. It is the main instrument of economic policy and considerable significance is attached to whether the government has a budget surplus or deficit and the size of the surplus or deficit. When the government achieves a budget surplus its estimated revenue exceeds its estimated expenditure and this surplus can be used to redeem part of the National Debt (see page 210). However, when the government has a budget deficit, its planned expenditure is greater than its estimated revenue and the difference must be made good by borrowing. Such borrowing becomes part of the Public Sector Borrowing Requirement (PSBR see page 207) and adds to the National Debt.

It used to be argued that the Chancellor should deliberately aim for a budget surplus or deficit as a means of varying injections and leakages into the circular flow of income so as to achieve certain economic objectives. In particular it was argued that, if aggregate demand was insufficient to generate the full employment level of national income, the government should aim at a budget deficit so as to increase injections thus raising income and employment. However, the effect of the Budget on injections and leakages is no longer considered as important as its effect on the money supply. In particular when the government has a budget deficit, the way in which this is financed can have a profound impact on the growth of the money supply. This issue is considered fully on pages 208–210.

### The regulator

Although rates of direct taxation can only be changed in the annual Budget with Parliamentary approval, the Chancellor has much more flexibility in varying the rates of certain indirect taxes. Specifically, export and import duties can be changed by up to 10 per cent of the *current* rate and VAT by up to 25 per cent of the current rate. The Chancellor can therefore change the *current rate* of VAT (17½%) to a lower limit of 11.25 per cent, or to an upper limit of 18.75 per cent without parliamentary approval.

### The central government borrowing requirement (CGBR)

The main component of the CGBR is the overall budget deficit. However, the CGBR is not exactly equal to the government's budget deficit because it includes certain items of expenditure such as the National Insurance Fund which are not part of the Budget. We shall see later that the size of the CGBR has an important bearing on the growth of the money supply because it is the largest component of the PSBR. This explains why the size of the budget deficit has acquired great significance in recent years.

### The public sector borrowing requirement/public sector debt repayment

The PSBR is the total amount the public sector needs to borrow from the private sector and from overseas for the year ahead. It therefore consists of borrowing by the central government, by the local authorities and by the public corporations. When the PSBR is negative part of the national debt is redeemed. A negative PSBR is therefore referred to as Public Sector Debt Repayment (PSDR). However, care must be taken here because part of central government borrowing is on-lent to other institutions *within* the public sector. To the extent that the CGBR is on-lent in this way it reduces the amount the rest of the public sector needs to borrow from the private sector and from overseas. In other words, it has already been included in total public sector borrowing. Only that part of borrowing by local authorities and public corporations that has *not* been on-lent by the central government adds to the PSBR. The structure and financing of the PSBR for 1989–90 are summarised in Table 18.2.

## The PSBR and the money supply

The most publicised aspect of the PSBR is its effect on the money supply, and in particular its relationship with M4. In practice, the effect of an increase in the PSBR on the money supply is uncertain since its impact on M4 may be offset in whole or in part by a change in any of the other components which make up M4. Nevertheless, the authorities remain convinced that there is a central link, and it is possible to identify some of the ways in which the PSBR might lead to an increase in M4.

The extent to which the PSBR leads to an increase in M4 depends on the way in which the PSBR is financed. In fact, there are several methods of financing the PSBR:

(a) by borrowing from the non-bank private sector,
(b) by borrowing from the banking system,
(c) by borrowing from overseas or in foreign currency,
(d) by issuing more cash (notes and coin) to the public.

*Table 18.2* The structure and financing of the PSBR

| Structure | (£ million) |
|---|---|
| Central government borrowing requirement* | −12848 |
| *less* Central government lending to local authorities | 4968 |
| *less* Central government lending to public corporations | 984 |
| Central government borrowing requirement (own account) | −6896 |
| plus Local authority borrowing from other sources | −4506 |
| plus Public corporations from other sources | −2968 |
| Public sector borrowing requirement | −14370 |
| *Financing* | |
| Net borrowing from | |
| Financial institutions other than banks | −8332 |
| Industrial and financial companies | 1975 |
| Personal sector | −1554 |
| Sterling borrowing from banks | −3348 |
| Sterling deposits with banks | −3211 |
| Foreign currency borrowing from banks | 299 |
| Foreign currency deposits with banks | −62 |
| Direct external finance | −136 |
| | −14370 |

*Note:* * This mainly consists of the Budget deficit
*Source: Financial Statistics*, HMSO

The effect of these different methods of financing the PSBR on M4 is considered in turn.

**Method (a)**

When the PSBR is financed by borrowing from the *non-bank private sector* there will be no direct effect on M4. The sale of debt to the non-bank private sector simply transfers bank deposits from the private sector to the public sector. When the government spends this money, deposits move back to the private sector and the money supply is unchanged.

**Method (b)**

However, the same is not true when the PSBR is financed through the *banking sector*. When the banking sector buys public sector debt, their purchase will be paid for by a reduction in operational deposits at the Bank of England. At this stage there has been no change in the money supply. One asset has simply been substituted for another and the liabilities of the banking sector are unchanged. However, the government has *additional deposits* and when these are spent the funds will flow back into the banking sector. This will increase the assets and liabilities of the banking sector, and extra bank deposits are included in M4. Each additional deposit in government hands as a result of selling public sector debt to the banking sector therefore represents an increase in the money supply. The direct effect of sales of public sector debt to the banking sector is therefore an equivalent increase in bank deposits and hence in M4.

The *direct* effect on M4 of the banking sector purchasing public sector debt is the same whether short-term debt or long-term debt is purchased. However, the *indirect* effects are likely to be very different.

When the banking sector buys *short-term debt* such as Treasury Bills, their operational deposits at the Bank of England decrease, but there is no overall change in their liquidity position. They have simply substituted one liquid asset for another liquid asset. When the government spends its additional deposits and they flow back into the banking system, the money supply will increase in the way described above. However, the overall liquidity of the banking sector will have increased with the receipt of extra bank deposits, and the banks will increase their lending to the discount market (so as to meet legal requirements) and to private customers. The increased liquidity of the banking sector might thus lead to a multiple expansion of bank lending. The extent to which this happens depends partly on the availability of willing borrowers and partly on acquiescence by the authorities. In other words, we are assuming that the authorities take no off-setting action to 'mop up' the excess liquidity. The ways in which this might be done were discussed in Chapter 17. If there is a multiple expansion of bank deposits, financing the PSBR by the sale of short-term debt to the banking sector might ultimately lead to a more than proportional increase in the money supply.

The situation is different when the banking sector buys *long-term debt*. In this case, their operational deposits at the Bank of England decrease and their investments increase. In other words, they have exchanged a liquid asset (operational deposits) for an illiquid asset (investments). When the government spends the deposits it has borrowed and they flow back into the banking system the money supply will increase. However, to the extent that these deposits are lent to the discount market as money at call, there will simply be a restoration of the banking sector's original liquidity position. In other words, although the money supply increases via extra bank deposits, there will be no significant change in the overall liquidity position of the banking sector and no multiple expansion of the money supply.

Clearly, if the authorities aim to control the growth of the money supply, the issue of long-term securities is preferable to an increase of short-term securities. However, it is not always possible or desirable to sell long-term debt and in these circumstances the authorities are compelled to sell short-term debt. The reasons for this are discussed in Chapter 21.

**Method (c)**

When the government borrows from *overseas or in foreign currency* the receipts must be paid into the Exchange Equalisation Account at the Bank of England in exchange for an equal value of sterling. The sterling balance is then paid into the government's account at the Bank of England. When the government spends these deposits, cheques will be drawn against them, and when they are cleared operational deposits at the Bank of England will increase and M4 will have increased. However, if there is unsatisfied demand for loans and the government does not sell securities to the non-bank private sector so as to reduce operational deposits, there will also be a multiple increase in the money supply as bank lending increases.

**Method (d)**

Finally, to the extent that the PSBR is financed by an increase in the issue of *notes and coin*, the money supply will increase. This is rather obvious since one of the components of M4 is notes and coin in circulation with the public. However, the Bank of England makes no attempt to control the issue of notes and coin and simply responds passively to the public's demand for cash. This has never been an important means of financing the PSBR, at least in recent years, so that issuing more notes and coin has had little impact on the growth of M4.

The broad aim of policy for the forseeable future is that the PSBR/PSDR should be zero, and in these circumstances there will be no monetary implications of fiscal policy. In practice the PSBR/PSDR is likely to fluctuate from year to year. However, these fluctuations will not be the deliberate result of policy.

## The national debt

The national debt is the total accumulated sum of all outstanding central government debt. Table 18.3 shows that, in 1990, its value stood at £185,870m. It also shows the relative importance of different securities which make up the national debt.

In the UK most of the national debt is held by domestic residents. This is referred to as *internal debt*. That part of the national debt held by non-UK residents is referred to as *external debt*. Table 18.3 shows that at the end of March 1990 about 11.7 per cent of total sterling national debt was held externally.

## The burden of the national debt

It is sometimes alleged that the existence of the national debt imposes a burden on the community. This argument takes many forms, but the one most often quoted is that a burden is imposed via the community being taxed to meet interest payments on the debt. When any part of the debt is redeemed, this too must be met out of current tax receipts. The implication is that the overall level of taxation would be lower if the national debt did not exist.

In fact, the suggestion that a burden is transferred to the present generation from previous generations is largely groundless and does not stand up to close examination. The main issues are summarised below.

*Table 18.3* The distribution and composition of the national debt 31 March 1990

| Distribution | (£ million) |
|---|---|
| Market holdings | |
| Public corporations and local authorities | 1551 |
| Banking sector | 9126 |
| Building societies | 4829 |
| Other financial institutions | 57593 |
| Overseas holders | |
| International organisations | 4596 |
| Central banks | 8126 |
| Other | 9021 |
| Other holders | 59207 |
| Total market holdings | 153576 |
| Official holdings | 32293 |
| Total | 185870 |
| Composition | |
| Treasury bills | 11572 |
| Government stocks | 125017 |
| Non-marketable debt | 49281 |
| Total | 185870 |

Source: *Bank of England Quarterly Bulletin*, November 1990, Vol. 30, No. 4

1. When the government borrows it does so to increase its own expenditure above current tax yields. To borrow from its own residents implies that the rest of society is cutting back on consumption (i.e. saving) with the resources released being transferred to the public sector. In fact, as Table 18.3 shows, approximately 90 per cent of internal debt is in private hands (market holdings) so that increases in the national debt have largely implied a cut in private consumption. To the extent that society cuts its consumption, the burden of government borrowing falls on the generation alive at the time the borrowing takes place. It is then that consumption is cut in order to release resources for the public sector.
2. Although interest payments on the national debt are met out of tax revenue, this does not necessarily imply the existence of a burden. The generation which receives interest payments from holding the national debt is also the generation which pays taxes to meet those interest payments. To the extent that the national debt is held internally, there is simply a redistribution of income within the community. Taken as a *whole*, the community is neither better off nor worse off. The same argument applies when any part of internal debt is redeemed.

Nevertheless, there are three ways in which the national debt can impose some cost on the present generation:

1. To the extent that national debt is held *externally*, it does impose a burden on present and future generations. When the government borrows abroad, the nation as a whole is able at that time to import more than it exports. In other words, borrowing from abroad makes it possible for domestic consumption to exceed domestic output. However, subsequent interest payments on the debt, together with its final redemption, give foreigners claims on domestic output which can only be met from exports. In this case domestic consumption will be less than domestic output. A burden has therefore been transferred to future generations who must cut their consumption because of debts incurred in the past. In this sense, external debt imposes a very real burden on future generations.
2. There are costs of *administering* the national debt which are paid out of current tax receipts. If the national debt did not exist these costs would not be incurred and instead of administering the debt resources could be put to other uses. However, the cost of administering the national debt amounts to less than £200m. which is a small proportion of GNP (see page 86). Nevertheless this is the opportunity cost society bears.

3. The higher levels of taxation necessary to meet interest payments on the debt might have a disincentive effect on effort and initiative. If this is the case, it will reduce GDP below the level that would otherwise be attained. It will also adversely affect the rate of economic growth. The ways in which higher taxation might have a disincentive effect are discussed on pages 219–20 but the empirical evidence on the existence of disincentive effects is controversial.

All that can be said with certainty is that external debt does impose a burden on the community. Nevertheless, it is important to keep the extent of this burden in perspective. Table 18.3 shows that only about 11½ per cent of the national debt is held externally. Furthermore, the real value of this, like the real value of all debt, is eroded by inflation. Because of inflation, a smaller volume of output is given up when the debt is redeemed than is gained when it is incurred. Currently the sterling national debt has fallen to just over 30 per cent of GDP compared with a figure in excess of 100 per cent 30 years ago.

Finally, in assessing the extent of any burden it is necessary to consider the use to which borrowed funds have been put. If they have been put to some productive use, such as improving the infrastructure, then far from passing on a burden to future generations, the capacity for greater future output is created.

## The canons of taxation

In 1776 Adam Smith set down four canons of taxation. These are still important today and provide a set of conditions against which any tax can be judged. The canons of taxation are:

- *Certainty*. The type and timing of taxes should be known with certainty to those paying them.
- *Convenient*. A tax should be as convenient as possible for the tax payer.
- *Economy*. A tax should be as cheap to collect as possible. In more modern jargon we might say a tax should be as *cost effective* as possible.
- *Equity*. Taxation should be as equitable as possible in the sense that there is equality of sacrifice.

More recently another principle of taxation has been added. It is that a tax should be as neutral as possible. This simply means that the imposition of a tax should not adversely affect government economic policy. Such an effect might be counter-productive. For example, it is sometimes alleged that high rates of taxation have a disincentive effect (see pages 219–20). A tax which has disincentive effects cannot be neutral.

## The structure of taxation

Taxation in the UK is usually classified as *direct* or *indirect*. Direct taxes are collected by the Inland Revenue, and in the main are levied on incomes and transfers of capital. Indirect taxes, on the other hand, are collected by the Customs and Excise Department. They are sometimes referred to as expenditure taxes since they are levied mainly on spending. However, the traditional distinction between direct and indirect taxes is that the incidence, or burden of a direct tax is borne by the person on whom the tax is levied. This burden cannot be transferred to another person or party. However, as we shall see on page 216 the burden of an indirect tax can often be passed on to a third party.

**Direct taxes**

The main direct taxes levied in the UK are summarised below.

*Personal income tax*

For tax purposes in the UK both earned and unearned income are treated together. Tax is levied on gross income minus various allowances, such as the single person's allowance. After all deductions have been made, taxable income was subject to the following rates in 1989–90:

| *Rate (%)* | *Taxable income (£)* |
|---|---|
| 25 | 0–20,700 |
| 40 | Over 20,700 |

One feature of income tax in the UK is that it is *progressive*. In other words, *the marginal rate of taxation is greater than the average rate.* However, care must be taken here because the higher rates of tax only apply to *increments* above the upper limit of each tax band. Thus, for example, someone with a taxable income of £25,000 pays income tax at the rate of 25 per cent on the first £20,700 and 40 per cent on the remainder.

*Corporation tax*

This tax is levied on company profits, whether earned at home or abroad, after deducting allowances such as interest on loans. However, dividends to shareholders are *not* tax deductable, and corporation tax is levied on profits *before* any part is distributed to shareholders. The rates of corporation tax in 1989/90 stood at 25 per cent for firms with taxable profits under £150,000 and at 35 per cent for firms with taxable profits over £750,000. Intermediate rates operate between these two levels.

*Petroleum revenue tax (PRT)*

This is levied at different rates on the net incomes from each field in the North Sea after deducting royalties and operating costs. In fact, there are three elements of North Sea oil and gas taxation. A royalty of 12½ per cent is levied on the value of the well-head deposits of oil and gas. PRT is then levied on company incomes, and finally, corporation tax is levied on company profits.

*Capital gains tax*

This tax is levied on the increase in the value of capital assets between the time of purchase and the time of sale. There are exemptions such as a person's main dwelling residence, life assurance policies and so on. In addition, there is a non-taxable allowance, which stood at £5,000 in 1989–90. Only capital gains in any year above this basic allowance are subject to taxation though capital losses can be offset against any gains. The rate of capital gains tax depends on the rate at which income tax is paid. For those who pay income tax at the basic rate capital gains tax is levied at 25 per cent and for higher rate tax payers it is levied at 40 per cent.

*Inheritance tax*

This is a tax levied on transfers at time of death and is levied at the constant rate of 40 per cent on the excess of any transfers above £110,000. Inheritance tax is therefore a *proportional tax.*

Indirect taxes

Indirect taxes can either be *specific* or *ad valorem*. Specific taxes have a fixed money value per unit, whereas *ad valorem* taxes are levied as a percentage of value. In this case, the amount paid in tax varies directly with the value of purchases subject to taxation.

The main indirect taxes levied in the UK are VAT and the excise duties on tobacco, oil and alcohol. These are summarised below.

*Value added tax*

In terms of revenue raised, this is undoubtedly the most important of all indirect taxes in the UK and accounted for 14 per cent of total tax yield in 1989/90. It is a proportional or *ad valorem* tax and is currently levied at the rate of 15 per cent. The mechanics of VAT are set out in Table 18.4.

Basically, firms supplying products on which VAT is levied add VAT to the total value of their output, but deduct VAT already paid on inputs. In other words, tax is levied only on the *value added* at each stage of production.

Not all commodities are subject to VAT. Certain stages in the production of particular commodities are exempt from VAT, while others are zero-rated. Where an exemption applies, traders do not

*Table 18.4*

| Value added (£) | | Purchase price to seller excluding VAT (£) | Purchase price including VAT (£) | Selling price excluding VAT (£) | VAT liability (£) | VAT credit (£) | VAT due (£) |
|---|---|---|---|---|---|---|---|
| 100 | Manufacturer imports raw materials | 0 | 0 | 100 | 15 | 0 | 15 |
| 100 | Manufacturer sells to wholesaler | 100 | 115 | 200 | 30 | 15 | 15 |
| 50 | Wholesaler sells to retailer | 200 | 230 | 250 | 37.5 | 30 | 7.5 |
| 150 | Retailer sells to customer | 250 | 287.5 | 400 | 60 | 37.5 | 22.5 |

Cost to customer = £460, of which VAT = £60

charge VAT on their own output, but are unable to claim back any VAT charged on their inputs as in the case of postage, rent and insurance. Where commodities are zero-rated no VAT is levied and traders can claim back from the Customs and Excise Department any VAT already paid on their inputs as in the case of exports, children's clothing and food (except meals eaten out).

*Excise duties*

These are levied on domestic and imported goods with the *aim* of *raising revenue*. As Figure 18.1 on page 205 shows, of all the excise duties, most revenue is raised from tobacco, oil and alcohol. In all three cases, excise duty is a large proportion of the purchase price and the large sums raised from the sales of these products is therefore an indication that demand for them is relatively inelastic. It is certainly true that in recent years increases in price caused by higher excise duty have had little *lasting* impact on consumption!

## The incidence of taxation

Economists refer to the question of who actually bears the burden of taxation as the *tax incidence*. Despite this, it is not always easy to identify the person or organisation on whom the tax incidence usually falls. In some cases it is possible for those who make tax payments to the authorities to pass the burden of taxation on to others. This is especially true in the case of indirect taxation as Figure 18.2 shows.

The imposition of a tax on sales equal to $ac$ per unit shifts the supply curve for this commodity vertically upwards by the amount of tax, i.e. from $SS$ to $S_1S_1$. Prices rise from $OP$ to $OP_1$. However, the price increase is less than the full amount of the tax, showing that producers pass only part of the burden of the tax. In this case consumers bear $bc$ of the tax incidence, and producers bear $ab$.

For any given product, the distribution of the tax burden after the imposition of an indirect tax, i.e.

$$\frac{\text{consumers' share of tax burden}}{\text{producers' share of tax burden}} = \frac{\text{elasticity of supply}}{\text{elasticity of demand}}$$

Thus, if supply is more elastic than demand, the consumers' share of the tax burden will exceed the producers' share, and vice versa.

## Criticisms of taxation policy

We can broadly identify three main reasons why governments levy taxes:

(a) to finance the provision of public and merit goods,
(b) to provide a powerful tool of economic management policy,
(c) to redistribute income and wealth.

The first of these has been considered on pages 4 and 5 and the second and third are examined in Chapter 19. There is no doubt that taxation policy in the UK achieves all three aims. However, there is a great deal of controversy about whether present policy is the most *efficient* means of achieving these aims. The remainder of this section is devoted to a discussion of these areas of controversy.

For taxation to be economically efficient it should not lead individuals or companies to change their behaviour, except where such changes are the intended result of taxation. Since the majority of taxes are raised to provide the government with revenue, this implies that in general taxes should extract money from the economy in as 'neutral' a way as possible. In fact, there are several reasons why such neutrality might not be achieved.

## Taxation and incentives

The way in which taxation affects incentives is probably the most controversial of all the issues surrounding the operation of tax policy. This is mainly because it is difficult to test any of the hypotheses in such a way that the results clearly indicate how taxation affects incentives. Nevertheless, several possibilities can be identified.

### The Laffer Curve

The Laffer Curve is illustrated in Figure 18.3 and shows how tax revenue and tax rate are related.

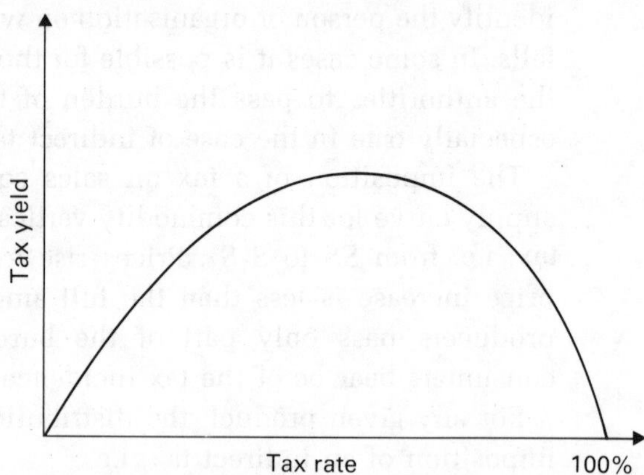


Figure 18.1 The Laffer curve

If there is no taxation, that is, the tax rate is zero, tax revenue must also be zero. At the other extreme if the tax rate is 100 per cent, tax revenue will again be zero because all production except that required for subsistence will cease. The tax rate of 100 per cent totally removes the incentive to work. Between these two extremes, different rates of taxation have a different effect on production. The problem for the authorities is to set the tax rate at that level which maximises tax revenue and therefore minimises the disincentive effect. Some studies for the UK suggest that a *composite* tax rate, that is, including direct and indirect taxes as well as social security payments, of 60 per cent will maximise tax revenue. The composite tax rate in the UK is currently estimated at about 40 per cent implying that *higher* taxes would have no disincentive effect. This is completely at odds with the government's belief, and that of most *supply side economists* (see page 230), that lower taxes are necessary to increase incentives!

### The poverty trap

A potentially serious disincentive effect arises when individuals are caught in the *poverty trap*. The poverty trap does not, as it is often thought, denote the existence of poverty. Indeed, it is the result of efforts to relieve poverty by providing benefits. Basically, the poverty trap arises because benefits are withdrawn the higher up the income scale a family moves. With higher income, therefore, a family faces both a rising tax bill *and* the reduction or withdrawal of its social security benefits. In cases where people pay income tax at the rate of 25 per cent and national insurance contributions at the rate of 9 per cent, the marginal rate of tax is 34 per cent. However, when the rate at which benefits are withdrawn is added to this, the *effective* marginal rate of tax is much higher and in certain income ranges it can exceed 100 per cent!

### The unemployment trap

The *unemployment trap* is similar to the poverty trap in that its existence is due to the availability of benefits. However, whereas the poverty trap affects those in employment, the unemployment trap affects those who are unemployed. In some cases the benefits available while unemployed are equal to or greater than the after-tax income that would be earned by accepting employment. When an unemployed person's disposable income falls by accepting employment, the effective marginal rate of tax on earnings is over 100 per cent. The effect of this is to create a serious disincentive for those who are currently unemployed to seek employment. Furthermore, the implication is that any attempt to price the unemployed into jobs by cutting wages actually worsens the unemployment trap. Indeed one reason put forward for taxing unemployment benefit is to reduce the extent of the unemployment trap by lowering the *effective* rate of benefit.

### Taxation and the incentive to work

It has been suggested that relatively high rates of income tax reduce the incentive to increase earnings through working overtime, accepting promotion and so on. There is also a view that high rates of taxation encourage a certain amount of absenteeism by reducing the loss of earnings which results from being absent. However, the available evidence on these matters is inconclusive and it is just as possible that relatively high rates of taxation will provide an incentive to work. This would be the case where individuals aim at a *given level* of after-tax income, and need to work overtime, accept more responsibility and so on, in order to achieve it.

### Taxation and investment

Taxation reduces the net return from investment and so might discourage enterprise and risk-taking. This is particularly likely when shareholders pay income tax at progressive rates.

Returns on high-risk investment are variable, and over any given period the total tax paid by shareholders is likely to be greater in this case than when returns are fairly constant from one year to the next.

This would happen because higher dividends paid in those years when profits permitted would push shareholders into higher taxable bands for income tax purposes.

### Stimulus to inflation

It has sometimes been suggested that the nature of income tax in the UK might increase inflationary pressure. The argument centres on the way relatively high rates of inflation and progressive taxation affect real income. Where pay awards rise in line with retail prices and workers continue to pay the same proportion of their income in taxation, real income will be constant. However, if wage awards push earnings into higher taxable bands, the *proportion* of income paid in tax will rise and real income will fall. The higher average rate of tax which results from incomes rising in a progressive tax system is referred to as *fiscal drag*. If workers demand further pay rises in response to falling real incomes the process will repeat itself; prices will rise still further and real income will fall as earnings are pushed into still higher taxable bands. In other words, prices will rise faster than after-tax income.

The following example illustrates the problem. Assume that the first £2,000 of earnings is untaxed. Thereafter the following rates of taxation apply.

| *Taxable earnings (£)* | *Tax Rate* |
|---|---|
| 1–1000 | 30 per cent |
| 1001–2000 | 40 per cent |
| 2001–3000 | 50 per cent |
| Over 3001 | 60 per cent |

If gross income rises from £5,000 in Year 1 to £7,000 in Year 2, we can see in Figure 18.2, how the amount paid in taxes rises.

Gross income increases by 40 per cent (2,000/5,000), but disposable income, or net income, increases by only 21 per cent (800/3,800). Suppose now that prices increase over the same period by 25 per cent. Disposable income at *constant prices* will fall from £3,800 in Year 1 to £3,680 (i.e. £4,600 × 100/125) in Year 2. In other words, *real income* will fall by over 3 per cent despite a rise in *gross income* of 40 per cent (Non-taxable allowances and taxable bands are usually increased in the Budget partly to avoid this effect, but where they are not adjusted in line with inflation some groups will experience a fall in real income).

This process whereby individuals are forced into higher tax bands because of rising income is referred to as *fiscal drag*. Governments have sometimes been accused of using fiscal drag as a means of financing their expenditures. If higher expenditures generate inflation they can be financed without increasing the rates of taxation because inflation will draw people into higher tax brackets and therefore

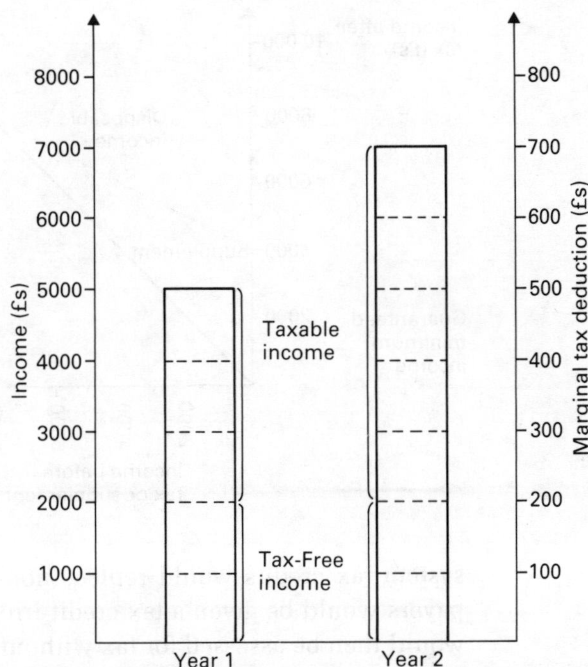


*Figure 18.2* Rising income and income tax

increase government revenue from taxation.

## Reform of the tax system

### A negative income tax

This proposal is sometimes referred to as a reverse income tax and aims to reduce the effect of the poverty and unemployment traps on the financial incentive to work.

There are many variations of the basic idea. One involves the establishment of a minimum income guarantee (the poverty line) which is fixed in cash terms according to the circumstances (number of dependants, etc.) of each particular family. The cash benefit, that is the minimum income guarantee, would be paid in full to those without any other form of income. It would therefore replace the present social security system. Thereafter tax would be levied on the whole of a person's earned income.

The operation of this system is explained using Figure 18.3 (page 220). We assume that the minimum income guarantee is £4,000 and that earned income is taxed (via loss of cash benefit) at the constant rate of 50 per cent.

When the family has no other income, it receives the full minimum income guarantee of £4,000. For each additional £1,000 earned, the rate of cash benefit falls by £500. This is equivalent to a marginal rate of tax of 50 per cent. The break-even point is £8,000. When family income reaches this level no cash benefit is received and no income tax is paid. For incomes above this level a positive rate of tax applies.

A slightly different proposal involving the establishment of tax credits has received most official support in the UK. Under this

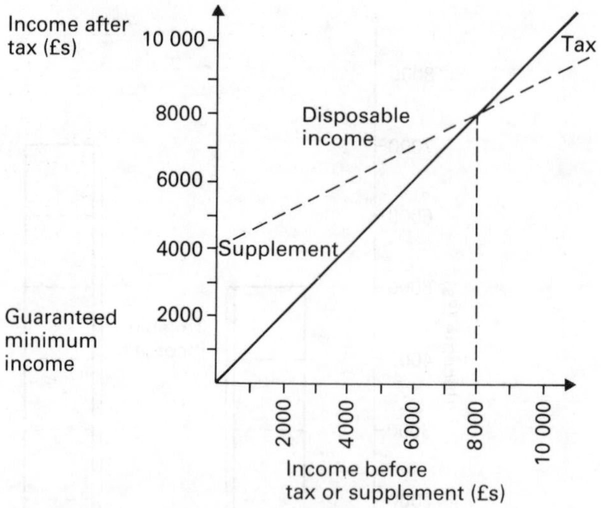

*Figure 18.3* A negative income tax

system tax credits would replace non-taxable allowances and all tax payers would be given a tax credit irrespective of income. All income would then be assessed for tax without exempting any initial amount.

If the tax credit exceeds the tax payable, the difference will be paid out of cash support; if the tax liability exceeds the tax credit, the difference is due in tax payment.

This system of taxation is easy to operate and therefore cheap to administer. For example, if the tax rate is 25 per cent, then an individual with a *tax credit* of £40 per week and no other source of income would receive £40 per week in state benefit. If this person now accepted employment at a *wage* of £40 per week, their tax liability would be (0.25)£40 = £10 per week. This person would therefore receive £30 per week in state benefit (i.e. the tax credit minus the tax liability) giving a total weekly income of £70. At a wage of £160 per week this person would receive no state benefit nor pay any tax since their tax credit exactly equals their tax liability. Positive income tax would only be paid when wages exceed £160 per week.

### Changing the tax base

There are three tax bases: wealth, income and expenditure. However, there are practical problems associated with the taxation of wealth particularly in terms of assessment and in recent years emphasis on tax reform has concentrated on shifting the tax base away from income and on to expenditure. In other words, it has been suggested that less revenue should be raised from taxing incomes and more from taxing expenditures. The advantages and disadvantages of indirect taxation are briefly considered.

### Advantages

- *Lower disincentive effect.* It has been argued that indirect taxes have a lower disincentive effect than direct taxes. If it is true this is an extremely important point because any disincentive effect implies lower growth of productivity and this in turn implies a slower growth in the standard of living. Any disincentive effect could manifest itself in several ways such as lower mobility of labour, a reduction in investment and so on. Perhaps the most obvious manifestation of the disincentive effect is the existence of the poverty and unemployment traps.

- *Indirect taxes can be used more specifically*. Indirect taxes can be used to achieve specific objectives. In particular, by placing taxes on demerit goods it is possible to force their price upwards and to reduce consumption. Direct taxes are much more sweeping in their effects.
- *Greater flexibility*. Indirect taxes are more flexible than direct taxes in the sense that rates of indirect taxation can be changed within certain limits by the Chancellor without parliamentary approval (i.e. without waiting for the Budget). This means they can be adjusted swiftly in response to some unanticipated event.

### Disadvantages

- *Regressive in operation*. Most direct taxes, and certainly personal income tax, operate progressively. This is particularly useful in redistributing income. Indirect taxes, on the other hand, operate regressively because they represent a larger proportion of the expenditure of lower income groups.
- *Effect on inflation*. Higher rates of indirect taxation have an immediate effect on the retail price index. This might be particularly serious if it leads to demands for higher wages because it might set in motion an inflationary spiral.

## Local taxation

Formerly local taxation was through a system of rates which were a tax on property values. This system has been replaced by a community charge or poll tax levied on the occupants of a household who are eighteen or over although there are some exceptions.

One reason for the introduction of the poll tax was dissatisfaction with the rating system. Rates were basically a tax which was related to the value of property. Because they were not related to current income they were criticised as acting regressively. (The type of property people occupy frequently reflects their *past* income rather than *current* income especially for many retired people.) They also varied widely between different rating authorities.

The poll tax widens the tax base and is more equitable in the sense that those who benefit from local expenditure now pay for it. Rates tended to be paid by house-owners rather than all adult occupants of a dwelling. It was estimated that only one third of the electorate paid rates in full! Moreover the business community will henceforth pay a single uniform tax set nationally. This implies that high spending municipal authorities will have to levy from its electors a higher rate of poll tax and in this way local authorities might become more accountable to local electors.

However, the poll tax is not related to income and is probably even more regressive than the local rates which it replaced. The cost of collecting the poll tax is relatively high and it is likely that there has been widespread evasion. (The rates were cheap to collect and difficult to evade!) In addition by levying taxes per person rather than per dwelling, the poll tax is likely to encourage low density occupation and discourage the sharing of large homes with other people. This could add to the shortage of accommodation in some areas particularly the south-east and reduce mobility of labour. Another factor is that removing a tax on property and replacing the rates with a poll tax is likely to contribute to raising house prices and again this could reduce mobility of labour.

## Test your understanding

1. What is the effect of a budget deficit on the level of aggregate demand?
2. How are the budget deficit, the PSBR and the national debt related?
3. How might an increase in the PSBR affect
   (i) the money supply
   (ii) interest rates

Question 4 is based on the following diagram.

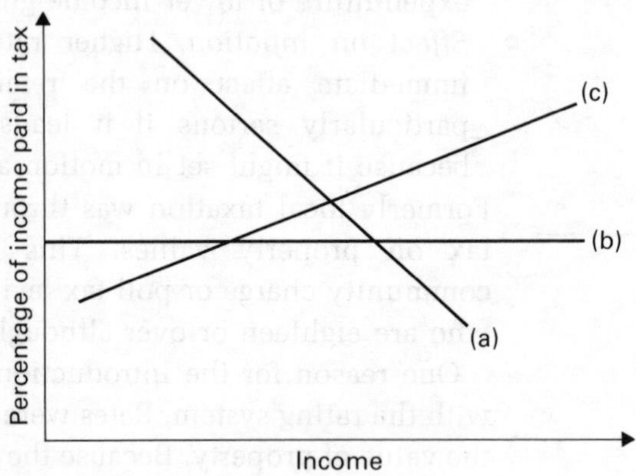


4. Which of the lines show
   (i) a proportional tax
   (ii) a progressive tax
   (iii) a regressive tax
5. What does the Laffer Curve show?
6. How might an increase in indirect taxes have a disincentive effect?
7. Can an increase in direct taxes ever have an incentive effect?
8. What would be the effect on the unemployment trap of an increase in
   (i) tax free allowances
   (ii) the basic rate of income tax
9. What is meant by the incidence of a tax?

# 19 The aims and methods of economic policy

In 1944 the government published a White Paper on Employment Policy which stated that: 'The Government believe that, once the war has been won, we can make a fresh approach, with better chances of success than ever before, to the task of maintaining a high and stable level of employment without sacrificing the essential liberties of a free society.' Since then there has been a change in the approach to achieving this objective, but there is no doubt that it remains an important *long-term* goal of all political parties. However, governments have other objectives which at times have taken precedence over employment levels as the main *short-term* goal. In recent years considerable importance has been attached to reducing the annual rate of inflation. At other times the balance of payments deficit has been the most pressing problem, and so on.

The overall aims of economic policy have not changed, but the means of achieving these aims have. For much of the post-war period governments pursued their aims by managing the level of aggregate monetary demand. Such an approach is essentially Keynesian, since it implies manipulating the level of aggregate demand (that is, C + I + G + X − M) so as to influence nominal income (Y). This approach is usually referred to as *demand management*.

More recently, and certainly since the late 1970s, the emphasis has changed from managing aggregate demand to what has come to be termed 'supply-side economics'. At its simplest, supply-side economics is the use of microeconomic incentives to achieve macroeconomic goals.

Supply-side economics thus reflects the view that the macroeconomic system can only operate efficiently if each microeconomic market (the labour market, the capital market and so on) operates efficiently. The emphasis of macroeconomic policy has therefore shifted away from simply managing the overall level of aggregate demand, to the pursuit of policies which will enable each microeconomic market to operate efficiently.

## The aims of economic policy

The economic aims of the government can be briefly stated as the maintenance of full employment, a relatively low and stable rate of inflation, equilibrium in the balance of payments and economic growth. Each is considered in turn.

### Full employment

A high and stable level of employment is a major aim of all governments. It has sometimes been argued that governments should aim at full employment. However, the concept of full employment is difficult to define because the minimum level of unemployment that can be achieved at any particular time is constantly subject to change and cannot be zero because, as the demand for various goods and services changes, so does the demand for the labour which produces them. The level of employment that can be achieved will depend on the distribution of that demand between different goods and services and on the mobility of labour. The more that demand is concentrated on labour intensive goods and services and the more mobile the population, the lower the level of unemployment that can be achieved. The government's aim in this area is therefore to achieve some level of employment which it considers acceptable. We shall later see that, because its aims are not independent of one another, what is considered to be an acceptable level of unemployment is to a certain extent dictated by the priorty governments give to achieving their other economic aims.

### Price stabiliy

This is another important objective of governments, although price stability does not necessarily imply a commitment to zero inflation. Changing supply and demand conditions for various products will lead to price changes in the various product markets and therefore a moderate rate of inflation might be thought acceptable, even healthy. Again, all that can be said is that it is for the government to decide what rate is acceptable, given the constraints imposed by its other aims. We should note that, when the government is aiming to reduce the rate of inflation, its choice of policy will at least be partly determined by whether inflation is due to excess demand (demand-pull inflation) or to rising costs (cost-push inflation) (see pages 160–162).

### Equilibrium in the balance of payments

This is not a concept that can be easily defined. However, since all imports must ultimately be paid for by exports, one definition is that the flow of *autonomous debits be equalled by the flow of autonomous credits*. At any moment in time, a country might have a surplus or deficit in its balance of payments so that autonomous debits and credits will not necessarily be equal. The concept of equilibrium must therefore be related to some time period over which a balance should be achieved.

There is a further problem, in that a balance between debits and credits will also depend on the exchange rate system which operates.

When exchange rates float, balance between autonomous transactions is guaranteed; at least it is under certain circumstances such as a 'pure' float. But when exchange rates are fixed autonomous transactions must either be encouraged or discouraged if balance is to be achieved. We have seen on pages 201–2 that attempts to manage the exchange rate have serious implications for policy in the domestic economy. Balance of payments equilibrium might therefore be said to exist when, over a given period of time, autonomous transactions cancel out in such a way that does *not impede* the government's efforts to achieve its other policy aims.

## Economic growth

Another important aim of governments is to manage the economy in such a way that economic growth will be fostered. There are many definitions of economic growth. It is sometimes taken to mean the growth of capacity of productive potential for the economy as a whole because in the long run this is the only way of increasing the size of real GDP. This definition implies an outward movement of the economy's production possibility curve. However, the usual definition of economic growth is an increase in real GNP.

Economic growth has been given high priority as a policy objective, because, if the growth of output exceeds the growth of population, per capita income will rise, i.e. the standard of living will rise. In the longer term, the compound effect on output of a constant rate of growth is impressive. For example, if output grows every year by 2 per cent, GDP will double in approximately thirty-six years; but if the growth of output can be increased to 3 per cent each year, output will double in approximately twenty-four years!

## Interdependence of aims

From the mid 1940s until the 1980s the traditional method adopted by governments to achieve their economic aims was variations in the level of aggregate demand or demand management. The use of demand management to achieve economic aims led to a major policy dilemma for successive governments. The problem was that it proved impossible to achieve all aims simultaneously, so that governments faced a conflict of policy objectives. We have already seen in Chapter 15 that the use of high levels of aggregate demand to achieve full employment often conflicted with price stability. However, it also conflicted with the balance-of-payments objective. As demand in the economy increased and incomes rose, so the demand for imports also rose. This was partly to be expected because of the high marginal propensity to import in the UK. However, the adverse impact of increased demand on the balance of payments was reinforced by higher domestic prices which made imports more competitive in the domestic market and exports less competitive in foreign markets. There is no doubt that increased home demand also resulted in goods initially produced for export being diverted to the domestic economy, where demand and prices were rising and where transport costs to market were lower. As a result, the level of unemployment a government could achieve was determined in part by the rate of inflation it was prepared to accept, and in part by its need to achieve balance-of-payments equilibrium. At times full employment was the major aim, while at others it was sacrificed to the more pressing problems of containing inflation and restoring equilibrium to the balance of payments.

## The stop-go cycle

This switch of policy objectives became known as the stop-go cycle. The stop phase of the cycle occurred when aggregate demand was reduced to combat inflation and/or the balance-of-payments deficit. As the economy slowed down and unemployment developed, these particular problems seemed to disappear; the government would then embark on the go phase of the cycle, expanding aggregate demand to bring unemployment down. As unemployment fell, the problems of inflation and the balance-of-payments deficit would re-emerge, and the cycle would be repeated. It has been argued that the stop-go cycle can be explained as the consequence of governments trying to reduce the level of unemployment below the natural rate. Each injection of demand temporarily reduced unemployment, but ultimately resulted in a higher rate of inflation and no permanent reduction in unemployment as the economy returned to the natural rate.

During the 1960s and 1970s in an attempt to break out of this cycle governments ceased to rely solely on managing the level of aggregate demand to achieve their aims, and began to make greater use of incomes policy and exchange rate adjustment as policy instruments. It was not until 1979, with the election of Mrs Thatcher as Prime Minister, that there was any radical change in the conduct of policy. These changes and the conduct of current macroeconomic policy are discussed further on pages 228–236.

Demand management also led to another problem. Successive governments believed that economic growth could be encouraged by greater investment and that this was more likely to be forthcoming when aggregate demand was rising. The reason for this was simple: rising demand would create a growing market in which the additional output that resulted from increased investment could be sold. However, the management of demand to encourage growth was rarely, if ever, the major policy objective of the authorities; more often price stability and balance-of-payments equilibrium took precedence over other aims. It is possible that the variable and unpredictable nature of aggregate demand discouraged the private sector from investing because of increased uncertainty.

## Instruments of policy

### Fiscal policy

This consists of variations in government income and expenditure. The main fiscal stance of the authorities is implied in the annual budget when the government outlines its income and expenditure plans for the coming financial year. However, in recent years it has become standard practice for chancellors to present an 'autumn statement' which, in exceptional circumstances, might include changes in the rates of indirect taxation.

For most of the post-war period fiscal policy was the instrument used to bring about major changes in aggregate demand. Until the mid/late 1970s comparatively little attention was paid to the size of the PSBR. Indeed, the size of the PSBR was regarded as a *consequence* of fiscal policy and not a *target* in itself. In other words, the government set its expenditure and taxation levels to achieve that particular level of GDP which it considered consistent with its various economic objectives. It therefore regarded its own budget deficit as simply a residual which had to be financed in order to achieve that level of GDP.

### Monetary policy

This consists of policies designed to influence the supply of money and/or its 'price', i.e. the rate of interest. As an instrument of demand management, monetary policy was regarded as subordinate to fiscal policy (until the mid/late 1970s). Whereas fiscal policy could bring about major changes in aggregate demand, the potency of monetary policy was questioned and it was relegated to the role of 'fine-tuning' the economy. In other words, its role was to bring about minor changes in aggregate demand which could not be achieved with fiscal policy. For example, the view was taken that when the economy approached the target level of output it might be necessary to adjust aggregate demand slightly upwards to achieve the employment target, or downwards to avoid any excess pressure which might generate inflation. Fiscal policy was considered unsuitable for such fine-tuning, because it produced major changes in aggregate demand and also takes longer to exert its full effect; on the other hand, monetary policy was considered capable of achieving the minor adjustments required.

Since the mid-1970s, and especially during the 1980s, the role of monetary policy has been elevated and it now plays a major part in the conduct of economic policy. This is discussed in more detail later in this chapter on page 228.

### Exchange rate policy

Since entry into the ERM this is not an option for the UK at present. However, if sterling withdraws from the ERM in the future, exchange rate changes will again become a policy option. If exchange rates are allowed to float market forces will have greater influence in determining exchange rates. This implies that domestic policy will no longer have to be directed to achieving a particular balance of payments position. To the extent that exchange rate changes offset a relatively high rate of inflation in one country compared to others (see page 192), the balance of payments will prove less of a constraint thus freeing economic policy to be directed to achieving other economic objectives.

### Incomes policy

The final instrument the authorities have at their disposal is a statutory incomes policy, although they have sometimes preferred to negotiate a voluntary policy. In the UK, the term 'incomes policy' has often been synonomous with wages policy, since it has mainly applied to wage increases. Although incomes policy can be used to redistribute income it has mainly been applied as an anti-inflationary measure in the UK. By establishing a norm for wage increases, incomes policy has sought to ensure that wage awards accord more closely with the growth of output, that is, productivity. If wages and productivity grow at the same rate, wage increases will have no effect on costs of production. Consequently they will have little, if any, effect on inflation.

In the UK incomes policies have not been particularly successful as a long-run anti-inflationary measure, although there is no doubt that they have sometimes been successful in the short run. One reason for their lack of success is that the norm has tended to be regarded as a minimum wage award on which more powerful unions have built further claims. Even when policy has been applied with the force of law so that wage increases have been limited, as soon as controls have been relaxed there has tended to be a 'catching up' phase with wage awards well above the growth of output.

Nevertheless, perhaps the main objections to incomes policy are that by establishing a norm they have reduced the incentive for workers to increase productivity, and that by removing flexibility in wage differentials they have led to lower mobility of labour. The price mechanism works in the labour market as well as in product markets, and by limiting the growth of wages in those occupations which are expanding and which require more workers, incomes policy reduces the incentive for workers to move. Again, this could limit the growth of productivity.

Because of these factors the present government believes that, in the long run, incomes policy has no particular advantages but that it does have serious disadvantages. However, this view is not shared by all and it is probable that incomes policy will again be used as a policy instrument at some stage in the future.

### The medium-term financial strategy (MTFS)

The conduct of economic policy changed decisively in 1980 when MTFS was introduced. The aims of the MTFS were to reduce the rate of inflation and to reduce the proportion of resources taken by the public sector.

Inflation was to be reduced primarily by a reduction in the rate of growth of the money supply and the reduction in the proportion of resources taken by the public sector was to be achieved by a reduction in the absolute size of the PSBR, as well as by reducing it as a percentage of GDP. It was thought that reducing the PSBR would not only reduce the extent of crowding out, it was also anticipated that it would lead to lower interest rates because of the implied reduction in the demand for funds.

This was a decisive change in policy in two ways. First it implied that the government accepted that the rate of growth of the money supply *determined* the rate of inflation and that *control of inflation could only be achieved by controlling the money supply.* It also implied an acceptance that the private sector used resources more efficiently than the public sector and therefore that economic growth was more likely to be encouraged by reducing the size of the public sector. This view remains important and privatisation, along with deregulation of markets, form an integral part of the government's supply-side strategy.

## Current macroeconomic policy

The main aim of macroeconomic policy remains a reduction in the rate of inflation so that the rate in the UK converges with that achieved by our EMS partners. This is to be achieved mainly by restricting money growth. Macroeconomic policy has partly been dealt with in chapters 17 and 18. However, it is important to note that the conduct of policy will undoubtedly change fundamentally in the future. In particular, instead of relying on interest rates to control consumer spending, greater emphasis will now be placed on the use of interest rates to influence the exchange rate for sterling so as to maintain its value within the ERM limits.

The conduct of policy will also continue to reflect the emphasis placed on the supply side of the economy. The aim of supply-side policy is to remove obstacles which prevent or discourage people and firms from adapting quickly to changing conditions of market demand and changing techniques of production. It is argued that the implied increase in efficiency will encourage economic growth. Two aspects of supply-side policies, *privatisation* and *deregulation* are considered under separate headings.

The emphasis on supply-side policies stems from a belief that, if markets can be made to operate more efficiently, this will encourage economic growth and employment without adding to the risk of inflation. We can see the effect of an increase in efficiency on aggregate supply in Figure 19.1.

If all other things remain equal, an increase in efficiency at all levels of output will shift the aggregate supply curve from $AS$ to $AS_1$. Any given level of output now has a lower supply price, and a greater

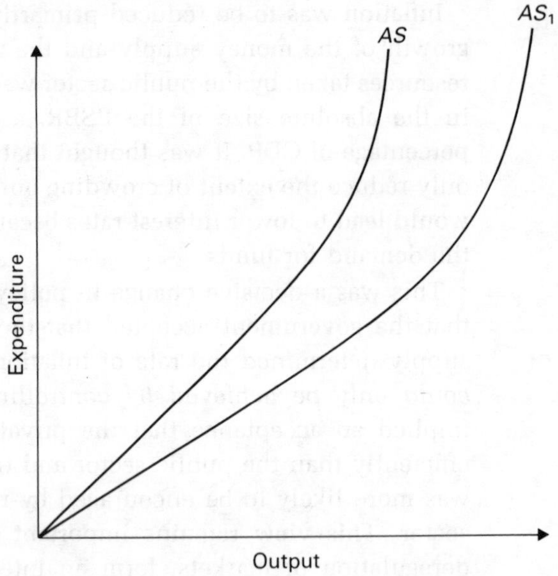


Figure 19.1 The effect of an increase in efficiency on aggregate supply

amount of output can be produced at full employment than previously. In the absence of any improvement in efficiency, attempts to achieve economic growth and full employment by increasing aggregate demand will not be sustainable because they will generate inflation and a balance of payments deficit.

The various methods by which the government has attempted to improve the supply side of the economy can be discussed under the following headings.

### Taxation

Measures have been introduced to ensure that, in general, people are better off in work than out of work. In particular, the basic rate of income tax has been reduced from 33 per cent in 1978 to a current level of 25 per cent. Further reductions are planned in the future. The threshold above which people start paying tax has been also increased by more than the rate of inflation. Additionally, unemployment benefit is now taxed. It is hoped that, among other effects, this will have a positive effect on the unemployment trap.

Corporation tax has also been reduced from 52 per cent to a lower rate of 25 per cent for smaller firms and a rate of 35 per cent for larger firms. The aim here is to encourage firms to invest in more productive capital by reducing the taxation of profits.

### The labour market

Alongside these changes the government has introduced several training schemes, the most important of which is the Youth Training Scheme (YTS) which provides one-year and two-year training placements for sixteen and seventeen-year-olds respectively who leave school or college (or who cannot find employment). On completion of their YTS scheme, an estimated 60 per cent of trainees find emplyment or go into further education.

Other important labour market measures are the Employment Acts of 1980 and 1982 and the Trade Union Act of 1984 which have attempted to safeguard the interests of individual employees and to encourage more effective democracy within trade unions. Some of the main measures introduced are:

- Removal of legal immunities both for picketing, other than by employees at their place of work, and for secondary industrial action.
- Introduction and strengthening of the rights of employees dismissed for refusing to join closed shops.
- Removal of legal immunities from civil actions so as to make trade unions subject to injunctions and damages when they are responsible for unlawful industrial action.
- Removal of legal immunities from civil action in any industrial action which has not been agreed in advance by a secret ballot of the membership.

The aim of this legislation is to create a more flexible labour market, since it is believed that lack of flexibility is one of the major reasons why real wages have risen to levels which reduce employment.

**The capital market**

A whole range of controls have been abolished in the capital market. For example, in 1979 exchange controls were abolished; and in 1982 hire-purchase controls were abolished. The aim is to improve efficiency by allowing savings to go where there is the best combination of risk and return.

The *Big Bang* also increased competition in the capital market. The Stock Exchange now permits *dual capacity trading*, that is, it allows firms to simultaneously act as *principle* on their own account and as *agents* for their clients. Fixed commissions by brokers have also been abolished and full ownership of Stock Exchange firms by non-members has been permissable since 1 March 1986. All of these changes are seen as major ways of improving competition, and through this, efficiency.

**Markets for other goods and services**

Again, a whole range of measures have been introduced, and while they vary in significance their aim is to create the conditions in which the freer play of market forces can stimulate the economy to work more efficiently. Two measures are particularly important: The Competition Act (1980) and the programme of privatisation and deregulation (see pages 232–236). The former gives the Monopolies and Mergers Commission power to investigate individual firms suspected of operating 'anti-competitive practices' referred to it by the Director-General of Fair Trading. The latter reflects the government's view that economic performance can be improved by subjecting firms and whole industries to the full rigours of the market – although the proceeds of privatisation have also helped to reduce the PSBR. The implicit assumption is that organisations in the public sector are sheltered from competition and that this leads to inefficiency. Whether this is true or not is debatable, but it certainly is true that on average the rate of return on capital employed in nationalised industries has for many years been lower than the rate of return in the private sector, while price increases have in general been higher.

In the financial sector the 1986 Building Societies Act has enabled them to compete more effectively with the retail banks. In particular they are now able to offer cheque books and cheque guarantee cards. Several now also offer cash point facilities. Other provisions of the Act allowed the building societies to abandon their status as Friendly Societies and form themselves into public limited companies as Abbey National has recently done. Building Socities are now also able to make unsecured loans up to certain limits for purposes other than house purchase and to compete for funds on the wholesale markets (see page 148). In 1986 a limit of 20 per cent of total borrowed funds was originally set on the amount that could be borrowed from the wholesale markets. However, in 1988 this was raised to 40 per cent further increasing their ability to compete with retail banks.

## Privatisation

The term *privatisation* is usually taken to imply the transfer of assets from the public sector to the private sector. In this sense privatisation refers to a change in the *ownership* of assets. However privatisation can cover other activities for example ceasing to provide such activities as refuse collection through the public sector and putting them out to private contract. Despite this, it is the transfer of assets from the public sector to the private sector which has attracted most attention and on which we focus in this section. Furthermore, although this might include activities such as the sale of council houses, it is the sale of nationalised industries as well as industries in which the state has a major shareholding with which we will be concerned.

One point to be aware of at the outset is that privatisation is not simply a British phenomenon. It is happening in many countries throughout the world. The USA, France, Germany, Spain, Singapore, Jamaica, Chile, Turkey and many other countries all have privatisation programmes. However, the reasons for privatisation in the UK are typical:

- A major aim of privatisation is to increase efficiency in the allocation and utilisation of resources.
- Another aim is to increase the extent of share ownership, partly for political reasons in the UK at least, but also because it is thought to affect the allocation and utilisation of resources.

- In the case of the UK, privatisation has been a major factor in cutting down borrowing by the government. Lower borrowing by the government, as we have seen on page 231, has been a major part of the government's macroeconomic strategy.

Let us consider each of these in turn:

Privatisation might encourage efficiency in privatised firms for several reasons. One is that there will be less government interference in pricing and investment decisions by these firms. Another reason is that there will be increased competition following privatisation.

It is certainly true that governments have often deliberately prevented nationalised industries from increasing their prices as a means of tackling inflation, and have altered investment in different industries as a means of varying aggregate demand. As privatised organisations, firms will be able to plan more effectively. However, efficiency in the allocation of resources might also be improved. When prices are prevented from rising, too much is consumed in relation to the optimum. Furthermore, it has been argued that increased investment in the nationalised industries has crowded out private sector investment, and the higher rate of return achieved in the private sector is taken as evidence that investment is more efficient when undertaken by the private sector.

However, there seems little evidence of increased competition following some privatisations. Indeed, some organisations such as British Gas have been sold as monopolies to increase their attractiveness to shareholders. It might be claimed that the government had little alternative since some industries are quite clearly natural monopolies (see page 64), and that in any case, as private sector organisations, they must compete for funds on the capital market with other private sector organisations. Nevertheless, critics have argued that monopolies do not have to be efficient to be profitable, and that profitability is the main determinant of a firm's ability to raise funds on the capital market. Furthermore, it would have been possible to sell these industries as regional units which would be allowed to compete for business in each other's regions as seems likely to happen when electricity and water are privatised.

Turning to the second aim of privatisation, the government has clearly had success in increasing the number of shareholders with over nine million private individuals in the UK owning shares in 1988. It has been argued that this will encourage efficiency because management are now accountable to shareholders with a vested interest in the efficiency and profitability of the companies in which they hold shares. However, few shareholders attend the AGM when the Board of Directors is elected and when they must account for the policies of the previous 12 months.

*Table 19.1* Major UK Privatisations

| Company | Date | £m |
|---|---|---|
| British Aerospace | 1981/82, 1984/85 | 389 |
| Cable and Wireless | 1981/82, 1984/85 | 1020 |
| Britoil | 1982/83, 1983/84, 1985/86 | 1053 |
| Enterprise Oil | 1984/85 | 382 |
| British Telecom | 1984/85, 1985/86, 1986/87 | 3682 |
| British Gas | 1986/87 | 5600 |
| British Petroleum | 1979/80, 1981/82, 1983/84, 1987/88 | 8054 |
| British Airports Authority | 1987/88 | 1275 |
| Rolls Royce Aero Engines | 1987/88 | 1080 |
| Other | | 2256 |
| Total | | 24791 |

As for the third aim of privatisation, there is no doubt that the government has achieved success in raising revenue through privatisation as Table 19.1 shows.

Nevertheless it has been suggested that the government might have met with even more success if it had not underpriced some of the shares it has issued. For example, shares in British Telecom were issued at a price of £1.30, but by the end of the first day's trading they were quoted at £1.73, thus depriving the government of potentially an extra £1.295m. revenue.

However, deciding on the price at which to issue shares so as to ensure that a sufficient quantity is sold is a notoriously difficult problem. Some have criticised the government for not issuing shares by tender. This was certainly a possibility open to the government, but was rejected probably because it was felt that this would not attract small investors with little or no experience of buying shares, to anything like the extent required to significantly increase the number of share-owning individuals.

## Deregulation

*Deregulation* is the term used to describe the process of dismantling state regulations on the activities of the business sector. Like privatisation, deregulation is a world-wide phenomenon, though in this chapter we are only concerned with deregulation in the UK. It is useful to note, however, that while privatisation and deregulation sometimes overlap, as when an industry is denationalised and is also opened up to competition, this is not always the case. Before we consider the issue of deregulation the reasons for regulating industry in the first place are considered.

### The reasons for regulation

It is usually suggested that the main reason for regulation is to safeguard the *public interest*, although what constitutes the public interest differs from case to case. For example, the banks have been subject to regulation mainly because of the possibility of default, if there was a sudden large withdrawal of deposits by customers. A bank that was unable to honour withdrawals might well precipitate a run on other banks as well as itself. Air transport, as well as buses and coaches, have been subject to regulation for safety reasons. Television and radio broadcasting have been regulated, partly because it was felt that competition would reduce the quality of reception by causing interference. The regulation of agriculture has been partly to ensure that harmful chemicals are not used to increase yields, and partly to ensure that, as an industry, agriculture survives so that food supplies cannot be cut off by a foreign supplier.

Despite these cases the most complete regulations are those governing the nationalised industries which are given sole rights of supply. One of the most important arguments for nationalisation was that in some cases, such as gas, water and electricity, a natural monopoly existed, and that nationalisation was necessary to ensure the public were not exploited by a private monopolist.

## The reasons for deregulation

The major reason for deregulation is that it is now thought that the public interest is better served by *competition* and that regulations not only restrict competition, but also impose higher costs on the firms subject to regulation. However, another factor is *technological advances* which have sometimes made deregulation essential if an industry is to survive the growth of foreign competition. For example, technological advances made automated dealing possible on the world's stock exchanges which substantially reduced the cost of transacting business. Technological progress also made it possible for a dealer in one financial centre, such as London, to transact business with another dealer in a different financial centre somewhere else in the world, with the latest dealing rates available on screen. When minimum dealing rates were abolished in New York, this precipitated reform of the London Stock Exchange (the Big Bang), because almost overnight it became cheaper to buy and sell securities in New York than in London! Without reform (see page 231) the London Stock Exchange would have ceased to be one of the world's leading financial centres.

If you refer back to the reasons for imposing regulations on industry it is hardly surprising that it has been suggested that efficiency in the allocation of resources is now given priority over safety standards. In fact there is no evidence that this is true and safety is still an important issue. What is different is the view that efficiency in the allocation of resources is better promoted by competition than by government controls on the behaviour of industry!

## Test your understanding

1. What are the economic aims of the government?
2. Why do the government's economic aims often seem to conflict?

3. What is meant by balance-of-payments equilibrium?
4. Why does the size of the PSBR depend mainly on the state of the Budget?
5. What are the problems with implementing an incomes policy?
6. Distinguish between demand-side economics and supply-side economics.
7. How does the government engineer a rise in interest rates?
8. What is the difference between *privatisation* and *deregulation*?

# Examination techniques

Most examinations include an essay, or free response, paper. Many also include a multiple-choice paper and a stimulus, or data response, paper. The aim of this chapter is to provide guidance on how to prepare for your own examination and how to cope with the different types of examination question.

## Exam preparation

Although all examinees are assessed on their performance in the examination room in what is a relatively short period of time, there is no short cut to success. Success will only come as the result of consistent effort, thorough preparation and careful revision. A surprising number of students pay only lip service to this important point.

Most syllabuses in introductory economics cover broadly the same material. There might be differences in emphasis but most syllabuses are quite general. Nevertheless it is a good idea to have a copy of whatever syllabus you are following so that you are aware of what topics must be covered. However, past examination papers are probably the best guide you can obtain to the way the chief examiner interprets the syllabus. It is always useful to obtain several of these and to study the different types of question set and the different ways a particular topic can be examined.

Past examination papers are extremely useful but you should never use them to try and question spot. This is a very dangerous game and chief examiners are well aware that many examinees scan past examination papers for clues about what might be on their own paper. Unfortunately it is most unlikely you will be able to correctly predict what is examined on your paper from scanning past papers; so if you plan your revision on such predictions you are likely to regret your actions! A more useful exercise is to attempt to answer past examination questions and to compare your answer with any information given in the examiners reports which most boards publish.

## Essay-writing techniques

During your course you will probably be required to produce essays for marking by the course tutor. Sometimes the marks obtained will count towards the final grade awarded on completion of the course, but more often essays (and other assignments) are simply set as an aid to understanding and learning. In either case you should ensure that each essay is written to the highest standard you are capable of achieving at that time.

Remember that writing essays sometimes involves drawing on knowledge from several parts of the course. The only way to be sure that you are answering a question fully is to understand all of the topics that have been covered. To do this you must regularly revise those topics that have been covered in class. A good rule of thumb is to spend about half an hour each week revising and testing your understanding of topics already covered.

Writing essays which are consistently of a high standard does not simply involve taking pride in your work, although this is obviously important. It also involves paying careful attention to many other points, and the remainder of this section is devoted to a discussion of these.

## Preparation

Obtain the essay title as early as possible and consider it carefully. Think what it means and what it is asking you do do. If you are unsure, a useful tip is to try and write in your own words on a sheet of rough paper what you think the essay title means. For example, if the essay title is: 'What are the reasons for government intervention in a market economy?' it is asking you 'Why do governments interfere with a market economy?', and to answer this you must state and explain these reasons.

## Planning your essay

Once you have decided what the title means, you can plan what to put in your answer. Make a list of the following things.

(a) What to put in your introduction.

In general, this should be very brief and to the point. It is best to include a definition of the central topic of your essay where this is appropriate. For example, if an essay title asks you to 'Explain, what is meant by . . .' or 'Define . . .', then it is best to start with a definition. Thus, in answer to the question 'Explain, with the use of relevant examples, what is meant by the term 'opportunity cost', you might begin by writing: 'Opportunity cost is usually defined as . . .'

Even where you are not specifically asked to define or describe something, it is good sense to do so: look out for this. For example, the title 'Economic goods are scarce goods – explain the meaning of this statement.', doesn't actually ask you to define 'economic goods' but you must do so if you are to explain the meaning of the sentence.

As well as a definition, it is usually helpful to outline the stages that will appear in your argument, in the introduction.

(b) What to put in the body of your essay.
Note down the major items you will be dealing with. Consider how to divide these up into separate paragraphs. Remember each separate item should be dealt with in a separate paragraph. At this stage you should note down examples or facts that you intend to use, diagrams that you will draw, and additional definitions that you will state.
(c) Whether a separate conclusion is needed.
In general, put one in. It will in any case serve as a useful summary of what you have said in your answer. For example, if you are asked 'Give the reasons for government intervention in a market economy', in your final paragraph you could write: 'We have outlined five reasons for government intervention in a market economy. These are: the instability that might arise in a market economy; the possibility of exploitation by monopolies; the extent to which inequalities occur; the hardship caused by economic change; and the desire to alter the use of resources when social and private values are different.' Sometimes the essay title itself will be a question, so that in your conclusion you must actually state what your answer has been.

## Writing your essay

Write neatly and legibly. Follow your plan. Take care to express your ideas correctly and in a way that is intelligible to others. Remember that all the sentences in one paragraph should be concerned with the same point and should follow logically from each other when you are outlining the argument.

In general, do not use abbreviations. Do, however, make sure that you phrase things in a way that is appropriate to the title, so that it is clear that you are answering the question. Avoid making a numbered list of items; each point must be described in a complete sentence. For example, where you are describing the measures used in regional policy, one sentence could begin: 'One measure used in regional policy is . . .' The second measure might be described in a sentence that starts: 'Another measure used is . . .' and so on.

Always try to write an essay to the best of your ability. If you do this, your essay technique will gradually improve. This is very important because if you do not learn to write clear, logical and well-reasoned essays in class or at home, success will be more difficult to achieve in the examination itself.

## Checking

Once you have finished writing, do not think the essay is ready to be handed in; first it must be checked by you.

Look at your plan and check that you included in your essay everything you intended to. It is amazing how easy it is to overlook something when you are busy writing.

Lastly, check that you have really written a full and complete answer to the question. Have you dealt with all the parts to the question? Have you explained and described everything as fully as you could? It is a good idea to do this check some time after you have written the essay. Coming to it afresh will allow you to consider it more carefully.

## Learning from your mistakes

When the marked essay is returned to you, don't file it away and forget about it. You will find it difficult to improve your technique unless you learn from your mistakes. This means reading over your essay after it has been marked, taking note of the comments that have been added and thinking about how it could be improved. This will dramatically reduce the likelihood of your making the same mistake twice and, coupled with regular revision, will markedly increase your chance of success in the examination.

## Data response techniques

Many of the major examining boards now include data response (i.e. stimulus-based) questions on their economic papers. In some cases there is a compulsory data response paper, but often they are set in the body of the question paper and are optional.

Broadly there are three types of data response question:

1. those which are based on hypothetical data,
2. those which are based on factual data,
3. those which are based on newspaper articles, or on extracts from official reports, etc.

Much of what has been written above about essays is still important, but because of the nature of data response questions it is impossible to give specific guidance on how to construct an answer. For example, in some cases it might be appropriate to include an introduction, but in others, where the question is highly structured and consists of several different parts, this might not be necessary.

What can be said is that in all types of data response question the purpose of giving data is to enable you to demonstrate an understanding of the principles contained in the data. In order to demonstrate understanding you must consider both the assumptions implicit in the data and the implications of any trends shown in the data.

This is very important because it enables examiners to distinguish between candidates who understand economic principles and can apply them, and candidates who have simply memorised them. When answering data response questions, examples should be taken from the data in order to illustrate your answer. This can sometimes be done by extracting the appropriate figures from the material given. At other times it is necessary to manipulate figures to obtain examples or to highlight trends in the data.

One point you should remember is that data response questions which involve arithmetic calculations are often easier than they at first appear. The best way to approach these is to use the information you are given to obtain, by calculation, as much additional information as will be helpful to you in tackling the question. Once you have obtained this it is often very easy to see the answer to particular parts of the question. However, do not neglect to mention the economic principles on which your answer is based. It is not your arithmetic ability which is being tested, but your ability to understand and apply economic principles.

## Multiple-choice techniques

Like data response questions, multiple-choice questions (sometimes called items) are becoming an increasingly common feature of examinations in economics. The most widely used type of multiple-choice question is the simple completion question. This consists of an opening statement (referred to as the stem) followed by a series of responses. Only one response (the key) correctly completes the statement in the stem, or answers the question it poses. The remaining responses are simply distractors. On the face of it, they appear as though they could be correct, but they are not. They are there simply to attract the unwary or the ill-prepared.

In the examination, the multiple-choice paper will consist of a relatively large number of questions (usually 30 or 50) to be answered in a relatively short period of time. As a method of examining, this is the major advantage of multiple-choice questions. They make it possible to test in an examination a wide range of subject knowledge and understanding. Such breadth of coverage is impossible to achieve in any other way under examination conditions.

Because multiple-choice questions can test both descriptive knowledge and analytical ability, they are not only a useful method of examining, but also an invaluable aid to learning. During your course you will find it very useful to assess your progress by using multiple-choice questions, whether you take a multiple-choice paper in the examination or not. Remember that each question has only one key, so that a good check of your understanding is being aware not only of why the key is correct, but also why the other responses are incorrect.

## Revision

There are no hard and fast rules about when to begin final revision for the examination. This depends on the individual, the type of examination, the time available, and so on. All that can be said is that if you are to give yourself maximum chance of success, thorough revision of all the syllabus is required. Nothing can be left out, otherwise you might find that there are compulsory questions you cannot answer, and that your choice of essay or data response questions is restricted. You should therefore begin revision at a fairly early stage and indeed final revision should simply build on an already solid foundation established by regular revision during your course.

It is probably best to begin final revision by making a detailed plan of when each topic is to be covered. You should make every effort to stick to this plan, but remember you are likely to find revision relatively easy at the start, but more difficult towards the end. Your plan should allow for this, and also for the fact that the more difficult topics will take longer to revise than others. You should take great care, therefore, to ensure that your plan sets realistic targets. Sticking to the plan will lead to growing confidence as you progress from one topic to the next and as your understanding of the subject as a whole grows.

How to revise is very much a personal matter, but you might find the following practical hints useful.

1. Rewrite your course notes in shortened form, using headings and making lists of points.
2. Learn these lists; it is useful to remember how many points there are in each list, e.g. learn that there are three types of injection into the circular flow of income.
3. Make a separate list of clear and concise definitions.
4. Learn these definitions by rewriting from memory and then checking against your notes.
5. Practise examination questions and especially multiple-choice items and data response questions. For essays, remember there are two things to practise: planning your answer, and writing it in the time allowed.

## In the examination

The final thing you must do before attempting any examination paper is to carefully read the rubric on the front of the examination paper. You must follow these instructions to the letter, noting in particular the total number of questions which must be attempted, and the number that should be attempted from each section. You should also note the total time allowed for completing the paper and bear this in mind when allocating time between questions. The remainder of this section provides guidance on how to cope with the different types of examination question, each of which may appear in a separate paper.

## Essays

### Choosing questions

Choose essay questions very carefully: First, read through all the questions, marking those that you think you might be able to answer. Next, for these questions, consider whether you can actually answer all the parts. There is usually little point in attempting a question if you cannot answer all of it. Finally, choose the appropriate number of questions out of those that you can answer, selecting those that you feel you can answer best. Remember that your aim is to show the examiner that you know and understand economics, and it will be your ability to do this in a question which will make it one of your 'best answers'; don't think that you can give a good answer to a question just because it is easy to answer without using economics.

### Answer plan

Plan what to put in your answer, and write this down, so that you can follow your plan. Think very carefully about actually answering the question. Note how many marks are allocated to each part of the answer. This is a guide as to how important each part is, so that it tells you how long to spend on each part.

**Answer carefully**

Write your answer carefully, expressing ideas precisely, using supporting evidence whenever available. Don't be vague and do give examples. Follow the rubric, i.e. set out your answer in the same way that the question has been set out; if the question is divided into two parts, (a) and (b), so must your answer be. Make a note of the time you begin each question and spend only the appropriate amount of time on it. This is important because if you are to succeed to the best of your ability you must complete the paper.

**Referring back**

Keep referring back to the question and to your plan. It is easy under examination conditions to wander off the point and to include irrelevant material. Marks are not usually deducted for this, but economists will know that the opportunity cost is very high. Time spent discussing irrelevant material is no longer available to discuss relevant material. The penalty for this kind of error might therefore be very serious. It only takes a short while to check that you are following your plan and that what you have written is relevant to the question.

**Answer check**

If you have any time left after completing your answers, check your work for errors and omissions. These can easily creep in under examination conditions.

**Data response**

Again, much of the suggested approach to the essay paper is still relevant here. However, in addition to thinking about the questions, it is necessary to consider how, in each case, the data can be used to answer the question. This almost certainly means recognising the economic principles illustrated by, or contained within, the data. On a first reading this is not an easy task and you should not abandon the idea of attempting a question merely because it is not immediately apparent how to answer it. A second or third reading will often provide you with insights that a first reading does not.

**Multiple choice**

All questions on the multiple-choice paper are compulsory, and you will have to work fairly rapidly through them to complete this paper. Despite this, don't try to do too much in your head. If you do, you are likely to become confused or to overlook some important point. Instead, draw diagrams, write down formulae to help you, and work fully through calculations. Because you must work quickly through this paper, it is particularly important to read the stem carefully. Under examination pressure it is easy to overlook a vital word. This is especially true where questions begin with a negative stem such as: 'Which one of the following is not an invisible export?' Before putting down your answer on the examination paper, therefore, you should quickly glance at the stem to ensure that you have not made an obvious error in your choice of response.

On this type of paper there will inevitably be some questions which are easier than others. Because of this you should not spend too much time on one question. If you are struggling with a particular question, it is best to miss it out and go on to the next one. Remember to mark the question you have missed out, and be careful not to put the answer to succeeding questions in the wrong place. This is very easily done when you are using a computer marked card to record your answers. The only certain way to avoid doing this is to check the question number and answer number before recording your response. Do not forget to go back and answer any questions you have missed out. If you are still unable to answer them, eliminate any responses you know to be incorrect and make a guess from the remainder. You have at least a 20 per cent chance of being right where the question has five responses, and at least a 25 per cent chance where it has four! Eliminating incorrect data responses increases the percentages still further.

## A final word

When you first start your course, set your sights on obtaining the highest grade. Stick to your aim throughout the course and gear the level of your effort accordingly. Pay particular attention to those topics which you do not fully understand and never assume that an individual topic is unimportant. In a subject like Economics, topics often interrelate and a full understanding of one topic is impossible without a full understanding of others. Remember that if you do find a topic difficult, other students will also find it difficult. This is why it is important to persevere. Not everyone succeeds in the examination, but those who persevere in seeking to overcome their problems have a clear advantage. At the end of the day, the highest grade is particularly important because few people achieve it. This book cannot guarantee success, but if used correctly it should prove to be a valuable aid.

# A guide to source material and further reading

Begg, D., Fischer, S., and Dornsbusch, R., *Economics* (3rd edition), McGraw-Hill 1990

Curwen, P.J., *Understanding the UK Economy*, Macmillan 1990

Hardwick, P., Khan, B., and Langmead, J. *In Introduction to Modern Economics* (3rd edition), Longman 1990

Parkin, M., *Economics*, Addison-Wesley 1990

Samuelson, P.A., and Nordhaus, W.D., *Economics* (14th edition), McGraw-Hill 1989

Griffiths, A., and Wall, S. (eds), *Applied Economics: An Introductory Course* (4th edition), Longman 1991

For up to date statistical data on the UK economy, the reader might find the following useful:

*Economic Trends* published monthly by the Central Statistical Office, HMSO

*Financial Statistics* also published monthly by the Central Statistical Office, HMSO

*Employment Gazette*, published monthly by the Department of Employment

For articles on economic theory and/or applied economics the reader might find the following useful:

*The Economic Review*, Philip Allan

*The Bank of England Quarterly Bulletin*

*The National Westminster Bank Review*

*Lloyds Bank Economic Bulletin*

# Solutions

## Chapter 1

1 Something is scarce when society desires more than it currently has. This is true of most goods and services. Something is rare when there are few in existence. To the economist such goods as motor cars are scarce, but they are hardly rare.

2 (a) because this is the only good which is produced from scarce resources. Note fish and ice at the fishmonger are scarce because they are produced from scarce resources.

3 'next most desired'

4 No. The economic problem exists because of scarcity. Some countries might well be richer than others, but scarcity is neither greater nor less in one country compared with another.

5 There is less likelihood of other members of society contracting the disease.

6 There are health problems associated with passive smoking. There are also costs involved in treating illnesses which are caused by cigarette smoking along with the loss in output from absences due to smoking relating illnesses.

7 (a) (i) F of X and E of Y (ii) G of X and D of Y
(b) ED of Y
(c) There is no opportunity cost because society is producing more by using resources that were previously unemployed
(d) The entire production possibility would move outwards from the origin.

## Chapter 2

1 (a) Price rises; (b) the existence of queues

2 A Pareto Optimal allocation of resources exists when the value society places on the last unit consumed exactly equals the opportunity cost of producing that unit. This concept is extremely important because when resources are allocated in a Pareto Optimally efficient manner, society's welfare is maximised because it is impossible to make one person better off without making someone else worse off.

3 The price mechanism will fail to achieve a Pareto Optimal

allocation of resources whenever prices do not fully reflect the full social costs and benefits of production and consumption. This will occur when there are externalities (positive or negative) associated with production and consumption. The existence of public and merit goods will also prevent the price mechanism from achieving a Pareto Optimal allocation of resources.

4 Public Goods: National defence (non-excludable and non-rival)
Merit Goods: A motorway, public libraries (social benefits exceed private costs)
Private Goods: A season ticket for a football club, a motor car (These goods are both excludable and rival and there are no externalities to consider)

5 See answer to Q2. Price controls prevent market price reflecting the full social cost of production.

6 (a) This will lead to a change in the allocation of resources because it will cause a change in demand for different goods and services.
(b) No effect because externalities have no effect on prices in free market economies.
(c) This will lead to a fall in income for those who become unemployed and in consequence they will change their demands for different goods and services.

7 In free market economies there is no government intervention.

8 The allocation of resources, that is, the output of organisations within the economy.

9 Because those involved in planning could be producing the output which is foregone when they are involved in drawing up a plan for the economy.

## Chapter 3

1 The entrepreneurial function is split between the shareholders who own the organisation, and salaried managers who run the organisation.

2 Saving.

3 Risk-taking (because they risk their funds) and decision-taking (because they decide the proportions in which the factors of production are to be combined).

4 The nature of repair work is such that each television set will require individual attention. It is impossible to break the work down into component parts the way that manufacturing a television set can be broken down into a series of different operations, each capable of being performed by a single person.

5 As factors of production become more specialised their skills become more and more specific and therefore the mobility of the factor declines.

6 Division of labour makes possible large-scale production.

However, if the market is small it will be uneconomic to produce on a large scale.

7 Average product will also be falling. In fact, average product will always fall whenever marginal product is less than the existing average product.

8 Marginal product is rising. See answer to Q7.

9 If marginal product is constant, total product will be rising at a constant rate.

10 (a) Productivity is measured by changes in average product. In this case labour input (no. of hours × no. of workers) falls but output rises. There has therefore been an increase in productivity.

(b) Since labour input has fallen, but hourly output has increased, labour costs per unit have fallen.

11 (a) Increasing returns to capital,

(b) decreasing returns to labour,

(c) economies of scale.

12

| No. of workers employed | Total product | Marginal product | Average product |
|---|---|---|---|
| 1 | 4 | 4 | 4.0 |
| 2 | 9 | 5 | 4.5 |
| 3 | 16 | 7 | 5.3 |
| 4 | 28 | 12 | 7.0 |
| 5 | 38 | 10 | 7.6 |
| 6 | 40 | 2 | 6.67 |

(a) After the employment of the fourth worker because the marginal product of the fifth worker is less than the marginal product of the fourth worker.

(b) After the employment of the fifth worker because the marginal product of the sixth worker is less than that of the fifth worker.

13 (a) and (b) only. (c) is the *purpose* of production!

## Chapter 4

1 Capital depreciation is the loss in value of a capital asset over time. The main reason for depreciation is technological advances. Technology leads to obsolescence even though machinery is often still working at maximum efficiency.

2 $TC_n - TC_{n-1} = MC$

3 Fixed costs are fixed with respect to output. In other words fixed costs do not change as output changes. Even when the firm produces no output, it still incurs fixed costs of production.

4 The long run is a period of time necessary to change all factor

inputs. If all factor inputs are variable, all costs, by definition, must be variable.

5 Fixed costs: Insurance charges, depreciation on capital.

6 The shape of the marginal curve is determined by the nature of returns as output changes. Typically firms initially experience increasing returns, that is, marginal product rises and marginal cost falls. Subsequently, as diminishing returns set in, marginal product falls and marginal cost therefore rises.

7 If marginal cost is falling, total cost will rise at a *slower rate* as output increases.

8

| Output | Total Cost | Fixed Cost | Variable Cost | Average Total Cost | Average Variable Cost | Marginal Cost |
|---|---|---|---|---|---|---|
| 0 | 100 | 100 | 0 | 00 | — | |
| 1 | 140 | 100 | 40 | 140 | 40 | 40 |
| 2 | 170 | 100 | 70 | 85 | 35 | 30 |
| 3 | 190 | 100 | 90 | 63.3 | 30 | 20 |
| 4 | 200 | 100 | 100 | 50 | 25 | 10 |
| 5 | 220 | 100 | 120 | 55 | 24 | 20 |
| 6 | 270 | 100 | 170 | 45 | 28.3 | 30 |

The firm begins to experience diminishing marginal returns when the fifth unit is produced, that is, after the production of the fourth unit.

## Chapter 5

1 In equilibrium $MU_A/P_A = MU_e/P_e$. $MU_A$ is therefore 4.

2 It shows an inverse relationship between price and quantity demanded. We would expect to find this because a fall in price implies that a higher level of utility can now be obtained from a given level of income.

3 (a) A movement *along* a demand curve is always caused by a reduction in the price of the product. Nothing else can cause a movement along a demand curve.

(b) A movement *of* a demand curve is caused by a change in at least one of the conditions of demand such as a change in: income, the distribution of income, the prices of complements or substitutes, advertising expenditure, population and so on. A change in price does not *cause* a shift of the demand curve.

4 (a) £20, (b) 24.

5 4p.

6 X and Y are complements; Y and Z are substitutes.

7 (a) 74p.
(b) 72p.
(c) 78p.

## Chapter 6

1 (a) Elasticity of demand would indicate the effect on quantity demanded of a change in price. This is important to any manager contemplating a price change since it is possible to estimate the effect on total revenue and profit of any change in price. Note, for a price reduction a manager would also be able to estimate whether it would be possible to increase output sufficiently to meet the increase in demand and the extent to which additional supplies of raw materials would need to be bought in, labour hired and so on.

(b) Knowledge of elasticity of demand would be useful to a Chancellor of the Exchequer contemplating changing the rate of indirect tax on goods and services since it would provide the basis for estimating the effect on government revenue. Similarly where a change in the rate of duty on imported goods is contemplated, knowledge of elasticity of demand for imports would provide the basis for estimating how much revenue would be earned and the possible effect on the balance of payments of a change in the rate of duty.

2 Profit will rise because sales will fall (unless elasticity of demand is zero). In response firms will cut output, costs will fall but total revenue will increase (see page 51.) If elasticity of demand is zero output will be unchanged but will sell at a higher price.

3 (a) 0.33, (b) they are substitutes (cross elasticity of demand is positive).

4 The supply of fresh vegetables will be less elastic than the supply of processed vegetables mainly because processed vegetables can be stored.

5 (a) 0.8.

6 Other things equal, the more mobile the factors of production the greater the elasticity of supply since additional factors of production can be obtained or transferred without difficulty in response to changes in price.

## Chapter 7

1 Perfect competition implies that there are no obstacles which impede competition between firms. For example, there is no consumer loyalty or any possibility that one firm has an advantage over other firms.

2 If there were significant economies of scale, firms would grow to take advantage of these and this would give them the ability to influence market price.

3 (a) 9 units (This is where the difference between total revenue and total cost is greatest.)

(b) (i) £5.60 (This is the minimum average variable cost.)
(ii) £10.00 (This is the minimum average total cost.)

4 Some consumers pay a lower price; price discrimination might

ensure continued production when it is impossible to at least break-even by charging a single price.

5 Because it is necessary to reduce the price of *all* units to increase sales.

6 'Higher'.

7 (a), (b) and (e) are true of monopoly *and* perfect competition.

8 No. Equilibrium output always occurs when average cost is falling, that is, firms in monopolistic competition operate with excess capacity.

9 The supply of their own brand of the product.

10 Oligopolistic markets are characterised by interdependence between firms. In other words the actions of one firm have effects on other firms in the industry.

11 No. The kinked demand curve has been suggested as an explanation of price stability in oligopolistic markets. It is not a theory of oligopoly because it does not tell us *how* price is determined.

12 (a) Monopolistic – because the firm can increase sales by reducing price.
(b) Supernormal profit
(c) OQ – because this is where MR = MC
(d) OP – because this is where MR = MC
(e) $OP_1$ and $OP_2$
(f) $OP_3$ = minimum average variable cost.

## Chapter 8

1 There is no limit on the number of establishments a firm can have.

2 A firm is a unit of ownership. An establishment is a unit where production is carried out. An industry consists of all firms engaged in the same productive activity.

3 To create a more balanced distribution of industry and employment and to narrow regional differentials in income.

4 Many small firms undertake individual jobs such as house extensions and so on.

5 A merger exists when two or more firms voluntarily pool their assets. An acquisition exists when one firm takes a controlling interest in another firm by obtaining over 50 per cent of its equity.

6 (b) and (c)

## Chapter 9

1 Net property income from abroad.

2 (i) When net property income from abroad is positive; (ii) when net property income from abroad is negative.

3 (a), (c) and (e).

4 (a) GNP rises by £68m.
(b) GDP rises by £70m.
(c) NNP rises by £67m.

5 Real national income rises by 125/110 = 13.6%.

6 Not necessarily. The increase in GNP might simply be the result

of a rise in prices. Even if it is the result of an increase in real income the standard of living will only increase if the rise in real income exceeds the rise in population.

7 When it results in higher social costs being imposed on the community; when it consists mainly of net property income paid abroad.

8 Wealth is a stock and income is a flow.

9 The former is simply a transfer payment. The latter gives a claim on the output of another country. It therefore adds to net property income from abroad.

10 Real national income is the volume of output a nation produces within a given period of time.

## Chapter 10

1 The equilibrium level occurs when there is no tendency for income to change, that is, when planned injections equal planned leakages.

2 (a) £7500m.
(b) k = 1/MPS = 5.
(c) £500m.

3 Because stock levels change whenever there is a discrepancy between planned injections and planned leakages. This ensures that realised injections are always equal to realised leakages.

4 Because a rise in taxation reduces the amount of income that is passed on at each stage.

5 This statement is incorrect. In reality a reduction in saving implies an increase in expenditure which will generate an increase in income. This is likely to lead to an increase in investment and, in a two sector economy, the higher level of income will lead to a higher level of savings.

6 It will most likely increase the size of the multiplier because it will increase the MPC.

7 An increase in government spending will have the greater effect on income because part of any reduction in taxation will be saved.

8 £1000m. (Note: transfer payments have no effect on income and only £500m. is initially spent.)

## Chapter 11

1 Strictly investment is the flow of expenditures devoted to projects producing goods which are not intended for immediate consumption.

2 An increase in population would be likely to shift the MEC schedule outwards because by increasing the demand for goods and services it will most likely raise the profitability of investment.

3 Stocks are classed as investment and therefore when stocks increase, investment increases.

4 The discounted present value of revenue is approximately £4.55m. The machine would therefore be expected to yield a profit of approximately £3.55.

5 These factors will tend to reduce the accelerator coefficient.

6 If two units of capital produce four units of output per period, the capital/output ratio is 1:2.

7 £200m.

## Chapter 12

1 The demand for labour is derived from the demand for the goods and services that labour produces.

2 No. Some occupations will be more desirable or less dangerous than others. The least desirable or most dangerous occupations would offer the highest wages in order to attract labour.

3 Demand for skilled labour is likely to be less elastic because it will be more difficult to obtain substitutes for labour. Note: the length of time required to train labour affects the elasticity of supply.

4 Wage differentials perform the same function in the labour market that price differentials perform in the product markets. In other words they perform an allocative function.

5 If a wage increase in one industry disturbs the existing pattern of differentials it might lead to wage demands in other industries to restore the pattern of differentials.

6 It would narrow wage differentials and thus remove the main incentive for labour to move to alternative occupations.

7 Trade unions bargain collectively on behalf of their members over pay and conditions rather than leaving each individual to negotiate with their employer.

## Chapter 13

1 This enables comparison between rates of interest quoted by different institutions.

2 (i) £50; (ii) £38.89 (approx).

3 Active balances are held with the intention of making purchases as and when necessary. Idle balances are held as a store of wealth.

4 It shows that the securities with longer to run to maturity have the highest yield.

5 A rise in nominal income is the most likely cause of a shift in the liquidity preference function but other occurences such as a loss in confidence in financial institutions would also increase liquidity preference. A reduction in the rate of interest will cause a movement along the liquidity preference function.

6 Transfer earnings are the minimum acceptable reward necessary to keep a factor of production in its present occupation. Economic rent is earnings in excess of transfer earnings. Quasi-rent is economic rent which is only earned in the short run.

7 The main argument is that since economic rent represents a surplus over transfer earnings, a tax on economic rent would have no effect of supply. In practice it is difficult to estimate the proportion of earnings which constitutes economic rent.

8 Normal profit.

## Chapter 14

1 This is the way economists define money. It simply means that anything which performs the functions of money is money.

2 (i), (iii), (ii).

3 Investments can be sold on the capital market. A financial intermediary cannot insist on repayments of an advance until maturity.

4 Narrow money is regarded as those assets used as a medium of exchange. Broad money includes assets which function as a store of value.

5 The authorities decide when they will be called and repaid. They are deposits which are frozen at the Bank of England and which cannot be used by those organisations which have paid them.

6 They compete for funds which they can then lend at a higher rate of interest than they pay to attract them.

## Chapter 15

1 Because a given amount of money now exchanges for fewer goods and services.

2 Sum of weighted index = 1160. Dividing this by the sum of the weights gives the current value of the RPI = 116.

3 Once an inflationary spiral is underway it is difficult to identify the cause. For example, a rise in wages leads to a rise in income and hence demand. If prices rise there might well be further demands for pay rises.

4 The equation of exchange is simply an identity that says nothing about causation. The quantity theory of money suggests that an increase in money growth causes an increase in the rate of inflation.

5 (a) demand for money will fall; (b) demand for money will increase; (c) demand for money will increase.

6 It is the rate of unemployment to which the economy will tend in the long run. It is therefore the equilibrium rate of unemployment.

7 (a) natural rate of unemployment will fall; (b) natural rate of unemployment will fall; (c) natural rate will be unaffected.

8 It is argued that an increase in government expenditure will crowd out or displace private sector expenditure, some economists argue in the ratio 1:1. It is important because it implies government expenditure has a less than proportionate effect on real income.

9 (a) through a reduction in the rate of interest; (b) through an increase in expenditure on goods and services.

## Chapter 16

1 Absolute advantage refers to a situation that exists when a country can produce a greater amount of one good than another country using the same amount of inputs. Comparative advantage refers to a situation that exists when a country has an absolute disadvantage, but a lower opportunity cost when producing one good than another country producing the same good.

2 To take advantage of comparative cost advantages; to obtain

goods that might not otherwise be available; in fulfilment of agreements between nations.

3 Size of the market, willingness to rely on other countries to supply goods and services which might be strategically important, existence of barriers such as tariffs.

4 Mutually beneficial trade is not possible because both countries have the same domestic opportunity cost ratios.

5 It is impossible to measure the rate at which all individual goods exchange against each other. Using an index expresses changes in the average rate at which goods and services exchange against each other.

6 A rise in the price of exports with import prices rising by a smaller percentage, falling or remaining constant. A fall in the price of exports with import prices falling by a greater percentage.

7 A tariff is a tax on imports. A quota fixes an upper limit on the amount of goods that can be imported.

8 The government gains revenue and domestic producers increase sales. Foreign producers loose sales and domestic consumers pay higher prices. Society in general looses because resources are allocated less efficiently.

## Chapter 17

1 (i) The balance of trade is the sum of visible exports minus the sum of visible imports. The terms of trade is an index of the ratio of export prices to import prices.

(ii) The visible balance is the sum of visible exports minus the sum of visible imports, that is, it is the balance of trade. The invisible balance is the difference between exports of services, plus interest profits and dividends and remittances by UK nationals living abroad and imports of services plus interest profits and dividends and remittances by foreign nationals living in the UK.

2 It is the sum of all errors and omissions in the balance of payments. It therefore balances recorded transactions with flows of foreign currency as recorded by the Bank of England.

3 They buy and sell domestic currency on the foreign exchange market. They also alter the rate of interest to attract or discourage short term investment flows into the domestic economy.

4 The price of foreign currency is fixed. The price of goods and services traded can rise or fall in response to changes in supply and demand.

5 Because each transaction is recorded twice. Once as a credit entry and once as a debit entry.

6 A clean float occurs when there is no intervention in the foreign exchange market by the authorities. A dirty float implies that the authorities intervene to influence the exchange rate for their currency but do not declare the extent of their intervention or their target value for the exchange rate.

7 If all other things remain equal a smaller level of reserves is required if the authorities are willing to accept more severe deflation to remove a balance-of-payments deficit.

8 Hot money is short term investment flows attracted by the expectation higher rates of interest or currency appreciation.

9 (i) By raising the cost of investment it might make manufacturing output less competitive in the long run. It has no short-run effects on the current account.

(ii) It attracts hot money.

10 Depreciation in these circumstances will cause a deterioration in the current account.

## Chapter 18

1 A budget deficit raises the level of aggregate demand because the government is spending more than it receives in taxation.

2 The main component of the PSBR is the central government's budget deficit. The PSBR adds directly to the national debt since it is borrowing by the public sector.

3 (i) Unless the PSBR is financed by borrowing from the non-bank private sector it will lead to an increase in the money supply.

(ii) Financing the PSBR implies that the public sector competes with the private sector for funds. It is usually argued that this will drive up interest rates.

4 (i) C
(ii) A
(iii) B

5 It shows the optimal rate of taxation in terms of revenue received.

6 Because it will raise prices and a given level of income will therefore buy less. The same thing happens when direct taxes are increased.

7 A rise in direct taxes implies that a higher income must be earned in order to maintain a given standard of living. Higher direct taxes therefore might provide an incentive to increase effort and initiative.

8 (i) This would tend to reduce the numbers caught in the unemployment trap since it would increase the amount of income they receive after tax.

(ii) This would tend to increase the numbers caught in the unemployment trap because it would reduce the amount of income they receive after tax.

9 The incidence of a tax falls on the person or organisation who actually pays the tax.

## Chapter 19

1 Full employment, price stability, stable exchange rate, economic growth, a reduction in income inequality, a sustainable balance-of-payments position.

2 Some aims such as increased economic growth and employment are often thought to depend on increasing aggregate demand.

However, this raises prices, puts downward pressure on the exchange rate and might cause a deficit in the balance of payments.

3 Balance-of-payments equilibrium is usually thought to exist when, over a period of time, autonomous credits equal autonomous debits.

4 The PSBR is the total borrowing by the public sector and by far the largest component of this is borrowing by the central government. A budget deficit adds considerably to central government borrowing.

5 Deciding a norm for pay rises, agreeing criteria against which to judge 'special cases', distortion of wage differentials thus impairing the allocative role of wage differentials.

6 Demand side refers to government attempts to manipulate aggregate demand so as to achieve economic aims. Supply side refers to attempts to improve efficiency by removing barriers to competition and in this way achieve economic aims.

7 It raises its dealing rate in the bill market and other organisations in the monetary sector raise their rates of interest.

8 Privatisation refers to the sale of public sector assets to the private sector. Deregulation simply involves removing those regulations which impede the growth of competition in particular markets.

# Index